PLAYING ON THE EDGE

PERFORMANCE, YOUTH CULTURE, AND THE U.S. CARNIVALESQUE

ADRIENNE MACIAIN, PHD

ACKNOWLEDGMENTS

My deepest thanks to Leo Cabranes-Grant and Catherine Cole, for believing in the project, and in my ability to carry it out, and for helping to nurture it as it grew from an idea, to a seminar paper, to a dissertation, and finally a book.

My thanks also go out to Harry Nelson, for his endless insights and enthusiasm, to Jody Enders for her excellent editing in the early stages, and to Naomi Iizuka for her close reading near the end of the process.

I am grateful to all the graduate and undergraduate students who helped me during the course of my research, but I offer my special thanks to those who went above and beyond to help keep me safe and sane: Ellen Anderson, Maria Constanza Berardi, Elli Resnavis, Jason Davids Scott, and Hank Willenbrink. I am equally grateful to those who supplied me with digital video footage of Halloween in Isla Vista: Bruce Gordon, Bob Lewis, and Matt Rundell.

Thank you to the many Isla Vista community members, both current and former, who contributed their memories, photographs, opinions, ideas, etc., especially Robert Bernstein, Stan Hoffman, Lieutenant Sol Linver (IVFP), Carmen and Genesis Lodise, Bob Potter,

Malcolm Gault-Williams, and Alison Zuber. Thank you also to all those who filled out one of my Halloween questionnaires, or who simply volunteered a tale or two upon learning of my project.

This couldn't have happened without you.

PART I
INTRODUCTION

PROBIENCE ON PARADE

FINDING NEMO ON DEL PLAYA DRIVE

October 31, 2003, approximately 11 p.m.: Del Playa Drive, precariously balanced between the student-heavy neighborhood of Isla Vista, California, and the Pacific Ocean, is swarming with costumed revelers.[1]

A young Latina in a skimpy Snow White costume, cheered on by her friends, is singing a sexually explicit song to a group of young men dressed as the Teenage Mutant Ninja Turtles.

Nearby, a doctor is attempting to convince his nurse that it's "okay" for her to remove her shirt because he is a licensed "boobyologist," while she counters that he has consumed too much alcohol to be practicing medicine at the moment.

Up on a balcony, a scantily-clad, tiara-topped Princess is mooning the crowd below, where a Caucasian man dressed as Speedy Gonzales in an exaggerated poncho and oversized sombrero, is chanting "Turn around! Turn around!" and encouraging others to join him.

On the sidewalk nearby, a costumeless teenager is arguing with the police officer who is handcuffing him, insisting that he had only joined the fight to save his brother, who was "seriously getting his ass kicked"; an unidentified passerby calls the officer a "pig" and tells him to, "leave the poor guy alone."

An apparently intoxicated, freckle-faced young woman in a Girl-scout uniform of exceedingly short length is arguing belligerently with an un-costumed friend, who is attempting to convince said Girl-scout that she has had enough tequila for one evening.

Suddenly, from the midst of this sea of chaotic revelry, a piercing cry arises. "NEMO!" a male voice calls out, "It's Nemo!" The crowd shifts as a sailor holding a video camera wades over toward where a young man dressed as "Nemo,"[2] is facing the opposite direction. The sailor, whose dark skin and black ponytail stand in stark contrast to his bright white uniform declares: "I have to find Nemo," partly as an explanation to those he must push out of the way, some of whom turn to follow him, joining the quest.

Having arrived, he calls out once more, "Nemo!" at which point the orange-and-black fish head turns to face the searching sailor and his camera, revealing an expression of genuine surprise. The newfound Nemo, sporting a loose-fitting orange tank-top and black jeans, holds up an open container of Jack Daniel's Tennessee Whiskey (in what, incidentally, should be his "gimpy" fin), declaring dramatically, "Oh my god, you fuckin' found me, Dude!"

The two strangers hug to the tune of a communal "awwwww": a conscious, collective parody of so many sentimentalized Hollywood-ending reunions. Having played out their scene, the two unceremoniously part, carried off in opposite directions by the chaotic currents of the chuckling crowd.[3]

Unlike at other annual festivals of comparable size, there are no planned events at Halloween in Isla Vista: no parades, no contests, no organized games to play or ceremonies to attend. The traditional activities are few – dressing up in a provocative costume, going door to door in search of alcohol and/or sexual adventure (the Isla Vistan perversion of "trick-or-treating") – and the rules of engagement are largely tacit and extraordinarily flexible.

That is not to say, however, that there are no noteworthy events taking place here on Del Playa; on the contrary, theatrical happenings are evident in every direction. No designated "performers" offer premeditated entertainment; instead, every participant is at once entertainer and spectator, exhibitionist and voyeur, constantly engaging in subversive sketches of varying lengths with fellow participants (and in this I include police officers, uniformed and otherwise).

Taken individually, these overlapping performances may not appear to be communicating any decipherable messages, either for the other participants, or for those non-participants who witness them (in person, or through the media). However, closer examination reveals common themes which begin to form a coherent narrative: the parodic perversion of childhood games and fantasies; an exaggerated indulgence in alcohol and other substances forbidden in childhood and adolescence in the U.S.; the flagrant foregrounding of sexuality; and a pervasive preoccupation with the creation and documentation of a sufficiently outrageous Halloween experience to carry into the increasingly isolated space of U.S. adulthood.

What once appeared to be an ordinary – if particularly popular – college party is thus revealed as a rite of passage marking the end of adolescence within a particular cultural and geographical context, as well as a cultural performance transmitting messages among, and about, a group of people representing the most important market within the global economy: United States youth.

At once a carnivalesque celebration of the fleeting freedom allowable before the onset of post-college productivity, and a funeral for the abandoned dreams of childhood and adolescence, Halloween in Isla Vista is much more than a gathering of costumed college students: it is an emblematic expression of what are commonly regarded to be "the best years" of a Westerner's life, performed by those who are assumed to be in a prime position to enjoy those years to the fullest.

THE SPECTER OF POST-ADOLESCENT YOUTH

"Youth is a fetishistic object that has an immaterial existence."

- Jan Jagodzinski[1]

Despite its centrality to the collective imaginary of the global capitalist marketplace as a time of unparalleled independence and pleasure-seeking, remarkably little has been written on the life phase that follows adolescence and precedes adulthood in the U.S. This is likely due in large part to the fact that it has only emerged as a distinct period of life within the past fifty or so years, and only in particular cultural and geographic contexts – largely, industrialized nations.

As Jeffrey Jensen Arnett argues in *Emerging Adulthood*, "In the past few decades, a quiet revolution has taken place for young people in U.S. society, so quiet that it has been noticed only gradually and incompletely."[2] The revolution to which Arnett refers is the prolongation of what was once a brief transitional period between adolescence and adulthood into a full-blown life-phase in its own right. This significant shift in the post-industrial life-cycle is partly due to the prolongation of education and delay of full-time employment, marriage, parenthood, and other sociological signifiers of adulthood, and partly due to shifting attitudes about those signifiers.

Although this particular shift has only become statistically significant since the 1960's or so, it must nonetheless be understood as part of a larger, and much earlier shift in the human developmental cycle: the creation of "adolescence" in its current usage. Marcel Danesi argues in *My Son is an Alien: A Cultural Portrait of Today's Youth*,[3] that the notion of adolescence as we understand it is the direct result of what he calls "a social experiment" which began in the early 19th century. After the onset of the industrial revolution, laws began to be put in place to protect children from the inhospitable working conditions of the new, industrialized workplace; no longer sent immediately out to work upon reaching puberty, more and more children were expected to continue their education past the attainment of sexual maturity. At that point "adolescent," a term which previously had referred to any young man who left home to pursue work in the city, took on a new meaning: any person remaining in school past the age of puberty.

In a psychoanalytic sense, the creation of "adolescence" could be described as a symptom of modernism's nostalgia for the loss of "childhood," an equally fantastic projection of bourgeois society. Here I invoke the Freudian concept of "nostalgia," which Lacanian cultural critic Jan Jagodzinski defines as: "a memory of loss," which, "for Freud, was not considered redemptive in its discovery, but constitutive of a desire that passes into a recollection of such an object whose status remains in doubt."[4] In other words, the recalled object, in this case "child," may never have existed in the form it now takes in nostalgic recollection.

This is the sense in which I will be using the term "nostalgia" throughout. "The child of modernity," argues Jagodzinski, "is a 'divine' fantasmatic object of desire [...], a transcendental signifier for bourgeois progress and modernization."[5] This object has been shaped "by the discourses of developmental psychology since the early twentieth century," which specified "developmental stages of progressive growth" that "turned out to be the same progressive stages of Western thought itself."[6] Adolescence emerged as one of these "empirically discovered" stages, precisely at the point when the romanticized object of "child" appeared to be threatened with extinction.

That is not to say that the fantasy object of "child" had previously existed in a more tangible form: within the discourse of nostalgia, the same feelings of mourning and melancholia can result from the perceived loss of a spectral object (i.e. an object that the subject only *believes* her/himself to have possessed) as from the loss of a tangible object, and that trauma of loss can be delayed, pre-empted, or repeated any number of times. The loss of childhood is a trauma that has been experienced repeatedly within industrializing Western society, each time provoking a new list of melancholic symptoms. Adolescence is one such symptom, a spectral object that provokes both fear and desire, both despair and hope, in those who continue to believe in it.

Adolescence, unlike the unequivocally romantic space of modernism's childhood, is a deeply ambiguous object. In many senses it is glorified as a time of carefree enjoyment and unbridled creativity. This image is in large part thanks to U.S. marketing companies which, by the 1960's, had begun creating products and advertisements geared specifically toward the adolescent market, emphasizing a connection between youth, fun, freedom, and consumerism. As Bill Osgerby argues in "'A Caste, a Culture, a Market:' Youth, Marketing, and Lifestyle in Postwar America"[7], it was these advertising campaigns aimed at teenagers that in large part solidified the mainstream U.S. point of view that youth is, or should ideally be, synonymous with enjoyment, leisure, and dispensable income. The enormous success of this type of marketing has had profound effects on U.S. society as a whole, solidifying a societal obsession with a hyper-sexualized, consumerist-oriented image of youth as a hot commodity.

And as commercial U.S. media supplants other cultural and educational institutions worldwide, it projects the unspoken ideal of a young, strong, sexy population. The result is that the markings of age are looked upon with increasing hostility, and considerable time and resources are poured into retaining an appearance and an approximation of youth, both in the U.S. and elsewhere.

Meanwhile adults continue to bemoan the loss of "childhood innocence" among their offspring, who do indeed appear increasingly eager to reach sexual maturity. This stands to reason since, as the majority of contemporary advertising campaigns will demonstrate, the sexually mature, attractive body is an extremely valuable commodity in the industrialized world. In the postmodern world, posits Jagodzinski, "to be desirable is to be a wanted body."[8] It should then come as little surprise that children in the U.S., who rank among the world's most highly-trained consumers, are impatient to possess the post-pubescent bliss promised them via the media. As Jagodzinski argues, "The postmodern trend of staying forever young is equivalent to the fantasy of the modern child never growing up."[9] Same melancholy, different symptom; and by no coincidence, both converge within the contested, contradictory space of adolescence.

Despite the ubiquitous glamorization of "youth" in the abstract, adolescence is simultaneously denigrated as a tumultuous time of emotional and physical turmoil. The list of movies, television shows, books, albums, etc. verifying that it is accepted and even expected that the average U.S. resident will be more or less miserable for the better part of his or her teenage years is too long and unwieldy to outline in detail, but would surely include the following examples: *The Breakfast Club* (John Hughes, 1985), *Pretty in Pink* (Howard Deutch, 1986), *Heathers* (Michael Lehmann, 1989), *My So-Called Life* (ABC television drama, aired 1993-1995), *Are You There God? It's Me, Margaret* (Judy Blume, 1970), and Nirvana's *Nevermind* (1991). The state of perpetual frustration and shame which we have come to associate with adolescence, so eloquently captured in all of the above examples, is anything but "natural." Rather, as Danesi points out, it is a direct consequence of forcing sexually mature individuals to ignore the biological transition of puberty. Danesi is explicit in his condemnation of the "social experiment" of adolescence, pointing out that it caused a host of unprecedented problems such as unwanted pregnancies, an increase in sexually transmitted diseases, and rampant alcoholism. "It was obvious to one and all," writes Danesi, "that sexually mature individuals could not be told *tout court* to ignore their sexual urges and concentrate on school as they did when they were children."[10] The inability of adolescents to conform to this unrealistic expectation inevitably leads to some degree of emotional and physical turmoil, thus creating the "teen angst" that has become accepted as a biological norm.

Although the age at which individuals attain the sociological markings of adulthood has continued to rise[11], "adolescence" still refers specifically to the period during which individuals who have reached sexual maturity continue to receive their primary (i.e. high school) education. Because these individuals are, for the most part, still subject to their parents' rules, and are often encouraged (or even ordered) to postpone sexual experimentation until after graduation, the socially "appropriate" time to deeply explore one's newly-discovered sexuality and independence has been pushed into the late teens and twenties. Thus it is now the period that follows adolescence, rather than adolescence itself, that has come to represent the transition into adulthood in the United States and many other industrialized nations. Having left the confines of parental surveillance and entered a social space where experimentation and personal discovery are often emphasized and encouraged, and frequently endowed with disposable income, this age range is increasingly looked upon as the luckiest of life-phases.

Meanwhile the working conditions in the U.S. are growing increasingly mechanized and profit-oriented, leaving little for potential workers to look forward to in terms of personal fulfillment. In the 1950's, Arnett points out, young people were eager to "settle down," possibly because of the massive upheavals they witnessed growing up – the Depression, World War II, and so forth. By contrast, people in their late teens and twenties today are much more likely to view the trappings of adulthood as undesirable yet inevitable eventualities rather than worthy goals to be achieved. Reared in stability, catered to by marketers and envied by their elders, many young people now take security for granted and instead seek to prolong the independent and spontaneous lifestyle popularly associated with youth.

1. (Re)Naming the subject

Although most social scientists and cultural critics will now admit that a new life phase has indeed emerged within the past few decades, and that it is situated between adolescence and an increasingly belated adulthood, there is little agreement about what this new phase ought to be called. Arnett has coined the phrase "emerging adulthood" to refer to the period that begins upon leaving one's childhood home, and ends when one establishes a relatively stable household of one's own. While I concur with Arnett that "youth" is too vague, and that "late adolescence" and "young adulthood" are misnomers, I worry that "emergent adulthood" falls into similar traps of ambiguity and inaccuracy. As Arnett himself points out, these so-called "emergent adults" are not particularly focused on the task of attaining adulthood. In fact, many of them are involved in a conscious struggle against the onset of adult norms and responsibilities. My research on Halloween in Isla Vista suggests that people in this age bracket are much more focused on detaching themselves from childhood and adolescence than on attaining any of the sociological markings of adulthood such as steady work, permanent residence in one place, marriage, and parenthood. In this sense, Danesi's adoption of the term "middlescence," which was coined, he says, in the latter in the mid-1990's by journalist Gail Sheehy, seems somewhat more appropriate. However, the interviews conducted by Arnett and others reveal that people who have left home feel that a significant shift has taken place, one which has impacted their lives, personalities, and so forth in profound and often unexpected ways. Any suggestion that these individuals are living in an extended period of adolescence, rather than a life-phase quite distinct from that which they experienced while living at home, is met with significant resistance, if not downright hostility. In short, the problem with conglomerate coinages like "middlescence" and "tweeniehood" (applied to the age group seven through twelve[12]) is that they place undue focus on the two surrounding life phases. This emphasis implies that the groups to which these terms refer have few defining qualities, aside from being located between two others.[13]

Much of what is unique to the life phase of adolescence, and to the phase that immediately follows it, remains obscured by commercial images designed to identify lack, rather than bounty. Part of my task here is to unearth and highlight the uniqueness of these phases, to define more clearly those qualities that make the two groups differentiable and noteworthy. In the case of adolescence, this extremely important work has begun to be undertaken in earnest by scholars such as Jonathan Epstein, Henry A. Giroux, Douglass Rushkoff, Marcel Danesi, and others.[14] Yet as Arnett notes, because it has only recently been accepted as a differentiable life-phase, the culture of slightly older people remains largely unexplored.

Although this study is focused on a specific subsection, namely college students, it will be indispensable to have a specific term by which I can refer to the larger group. For the reasons I have outlined above, I find the current terms to be inadequate. I am therefore moved to coin a new term, one that focuses on what is extraordinary about the lives of U.S. residents who have left their parents' home but have not yet set up a household of their own. Arnett, for example, names five main features of this phase:

- It is the age of *identity explorations*, of trying out various possibilities, especially in love and work.
- It is the age of *instability*.
- It is the most *self-focused* age of life.
- It is the age of *feeling in-between*, in transition, neither adolescent nor adult.
- It is the age of *possibilities*, when hopes flourish, when people have an unparalleled opportunity to transform their lives.[15]

Although I find all of these features to be insightful and relevant, features one, three, and five strike me as particularly telling. Western societal nostalgia over the perpetual loss and re-loss of a protected time of childhood insures that parents will most often treat adolescents as older children rather than younger adults. Therefore most identity exploration and experimentation is now postponed until after an individual has left the home of his or her parents. Meanwhile, decreasing opportunity and incentive to attain a settled state of adulthood has extended the time during which such self-transformation is accepted and even encouraged.

This is particularly true in the United States, as Thomas D. Cook and Frank F. Furstenburg Jr. argue in their article, "Explaining Aspects of the Transition to Adulthood in Italy, Sweden, Germany, and the United States: A Cross-Disciplinary Case Synthesis Approach." "Normatively," they write, "the United States offers second and third chances to young people" in the domains of education, employment, and even their personal lives.[16] Whereas in other nations, students are required to choose an educational and career path early on, U.S. residents are offered unparalleled opportunity to change direction well into their studies or even their career. Likewise, the stigma that surrounds cohabitation, divorce, and remarriage in many nations is on the wane in the U.S., offering young people a corrective measure in the domestic domain as well. U.S. residents – and particularly white, upper-middle class U.S. residents – in their late teens and twenties are therefore even more likely than their European counterparts to be rigorously engaged in identity exploration, to be self-focused, and to be blessed – and cursed – with a vast array of possible directions with which they may take their lives.

This is what I find to be most unique, and most important about this particular life phase in the United States: that it is a time of unprecedented self-exploration and experiment. It is therefore this explorative, experimental element which I most wish to evoke when choosing a term for the life phase that follows adolescence. Through a ritual succession of trial-and-error attempts at self-discernment, U.S. youngsters are expected to gain the necessary external experience and internal insight to become sovereign citizens. This trial-and-error method is particularly exaggerated within the university environment, where students are encouraged to explore different options before committing to a major, and even then they are allowed the opportunity to change majors at any point in their studies. Writes Arnett:

> "In many ways, the American college is the emerging adult environment par excellence. It is expressly designed for the *independent explorations* that are at the heart of emerging adulthood."[17] (Emphasis mine)

Because my study focuses on a student-driven event, I am inclined to seek a root word which highlights this tendency toward independent exploration. Terms like *experimental, explorative,* and *probationary,* for example, resonate not only for this age group generally, but for the chosen subgroup of college students particularly. "Ex," however, implies an outward movement, and much of the testing undergone during this life phase is internal. Therefore I will begin with the root "prob" from the Latin *probare* meaning to test or prove worthy. This seems particularly appropriate, since people in this life phase are not only engaged in self-testing, they are being continually tested by outside forces as to their worthiness: by peers, by professors, by employers, by police, by parents, and by society-in-general as embodied in the media.

As to the suffix, frankly I find "-escence" much more elegant and satisfying than "-hood." "Probescence" and "probescent," however, have the unfortunate distinction of connoting pre-pubescence, an era which most people who have successfully navigated the treacherous transition that is post-industrial puberty would much prefer to forget. Therefore I will shorten my neologisms to *probience,* referring to the life-phase between adolescence and adulthood, and *probient,* referring to those individuals experiencing said life-phase.

2. Isla Vista, identity laboratory

I readily admit that the sample of probients upon which my study will be focused is not intended to be representative, but rather is culturally and geographically specific. The unparalleled opportunities for individual transformation which Cook and Furstenburg attribute to young people in the U.S. generally are not in fact universally available, but are more or less reserved for those probients whose parents fall within the middle-to-upper economic brackets.[18]

Despite the slummish conditions in which many of them dwell in Isla Vista (see section four), the majority of students attending UC Santa Barbara come from relatively wealthy homes: the parents of approximately 60% of incoming freshmen in the years 2002, 2003, and 2004 made more than $60,000 per year.[19] According to Sal Castillo of the UCSB office of Institutional Research, UCSB has for many years held the distinction of attracting the most students whose parents belong to the highest income bracket ($100,000 or more). However, Castillo also noted that UCSB has been relatively successful (within the UC system) in recruiting students from the lowest income brackets, making UCSB's population unusually extreme in its class distinctions.[20]

The opportunity for identity exploration and self-transformation is therefore already well within the grasp of most UCSB students, while for a minority of students, particularly those whose attendance at UCSB is made possible through the Educational Opportunity Program (E.O.P.), their time at college may well mark their first, and perhaps their last chance to indulge in full-time self-exploration.

I will argue that Halloween is in large part a celebration and a seizing of that opportunity, and for some, an occasion on which to flaunt, or to mock, the self-absorption afforded by leisure and privilege. The majority of revelers having left high school (and, often, their parents' homes) within the last four years, they find within the university environment an opportunity to re-envision themselves; no longer surrounded by people who know them as they were, college students are able to consider new possibilities, to be as they might (like to) be. This exciting air of possibility-in-anonymity is amplified through the carnivalesque Halloween conventions of disguise and playacting, fostering feelings of freedom from social rules, expectations, and consequences.

Furthermore, as I will argue in my conclusion, the Halloween carnival in Isla Vista carries the potential not just for individual but for socio-cultural experimentation and exploration. Isla Vista has itself been considered an experimental community, a self-conscious breeding-ground for revolutionary thinkers and social activists (see section four). In this sense, the Del Playa street party may be seen not merely as an expression of what U.S. college culture *is*, but as an open-air laboratory for testing new possibilities of what it, and what U.S. culture more generally, *might* be.

That is not to say that the social experiments witnessed at Halloween time are undertaken in a consciously revolutionary spirit, nor that participants would be particularly pleased to hear me compare their activities to the academic research they believe themselves to have left on campus. On the contrary, I recognize identity formation to be a largely unconscious process, deeply rooted in fantasy and the collective imaginary.

As Jagodzinski explains, the ideological reproduction of the Symbolic Order (subjective reality) requires that subjects maintain a certain degree of ignorance of, or at least disregard to, what they are doing. This brings to mind the Heideggerian paradox that often, the closer we are to an object or concept, both in terms of proximity and familiarity, the farther we are from comprehending it. In his 1929 essay "Vom Wesen des Grundes" (The Essence of Reason), Martin Heidegger described human Dasein (being-present or consciousness) as nurtured by distance, and ironically posited that distance as the only true means of establishing true closeness to things and fellow beings.[21]

The revelers' immersion in the process of identity formation in many ways conceptually blinds them to that process: they are only aware of enjoying themselves. As Arnett acknowledges, "many of the identity explorations of the emerging adult years are simply for fun, *a kind of play*[...]." Nevertheless, he describes this kind of playful exploration as part of a gradual move toward the very serious task of self-definition.[22] Likewise, the conceptual blindness of the Isla Vistan revelers in no way hinders the effectiveness of the Halloween street party as a means of discerning individual and collective identity. On the contrary, as Jagodzinski suggests, it is a necessary component therein.

Nevertheless, this complex, multilayered college carnival is largely met with condescension – if not outright condemnation – from non-participants, who tend to dismiss the event as being little more than an annual excuse for binge drinking and destructive behavior. Considerable effort and resources have been poured into restricting the festivities over the years (see part two). That Halloween in Isla Vista has not merely survived, but actually flourished under extremely hostile conditions is significant in that it parallels the history of some of the most famous carnivalesque festivals world-wide.

In sifting through the archives at *The Daily Nexus*, UCSB's student-run newspaper, I was repeatedly struck by a dual sense of *déjà-vu*: not only did history seem to repeat itself in Isla Vista, it seemed to be reproducing quite a different history: that of the Trinidad Carnival.[23] Common to both festivals are: continual complaints from authorities and community members about the raucous festivities; repetitive, nostalgic declarations that this year's party was no match for the celebrations of "years past"; sporadic doomsday predictions that the festival is "dying out"; and an endless, strongly resisted struggle to regulate the more violent and vulgar aspects of the celebration by local authorities.

As a relatively young carnivalesque festival, Halloween in Isla Vista has not yet collected the kind of historical legacy characteristic of the world's best-known carnival masquerades, and therefore lacks the semiotic richness and organizational infrastructure under-girding these well-studied events. Yet the controversy generated by this annual public party suggests that it serves the same complex, often contradictory social functions as do the numerous Carnival celebrations throughout the Caribbean islands (see section two).

Like its Caribbean forebears, Halloween in Isla Vista has been continually maligned as unnecessary and a scourge upon local society. Following in the footsteps of those who have defended carnival celebrations in Europe, the Caribbean, and other parts of North America as being worthy of academic attention,[24] I hope to convince skeptics that Halloween in Isla Vista is much more than "just a party": it is a complex carnival that serves multiple functions within the social spaces of Isla Vista and the surrounding communities.

Let me be clear about this: I am not arguing that Halloween in Isla Vista should be viewed as "harmless" experimentation, or that its functional aspects somehow neutralize its negative impact on the community. On the contrary, like any laboratory, Del Playa is indeed a dangerous space: the volatile combination of impulsive expression and rejection of responsibility on the part of the revelers breeds both creativity and catastrophe. My intent is not to minimize the very real problems associated with Halloween in Isla Vista, but simply to approach the event, and the college culture of which it is a product and a reflection, as serious subjects of inquiry.

Research on student culture has thus far primarily regarded manifestations such as the Del Playa street party (when it has regarded them at all) as problems to be solved, or as radical political gestures to be glorified.[25] I argue that student-driven carnivalesque events like Halloween in Isla Vista should instead be regarded as opportunities to explore the interplay between the global carnivalesque and U.S. institutions of higher learning.

FORM FOLLOWS FUNCTION

METHODOLOGY

This being the first academic inquiry into both the past and the present of the Halloween event in Isla Vista, it was necessary to undertake a good deal of archival and field research in addition to consulting secondary sources. My most invaluable archival resource was the UC Santa Barbara student newspaper, *El Gaucho*, renamed *The Daily Nexus* in 1970. In addition to the *Gaucho/Nexus*, I perused back issues of the *Santa Barbara News Press*, as well as the University Archives, including several UCSB *La Cumbre* yearbooks, as well as administrative meeting minutes and planning reports. Also extremely useful was the video footage taken by participants (Bruce Gordon, Sevan Matossian and Greg Shields), by the Isla Vista Foot Patrol, and by local resident Robert "Bob" Lewis.

In addition to archival research, I made use of Oral Histories, conducting a number of tape-recorded interviews, telephone conversations, and/or email correspondence with people who lived in Isla Vista, were affiliated with the University, and/or attended the Halloween event at some point in its history.

I also conducted interviews—some formal, some informal—with current participants, police officers, UCSB administrators and professors, and Isla Vista residents, before, during, and after Halloween in

2003, 2004, and 2005. The list of those interviewed may be found in the Reference section. These interviews I supplemented with two questionnaires, one in 2003 and one in 2004. The 2003 questionnaire was distributed to random students during and after the Halloween celebration.

From this first experience I learned several things: first, students cannot be counted upon to voluntarily fill out and return a questionnaire unless they are given some incentive (i.e. extra credit for a class) to do so; second, the multiple choice set-up I had chosen for the first question was rather leading; and third, even such contrivedly random distribution did not guarantee a diverse sampling of responses. Thus I made the following changes the following year: I used more open-ended questions and encouraged students to share whatever thoughts or ideas they had about Halloween, and I collaborated with an instructor (Marc Shaw), who assigned the questionnaire as part of his class curriculum. The 2004 questionnaire was thus distributed to students in DA 60: Appreciation of Theatre, a large lecture course in Dramatic Arts aimed at non-majors. I chose DA 60 students as my sample population for two reasons: first, because Halloween in Isla Vista, with its proliferation of street theatre and enforced participation in ritual performance, fit neatly into the curriculum; second, because the course, which fulfills a "General Education" requirement at UCSB, attracts a wide variety of students, making for a relatively random cross-section of participants. The two questionnaires can be found in the Reference section.

Finally, I attended four Halloween celebrations in Isla Vista, between the years 2002 and 2005. During Halloween 2004 and 2005, I stayed "in the field" each night of a four-five night street party, observing interactions on Del Playa and nearby streets, and a number of private parties, until the streets began to empty in the wee hours of the morning. While observing and interacting with participants, I recorded extensive field notes into a miniature hand-held tape recorder, which I later transcribed and supplemented with retrospective insights. Additionally, in 2004 I was joined by a group of graduate students taking a Performance Studies seminar taught by Professor

Catherine Cole (Dramatic Arts). These students were assigned to observe the Halloween festivities for at least one hour on one of the three major nights of celebration (Friday, Saturday, Sunday), and to write up their observations in the form of Ethnographic field notes. Many of the students stayed for much longer than the requisite hour, and a couple of them returned for multiple nights. The resulting notes yielded multiple perspectives on the event, both in the sense that more pairs of eyes in more locations means more interactions observed, and in the sense that each observer brought to the event a unique reading of its functions and meanings. A list of participating graduate students can also be found in the Reference section.

THE LAY OF THE LAND

SECTION OVERVIEW

This study attempts to answer several broad questions about the relationship of the carnivalesque to college.

First: What is the carnivalesque, and how does it function in the contemporary United States? Part two is devoted to exploring this question, examining various theories of the carnivalesque and considering their applicability to millennial U.S. culture.

Second: Should events like Halloween in Isla Vista—i.e. large probient gatherings on or near college campuses—be considered carnivalesque? In other words, do such events fulfill the functions of a carnivalesque festival, as described in part two? In part three, I explore this question through the representative example of Halloween in Isla Vista, examining both the historical development of the event, and its current place within the local community.

Part four provides a short history of Isla Vista itself, in an effort to contextualize the Halloween event within this highly specific cultural-geographical milieu, and to clarify connections between the community's unusual social structure and the persistence of the annual bacchanal.

The third broad-ranging question my study attempts to answer is: What can be learned about contemporary U.S. college culture—as I have argued, an important key to comprehending global capitalist culture—by reading carnivalesque events like Halloween in Isla Vista as cultural performances? In other words: if the public performance of Halloween in Isla Vista is an expression of who the revelers are as a group (i.e. U.S. probients), what does that portrait look like when examined, and re-examined, from various theoretical perspectives? Part five takes a close reading of the costumes worn by the majority of the revelers, exploring their function within the celebration and probing into the kinds of messages the wearers are circulating, consciously or otherwise, through their physical appearance. Viewing Del Playa as a designated performance space during Halloween weekend, I argue that the costume choices made by participants may be interpreted just as those worn for any other theatrical event: they offer vital clues into what sort of world is being created, what kinds of people populate that world, and what kind of response is sought from audience members.

My conclusion aims to re-examine the function of U.S. institutions of higher learning by gazing at contemporary academia through the looking-glass of carnivalesque experimentation. Drawing parallels between Mardi Gras in New Orleans (specifically the 2006 celebration) and Halloween in Isla Vista, I propose a creative, intellectual function for the carnivalesque within U.S. society, and posit that this function is most sorely needed within the increasingly mechanized realm of contemporary U.S. higher education.

PART II
IN SEARCH OF THE U.S. CARNIVALESQUE

THE CARNIVALESQUE AS A GLOBAL PHENOMENON

"The carnivalesque has not disappeared from Western society. It persists in numerous scattered festivals, rites, and performances, ranging from ritualized, transvestite-costumed attendance at screenings of *The Rocky Horror Picture Show* to […] contemporary Halloween celebrations."

- Russell W. Belk [1]

A damn good Halloween

It is nearly four a.m., and the last night of the Isla Vista Halloween carnival for the year 2005 is in its final throes. Having been invited to observe a gathering at the home of a reveler whom I will call "Alice," I and a fellow graduate student, Hank, are fighting sleep as the last of the die-hard partiers evacuate the premises, much to Alice and her roommates' apparent relief. Hank offers to make fried peanut-butter and banana sandwiches – "Elvis' favorite food" he tells us – and no one refuses. As he cooks, Alice and her roommates go to their respective rooms to change out of their Victoria's Secret Angel costumes, and return to eat the oozing golden-brown triangles in their pajamas. "Well," says a roommate, holding up a glass of water as if to propose a toast, "we didn't get cited, we didn't get arrested, we didn't get hurt, and we walked around in our fucking underwear." "Yeah," Alice concurs, nodding sleepily and smiling, "It was a damn good Halloween."

What makes a "damn good Halloween" [carnival]? What is the carnivalesque and how is it manifest within the contemporary United States? In this chapter, I will seek a broad theoretical framework for the U.S. carnivalesque by interrogating existing carnival theories and exploring their applicability to post-millennial United States culture. I will then propose a specific event/location where I believe much carnivalesque energy to reside, and the remainder of the sections will be dedicated to examining that event as a representative example of the U.S. carnivalesque, using this new theoretical framework to help tease out its social-cultural features and functions.

Many a tree and countless cartridges of ink have been sacrificed in the name of scholarship on the carnivalesque in the Americas, particularly within the last decade or so.[2] However, the vast majority of that scholarship has concentrated on Caribbean carnival and its most immediate United States ancestors, Mardi Gras in New Orleans and Brooklyn's Labor Day Carnival.[3] In fact, there seems to be some doubt as to whether carnivalesque masquerade, as it exists and has been studied in Europe, the Caribbean, and elsewhere, has a recognizable United States equivalent that is not directly derivative of these other festivals. I will argue that there most certainly is such an equivalent, and that it deserves the same detailed degree of scholarly attention as that paid to its Caribbean, South American, and European cousins.

1. "AMERICAN CARNIVAL," or carnival in America?

The first problem when searching for the United States equivalent of "carnival" is the conceptual confusion surrounding the term itself.

The word "carnival" when used in the context of the United States has largely become synonymous with a specific kind of entertainment, often found at agricultural ("County") fairs, and with the traveling performers and side-show "freaks" who once inevitably accompanied such entertainments, popularly referred to as "Carnies." Yet even within that narrow "American" usage, the definition of "carnival" remains divided: it is simultaneously a reference to an antiquated practice, and to a contemporary practice, as well as a catch-all buzz-word intended to describe U.S. culture in general. Thus while Leslie Prosterman can elaborate for several pages on the reactions of Midwesterners to the inclusion of "carnival" in their county fair and draw clear distinctions between "fair" and "carnival" aesthetics, [4] pop cultural critic James B. Twitchell can use the term "Carnival Culture" as a shorthand way of describing the postmodern breakdown of the once-clear dividing line between "high" and "low" aesthetics in the United States in general.[5] Meanwhile, American cultural critic Philip McGowan reads "American carnival" as "a term connoting the capacity of US culture to employ a mode and method of seeing that operates along contours of race, ethnicity, and Otherness," and insists that "as a critical term, it resists categorization to Bakhtinian definitions of carnival."[6]

Within this wide-ranging usage, I do see a common thread binding the cultural phenomena described by Prosterman (a recognizable form of popular American entertainment), Twitchell (the disappearance of apparent distinctions between high and low cultural forms), and McGowan (the spectacular display of the subversive for the purpose of reifying mainstream American culture), and that is a conceptual link to *aesthetics*. In other words, "American carnival" is most commonly understood as a reference to a set of *aesthetic* practices associated with popular (i.e. "mainstream") United States culture. This understanding of carnival as a pop cultural aesthetic category is certainly useful, both as an analytical tool in the study of United States culture, and as a means of distinguishing between "American carnival" and carnival as it is understood in other parts of the world. However, it has had the unfortunate effect of relegating theories of carnival within the U.S. entirely to the aesthetic realm, and of severing conceptual links to the carnivalesque as a global phenomenon.

I do not question that the concept of carnival within the cultural context of the United States has taken on meanings that are specific to that milieu, nor do I question the validity and utility of those idiosyncratic meanings. However, I insist that their presence does not preclude the existence, within that same cultural-geographical milieu, of those cultural phenomena that have come to reside under the heading of carnival within global parlance. In short, my interest here is *not* in "American carnival," but in carnival—that is, *the carnivalesque* as a global phenomenon—as it is manifest in the United States at the turn of the millennium.

2. Bathing in the mud: law and the carnivalesque

"Without a valid law to break, carnival is impossible."

- Umberto Eco[7]

Before investigating the place of the carnivalesque in United States society, we must first tackle a more basic, and at the same time more problematical issue: What is the carnivalesque? How does it function, particularly in relation to authority and behavioral regulation within a given society? In this section, I will examine two major theoretical perspectives on this matter: the Bakhtinian, and the post-Bakhtinian.

The notion of the carnivalesque was most famously theorized by Russian writer Mikhail Bakhtin (1895-1975) as a celebration providing "temporary liberation from the prevailing truth and from the established order" that "marked the suspension of all hierarchical rank, privileges, norms, and prohibitions."

Although his scholarship focused specifically on carnival celebrations in medieval Europe, Bakhtin's ideas formed the basis of carnivalesque theory, the original assertions regarding what carnival is, how it functions, and why it is important.

> "Carnival," wrote Bakhtin, "was the true feast of time, the feast of becoming, change, and renewal. It was hostile to all that was immortalized and completed."[8]

Thus, to Bakhtin, carnival's main function was to celebrate change, renewal, and possibility within a seemingly fixed social order. He argued that through "gay relativity," or the temporary suspension of social hierarchy, and "grotesque realism," or an exaggerated emphasis on the materiality of the physical body, carnival is able to provide participants with a "second life," one "organized on the basis of laughter," and capable of challenging the sanctioned reality of the first.[9]

Bakhtin argued that carnivalesque performance could be, and often has been, an agent of permanent social change. He saw the inversions, subversions, degradations, and exaggerations of carnival as revolutionary in spirit, able to liberate participants through the ritualized reversal of accepted order. I define that accepted order, the "first" life against which carnival is staged, as *adherence to culturally-defined classifications*.

As Anthropologist Mary Douglas argues in her foundational text on taboo and pollution behavior, *Purity and Danger*, every culture has a series of "cherished classifications" which make up the basis of their schema or collective world-view.[10] In order to reinforce those classifications, a complex set of rules and conventions is created, as well as a system of dangers and/or punishments for those who fail to conform.

For example, extra-marital sex poses a direct threat to the institutions of marriage, (heteronormative) monogamy, and patriarchal lineage. Therefore, in many cultures (such as the Nuer in East Africa) adultery is considered dangerous and is attached to a whole host of pollution behaviors. In some places, it is believed that adulterers themselves will become sick, in other places it is the offended spouse who is said to fall sick because of their spouse's philandering, and in still other places, it is the children or parents of the adulterer who will suffer the consequences. In all cases, the threatening activity (in this case adultery) is believed to "pollute" the community, putting at least one person, and often many people, in danger.[11]

Another common trigger for pollution behavior is liminality (the condition of being in-between established stages or categories). People in transitional phases, such as fetuses in utero, older children entering puberty, women in the midst of menstruation, the ill or dying, etc., are often considered dangerous to the social order. For this reason they are frequently separated out from general society and marginalized until some recognizable shift in their status occurs, often accompanied by a ritual of re-integration.[12]

Douglas insists that industrialized society is far from immune to pollution behavior, but that our scientific understanding of microbes, etc., has divided our ideas about purity and contagion—our notion of "dirt"—into two distinct categories: "hygiene, and respect for conventions."[13] The rules of hygiene shift as our understanding of what makes us ill changes and expands, but the rules of non-pathogenic social decorum remain remarkably constant. Douglas describes the social, non-pathogenic understanding of dirt as simply "matter out of place," i.e. indoor things outdoors, outdoor things indoors, upstairs things downstairs, underclothes worn on the outside, etc. There is nothing inherently dirty about, say, a washing machine, until it is left out on a front lawn. Likewise, food is not dirty in the context of the kitchen or the dining room, but when discovered in the bedroom, or spattered on one's shirt, it triggers a pollution reaction, in that we often feel compelled to remove it.

> "In short, our pollution behavior is *the reaction which condemns any object or idea likely to confuse or contradict cherished classifications* " (emphasis mine).[14]

This system of cherished classifications is precisely the "sanctioned reality" to which Bakhtin refers. Carnival in Bakhtin's view, then, is the adult equivalent of children playing in the mud: a deliberate indulgence in "dirt," in those elements that have been rejected from the ordered social system. Yet because this public mud-bath is undertaken collectively and/or (theoretically) anonymously, the resulting pollution behavior is suspended: the usual reaction of fearing, condemning, and punishing transgression is transformed into collective delight in consciously defying convention.

In fact, it seems to me that by Bakhtin's description of the phenomenon, carnival could indeed be capable of *undermining* pollution behavior. By deliberately confusing and contradicting cherished classifications, carnivalesque behavior could alleviate irrational fear and condemnation of the unconventional, and create a space of possibility wherein new modes of being might be safely introduced into the social lexicon on a more permanent basis. For example, by this logic, the proliferation of drag during carnival time could eventually alleviate social anxieties surrounding the blurring of gender roles.

Bakhtin's theory is an attractive one. It is tempting indeed to view the carnivalesque, which is characterized by celebration, indulgence, and pleasure-taking, as an effective means of challenging the status quo, as indeed many subsequent theorists have done to some degree.[15] Yet Bakhtin's unbridled optimism is somewhat suspect, as the theoretical camp I have labeled "post-Bakhtinian" has effectively argued.

Theorists such as Simon Dentith, Terry Eagleton, Umberto Eco, V.V. Ivanov, Baz Kershaw, Brian Sutton-Smith, and Diana Kelly-Byrne call into question carnival's potential to incite meaningful social change, positing the temporary reversal of order during carnival as an ultimately conservative force. They view the feeling of liberation experienced by the revelers as illusory, a sanctioned game of make-believe designed to fool "the people" into believing that they are free agents and that change is possible, when in fact the balance of power remains unchanged, and social life will return to normal the moment carnival has ended.

Dentith, for example, emphasizes the mainstreaming function of historical carnivalesque celebrations such as the medieval *charivari*, whose focus was on humiliating those who had transgressed the norms of a given community. He writes:

> "The carnival inversions, the world-turned-upside-down of these festivities, were clearly not aimed at loosening people's sense of the rightness of the rules which kept the world the right way up, but on the contrary at reinforcing them."[16]

In other words, for Dentith, carnival serves as a warning, a periodical reminder of the danger of chaos, and actually *reinforces* the need for pollution behavior by publicly displaying the results – often grotesque and even terrifying – of going against the "natural" order.[17]

V.V. Ivanov also denies the revolutionary potential of the carnivalesque, describing the ostensibly transgressive enactments that take place during public festivals as direct inversions of binary oppositions, rather than as subversive re-alignments.[18] Brian Sutton-Smith and Diana Kelly-Byrne make a similar claim in *Masks of Play*, arguing that carnivalesque festivals provide a useful meta-communication about the society in which they take root by producing an "inverse text" of the community's norms and standards through their exaggerated reversal.[19] A useful image here might be a photographic negative: although the color scheme has been inverted, the picture remains intact, and may, in some instances, become clearer when viewed in reverse.

Umberto Eco argues even more emphatically that carnivalesque performances serve to fortify, rather than undermine, the existing order, drawing parallels between carnival and classical comic structure.

In comedy, notes Eco, there can be no irreversible consequences for the hero; rather, there is inevitably a "happy ending" in which all is put to rights, and his/her transgressions are forgiven and/or forgotten. In watching a comedy, the audience takes its delight in seeing someone get away with those things they would like to get away with, but don't dare attempt. Similarly, during carnival, each reveler gets to play the hero(ine) of his/her very own comical adventure, flouting taboos, bending rules, and, if all goes as planned, ending up approximately where her/his journey began.

Where would be the fun, Eco rhetorically inquires of us, if there were no rules to bend? He writes:

> "Carnival, in order to be enjoyed, requires that rules and rituals be parodied, and that these rules and rituals already be recognized and respected. One must [...] feel the majesty of the forbidding norm to appreciate their transgression. [...] In this sense, comedy and carnival [...] represent paramount examples of law reinforcement. They remind us of the existence of the rule."[20]

Eco further argues that the compliance of those in power confirms the underlying conservatism of carnivalesque reversals: by agreeing to be parodied, they are in fact affirming their dominant position. If, on the other hand, those in authority are taken by surprise, or some *un*authorized carnivalization unexpectedly occurs within the space-time of the "real" – i.e. quotidian life, "it is interpreted as a revolution," and quickly shut down.[21] In Eco's view, then, carnival is only carnival so long as it remains an *authorized* transgression; as such, it necessarily *reinforces authority*.

Yet, as I will argue in subsequent sections, the line between riot and revelry at carnivalesque events is often surprisingly thin. Sorting out which transgressions are authorized, and by whom, is not so simple in the context of a post-millennial United States. Therefore I find the assessment that carnival necessarily reinforces the status quo equally suspect to Bakhtin's belief that it necessarily disrupts it.

3. Dueling fathers: authority in the postmodern world

The two schools of thought I have thus far examined view the carnivalesque in black-and-white terms: either carnival is a revolutionary force, or it is a conservative force; either it undermines authority, or it reinforces authority. Neither conclusion feels accurate in the case of the contemporary United States.

The binary model on which both these schools of thought are based (carnival as agent of social change vs. carnival as opium of the masses) may well be useful in times and places where there is a distinct, repressive authority which is being reversed at carnival time. However, as Richard Schechner argues in his essay "Carnival (theory) after Bakhtin," contemporary North America is not the stratified, non-democratic society on which Bakhtin's observations were based. Rather, we are living in a dysfunctional "democracy" that is dependent upon the illusion of individual sovereignty, an illusion that must be perpetually reinforced through social and political rituals.

> "If people believe that they are collectively sovereign," asks Schechner, "then against whom is carnival staged? From what overall authority is carnival a relief?" [22]

This question of the "overall authority" against which revelers appear to be rebelling will be the central focus of this section: if we can recognize the specific power relationships being targeted for inversion in U.S. carnival, we can begin to understand the larger mechanisms that drive us as a society.

Yet as Schechner himself points out, the first half of his question makes a fairly vast assumption: do we contemporary U.S. residents genuinely believe ourselves to be collectively sovereign? This seems unlikely, considering our almost pathological need to be continually convinced of that sovereignty through rituals of democracy and consumerism, and through endlessly proliferating discourses of individualism and personal agency.

I tend to agree with radical performance theorist Baz Kershaw, who claims that "in the capitalist democracies, confidence in the legitimacy of established political processes is in a state of continual crisis." Kershaw connects this skepticism, ironically enough, with the apparent dearth of radical political theatre in the late 20th and early 21st centuries. "If few people really believe in the state," posits Kershaw, "then it is hardly worth attacking."[23]

The kind of spontaneous street theatre viewed at carnival time, however, appears to be on the rise in the contemporary United States. In following Kershaw's logic, if most people are convinced of their freedom and empowerment, they will hardly find it interesting or fulfilling to take part in rituals that provide a temporary feeling of power and liberation. So the proliferation of such rituals in the U.S. strongly suggests that a sizable contingent of U.S. citizens feel disempowered in one sense or another.

Writes Kershaw, "as a profoundly public genre, [street theatre] is inevitably thoroughly contaminated by its wider cultural context."[24] Hence, in a dysfunctional democracy categorized by widespread feelings of disempowerment, we can safely assume that carnivalesque street theatre will serve the double function of playing out democratic illusions and at the same time providing a sense of liberation from the oppressive forces they are intended to mask—in other words, from this mysterious "authority" against whom carnival is staged.

In light of this double-function of the carnivalesque within the contemporary U.S., the question will need to be rephrased: *what is the authority that encourages Americans to participate in carnivalesque rituals, and what is the authority against which they are rebelling through their participation?*

My answer is that these two authorities are in fact two aspects of the same cultural system, but in order to understand the way that system functions, it will be necessary to review the very concept of "authority" in 21st Century United States.

As Michel Foucault effectively argued in *Discipline and Punish*, the twin concepts of central authority and individual discipline were the defining principles of power relations in the 20th Century.[25] In the 21st Century, however, the concept of discipline has begun to disintegrate, throwing some of its primary institutions (the school, for instance) into crisis. A number of cultural critics have offered theories explaining this shift, and describing the new authoritative structures that have sprung up in place of the old.

In *Perform... Or Else!* Jon McKenzie argues that there is still an authoritative structure against which one might choose to rebel, albeit an increasingly decentralized, apolitical structure. McKenzie posits that performance, that is, the pressure to *perform* as a productive member of global capitalist society, has replaced the need for a (localized) political authority which must be deferred to and appeased.

> "Performance," argues McKenzie, "will be to the twentieth and twenty-first centuries what discipline was to the eighteenth and nineteenth, that is, an onto-historical formation of power and knowledge."[26]

This claim is supported by Kershaw, who argues for "the new importance of performance" as a key feature of "post-modernity," which he usefully defines as "an *as yet fictional* historical phase posited by post-modernism" or the theoretical perspectives developed by cultural critics in reaction to, and contestation of, modernity.[27] What he calls the "destabilisation of the cultural climate throughout the world" as the certainties of modernity disintegrate into debate, has increased the need for a continual stream of performance to establish and re-establish cultural stability, so that performance "becomes a major element in the continuous negotiations of power and authority."[28] This is largely accomplished through what Kershaw calls "mediatisation," or the dispersion of theatricality throughout the social fabric via television, film, and the internet.[29] This seepage of (theatrical) performance into everyday life means that social survival has become inextricably bound up with one's ability to *perform* any number of culturally-defined roles.

However, Kershaw stops short of connecting performance in the theatrical sense to the more technical usage of the term as a measure of adequacy for people, machines, and technologies. McKenzie's theory picks up where Kershaw leaves off, positing that *performance* has become a shorthand term for a vast array of normativising standards regarding how people and things (for he includes in this our increasingly personified technologies) are expected to *act* within postmodern society. We are no longer *told* what to do and how to behave: we are *shown* via performance, and it is made clear to us, without anyone having to explain as much, that if we do not perform up to standard, that contemporary society has no use for us.

Thus the concepts of discipline and punishment are still implicitly present within McKenzie's theory, as indeed the "...*Or Else*" of his title suggests. It seems that, in McKenzie's view, discipline and punishment have simply been recast from the authority of nation-states and other political entities to the increasingly diffuse and de-politicized corporate social machine.

Lacanian cultural critic Jan Jagodzinski is even more explicit about the disintegration of discipline in the postmodern era, describing postmodernity as "a radical time of decentering of authority" which he names "de-Oedipalization" or "post-Oedipalization." [30] He defines Oedipalization as "the pivotal process between the Imaginary order or primary narcissism of infancy and the establishment of the Symbolic Order"; in other words, the point at which the Law (conceptualized by Jagodzinski, after Lacan, in patriarchal terms as the "Oedipal father") replaces "the drives that batter on the Imaginary in the pre-Oedipal period."[31]

Oedipalization in the larger social realm might be understood as the process by which the Law is instilled into social interaction, deferring or delaying the immediate needs and desires of individuals in the name of a common or "greater" good; the process, in short, of *Civilization.*

In calling ours a "post-Oedipal" period, Jagodzinski does not mean to imply that we have somehow shed the patriarchal structure of modernity.

"The 'post' should not be read as a period following Oedipus," explains Jagodzinski, "but more as a disruption to patriarchy [from] within it which now takes a new form."[32] This "new form" of authority Jagodzinski names the "Jouissant" father, a pleasure-loving thrill-seeker who encourages his children to seek their hearts' desires, all others be damned.[33]

This disruption from within patriarchy has been made possible, argues Jagodzinski, by global capitalism, which has not only weakened the authority of the nation-state, it has undermined the very concept of obedience to any singular authority beyond one's own drives by setting up personal gratification as the greatest possible good. Indeed, the attainment of individual happiness via consumption is the sacred goal upon which postmodern capitalist culture is based; it therefore stands to reason that our (culturally-determined) desires have become the ultimate authority.

Given the carnivalesque's apparent emphasis on individual indulgence, it is difficult to view it as genuinely disruptive to capitalist values. Indeed, seen through the lens of Jagodzinski's theory, the extreme, excessive, decadent, self-indulgent behavior witnessed at carnival time is precisely *not* a reversal of capitalist culture, but rather its ultimate outcome.

Baz Kershaw links the contemporary carnivalesque, which he defines as "a cultural practice characterised by excess, immersion and the elimination of distance between subject and object," to "the development of post-industrial consumerism."[34] Carnival could thus be considered the postmodern cultural performance par excellence: a hedonistic, narcissistic celebration of the all-consuming Self as created in the image of the Jouissant father. This would seem to place Jagodzinski in the post-Bakhtinian theoretical camp, which views the temporary transgressions of carnival as upholding rather than undermining the dominant paradigm. But Jagodzinski does not view the transgressions of carnival as temporary, nor even as true transgressions.

"Designer capitalism," writes Jagodzinski, "is driven by an insatiable thirst of transgression."[35] In other words, within capitalist society, transgression becomes absorbed into the social economy to such a degree that it is neither disruptive of, nor even differentiable from quotidian existence. Rather, he posits carnivalesque revelry as a kind of public homage to that benevolent god of hedonistic pleasure, the Jouissant father. In fact, Jagodzinski claims that, under the rule of the Jouissant father, rebellion *of any kind* is impossible. "There is nothing to revolt against," he writes, "in a society that demands that satisfaction be met."[36] Hence, according to Jagodzinski, any apparent resistance or oppositional energy witnessed at carnival time should be viewed as a game of feigned transgression, the goal of which is to augment one's personal enjoyment while maintaining the illusion of an outside authority against which one may rebel.

Here again we find the rather questionable assumption that postmodern subjects are fully convinced and satisfied by the sense of individual sovereignty created through iterative rituals of consumption. We also find an interesting paradox given Jagodzinski's proclamation that the Oedipal and Jouissant fathers are "two sides of the same coin." Although they are perceived as binary opposites, writes Jagodzinski, "they flip from one to another at the very place where the Möbius band turns, [...] they exchange places when there is no longer a transcendent ideal to hold them apart and in tension."[37] If these two extremes, the father who always says "no / enough" and the father who always says "yes / more," are indeed one and the same, two different faces of the same inescapable Authority, then revolt would seem to be simultaneously impossible and *inevitable*, paradoxically absent and constantly present, since to rebel against one "father" is to do the bidding of the other.

The Oedipal father and the Jouissant father could not be said to *compete* with one another in the way that political candidates compete for votes, or suitors compete for the affections of a desired partner. Rather, they form an inseparable team, a highly functional "Good Cop-Bad Cop" partnership that has been extremely successful in shaping postmodern behavior, each instilling anxiety about the imminent takeover of his counterpart and the unbalanced dystopia that will surely result.

As global capitalism proliferates, the cultural reach of this twoheaded father-figure continues to expand. Argentine cultural theorist Beatriz Sarlo names the global market as having taken up "the baton dropped by authority."[38]

Rather than ruling through the threat of disempowerment (the psychoanalytic term would be "castration"), the global market rules by creating desire and promising gratification to those who conform to its aggressive ideal of relentless pleasure-seeking. To rephrase this idea in terms of *performance*: the market promises a culturally-defined ideal of personal enjoyment to those who can correctly perform their unending desire to attain that ideal. Like postmodern authority, the market, so argues Sarlo, "has two faces: It promises a form of ideal freedom as well as guaranteed exclusion." Within the discourse of the market, all consumers are created equal, and yet the reality is that "the market chooses those who are in a position to choose within it." [39] It is a circular, self-perpetuating system.

And as members of capitalist society are bombarded by images of others' cyclical performances of desire and enjoyment, they are aggressively compelled to perform their own desire and enjoyment with competing fervor. "The subject," writes Jagodzinski, "is constantly confronted by the Other's enjoyment, often in its most unbearable dimensions [...]; everywhere we see others satisfied, happy, and 'enjoying.' And so we are told to 'enjoy!'"[40] In fact, we are not only compelled to enjoy, we are haunted by the notion that we are not performing our enjoyment correctly. As Jagodzinski puts it:

> "We never feel as though we are [enjoying] adequately enough, nor feel that we have enough. Duty no longer lies in going to work and working hard—the boundaries between leisure and work become blurred for those who are "fully" enjoying. Money is earned so it can be spent on more pleasure."[41]

Thus production and consumption have merged into an undifferentiated mass of behavioral expectation, an endless cycle of competitive work and play that can be just as demanding as unquestioning adherence to a more overtly disciplinary authority. So upon closer inspection, the Jouissant father proves not only to be the partner of the Oedipal father, but to be equally as demanding and tyrannical. With all of this in mind, let us return to my earlier question:

> *What is the authority that encourages Americans to participate in carnivalesque rituals, and what is the authority against which they are rebelling through their participation?*

The authority that encourages participation in carnivalesque rituals is the Jouissant, pleasure-performing father; the authority against which participants rebel is the Oedipal, law-bound father.

Yet, as we have seen, these two "fathers" are not genuinely in opposition to one another. Rather, they two more-or-less interchangeable aspects of a single cultural system: the global capitalist market. Thus, within the market-driven cultural climate of the contemporary United States, the binary equation of adherence to authority versus rebellion against it is no longer a viable model for understanding the place and function of the carnivalesque.

New theoretical models must be sought out, models that do not conceptualize the carnivalesque in such binary terms (i.e. either they are supporting authority—inevitably understood as Oedipal, law-bound authority—or they are undermining it), but rather allow for a good deal of complexity and internal contradiction.

Fortunately, such models already exist, and a markedly large number of them have been created in response to a single event: the Trinidad Carnival. As I will demonstrate in chapter two, the history of the event I have chosen as my representative example of the U.S. carnivalesque (Halloween in Isla Vista, California) parallels that of the Trinidad Carnival in a number of ways. And as I will show in the next section, this history betrays a complex, contradictory relationship to authority, social regulation, and dominant ideologies that will be useful in seeking a theoretical model for carnivalesque events celebrated on U.S. soil.

4. Trinidad Carnival: a select history

The Trinidad Carnival has been marked, from its earliest days, by contradiction, paradox, and a dialectical tension between revelry and hierarchy, self-indulgence and social consciousness. As Milla Cozart Riggio and Richard Schechner argue in *Carnival: Culture in Action— The Trinidad Experience*, the Trinidad carnival "both critiques official culture and supports it."[42]

Marked by "multiplicity and contradictory intentions," the Trinidad Carnival, argue Schechner and Riggio, is a paradoxical balance of "top-down" (Oedipal) structure and "bottom-up" (Jouissant) impulse, a complex hybrid that reproduces the workaday world of hierarchy, competition, and territorialism, while at the same time inverting and mocking that world.[43]

Furthermore, the history of the event betrays a marked social anxiety surrounding its celebration, and a continual struggle to contain and control the festivities alongside contradictory rhetoric of permission for, and even support of, celebration of carnival. Much of this tension is centered around issues of identity and ownership, with the major fault lines arising between designations of race, gender, and especially class.

The Trinidad Carnival began in the early 19th century, with traditional pre-Lenten masquerading by homesick European settlers. As ex-police chief L.M. Fraser reported in 1881: "In former days and down to the period of the emancipation of the slaves the Carnival was kept up with much spirit by the upper classes" who could be seen driving through the streets of Port-of-Spain in elaborate masks and, in the evenings, making the rounds at the homes of other well-to-do Trinidadians, "which were all thrown open for the occasion." Although "Free Persons of Colour" were permitted to wear masks, they were "subjected to very stringent Regulations and [...] compelled to keep to themselves and never presumed to join in the amusements of the privileged class." Fraser describes the Indian population as keeping "entirely aloof," and the slaves as having "no share" in the festivities, "except as onlookers, or by special favor when required to take part."[44]

In this early era, the press spoke approvingly of Carnival as a festive, "high society affair," notes historian Errol Hill.[45]

But by the time the slaves were officially emancipated in August of 1834, Carnival had already begun to exhibit signs of a hostile takeover by those who had previously been banned from the celebration. It was clear there was no stopping the African (former slave) population from joining the festivities, or from adding their own traditions of masking, music, dance, satire, and ancestor worship to the Carnival celebrations. The resulting "creolized" Carnivals were greeted rather ambiguously, both by police and by upper-echelon Trinidadians, who felt they had been robbed of "their" Carnival.[46] Local papers teemed with editorials lamenting the raunchy behavior and indecent costuming of the working-class revelers. Take this public admonishment, printed in *New Era* on February 23rd, 1885:

> "It would be to the advantage of all parties, if *men dressed as women*, and *women in their bedroom costumes*, could be induced to turn their propensities for fun to better account."[47] (Emphasis mine)

As this editorial attests, cross-dressing was a popular source of complaint for high-society Trinidadians; deemed especially offensive was the practice of women dressing as men so as to indulge in unladylike behavior. In fact, some women were apparently prosecuted for cross-dressing in men's clothing, and/or for using indecent gestures, language, etc.[48]

Along with the annoyance of "women in their bedroom costumes," a long-standing pet peeve of the upstanding citizens of Trinidad was the unsettling practice of grown women dressing in schoolgirl uniforms which were far too small for them and therefore highly titillating to onlookers. On the island of Martinique, this "sexy schoolgirl" uniform evolved into the more "refined" tradition of the "bébé" costume: women dressed in the frilly trappings of baby dolls.[49]

The discomfort expressed by onlookers for all of the above listed costuming practices is reminiscent of Douglas's example of "under-clothing appearing where over-clothing should be" as an instance of conceptual "dirt" in Euro-American society.[50] Cross-dressing (i.e. drag), public display of clothing normally reserved for private space (i.e. the bedroom), adults dressed as children (or vice-versa), and cross-racial masquerading all share the common goal of deliberately confounding accepted classifications of identity. If a woman can put on a man's suit, the category of "man" is endangered. If a man can wear his private attire in public, the distinction between the public and private selves is imperiled. If a post-pubescent woman can wear the uniform of a schoolgirl, emphasizing its sexually alluring qualities, then the object "child" (as an innocent, pre-sexual being) is exposed as imaginary. And perhaps most dangerous within a racially segregated community, if a black man can put on a white mask, and a white man can paint himself black, the racial distinctions upon which the social hierarchy is based are necessarily called into question.

It is therefore unsurprising that the most reviled masking traditions were the racial transgressions witnessed at carnival time. White Trinidadians were known to dress as "Mulatresses" and "Negres de Jardin" (*Négue Jadin* in Creole), that is, black field workers, at their Masked Balls.[51] Worse still (in the opinion of the European elite, at least), black revelers shamelessly masqueraded as white folks. Cowley quotes a description by Charles William Day of the 1847 carnival:

> "Every negro, male and female, wore a white flesh-coloured mask, their wooly hair carefully concealed by handkerchiefs; this, contrasted with the black bosom and arms, was droll in the extreme. [...] The best embodiments were the Indians of South America, daubed with red ochre; personified by the Spanish peons from the Main, themselves half Indian, as testified by their exquisitely small feet and hands. Many of these had real Indian quivers and bows, as well as baskets; and doubtless, were very fair representatives of the characters they assumed. [...] I noticed that whenever a *black* mask appeared, it was sure to be a *white* man. [...] ...most of us were glad when the priestly saturnalia was over."[52]

Day expresses both discomfort and amusement at these cross-racial costuming practices: the "negro" ladies in white masks, and the "white" men in black masks, are treated as objects of derision ("droll in the extreme") and appear to be a large part of the reason (along with the noisy drumming and music that accompanied the revelry) so many of the (European) onlookers were relieved to see the end of "the priestly saturnalia." However, Day makes a noteworthy exception for the "Spanish peons," whose Indian embodiments he admires for their ostensible authenticity, although he admits that he has no real expertise on the subject.

His acceptance of the practice is apparently contingent on his ability to see these actors as authorized by blood right to portray

South American Indians in that they are, so he claims "themselves half Indian." He bases this claim on a physical trait, the "exquisite" smallness of their hands and feet, lending pseudo-scientific support to his theory and reinforcing the primacy of the "natural" body as the truth over which the revelers have layered their (ludicrous, misleading) cross-racial costumes.

In response to, or at any rate in tandem with, continued complaints from "upstanding" (read: upper-class, white) citizens, a series of police ordinances were instituted to try and regulate masking.[53] This did little to quash the spreading of Carnival fever, however, particularly among the black and East Indian populations, so that by 1846, the Trinidad police were moved to ban public masking altogether. The ban continued for many years, and by 1857 the belief began to circulate that Carnival was "dying out."[54]

The Trinidad doomsayers were, of course, incorrect: Carnival not only did not die out, it increased in both scope and popularity over the next few decades. However, much to the chagrin of its middle- and upper-class supporters, it also became an increasingly working-class affair during that period. Writes Anthropologist Philip W. Scher,

"Throughout the 1860s and 1870s and for much of the 1880s Carnival had been taken over by 'the lower orders.' Commonly known as the Jamette Carnival, the festival was the province of those people who dwelled below the 'diamètre,' the imaginary line that bisected society and divided it into the respectable and the criminal."[55]

These Jamette Carnivals were "often violent, sexually explicit affairs" that were equally offensive to the sensibilities of the ruling elite (white) and those of the middle class (mostly colored). Scher writes that "If there was one thing [both these groups] could agree upon, it was that something had to be done about Carnival. The difference lay in just what that was supposed to be."[56]

The white elite tended to favor strict reform measures, police ordinances in particular, while the colored middle-class press, writes Scher, "walked a fine line, criticizing ordinances intended to prohibit the event but supporting those ordinances designed to help control the event."[57] Colored Trinidadians were possessive of the Carnival tradition, which they viewed as the culmination of their combined European and African heritage. They therefore resented equally the underclass shenanigans, which they viewed as a threat to the respectability of "their" Carnival, and the police's perpetual threats to ban the festivities altogether.

A clear example were the reactions to the "Anti-Masquerader ordinance," passed in 1868, which banned the playing of instruments between midnight and six a.m.[58] The step was lauded by the white elite, who had long reviled the noisy, dusk-til-dawn revelry that had become traditional during Carnival time. The *Port of Spain Gazette*, for example, applauded the measure, insisting that Carnival was "essentially an un-English amusement" in any case, and should be "dealt with in the same manner as in the (European) countries from which it originated."[59] This was clearly a dig at the local French population, with whom the English perpetually quarreled, but also a disavowal of any desire for, or responsibility to, the current incarnation of Carnival on behalf of the ruling (English) elite.

The middle-class press, however, was more moderate in its reaction. The *Star of the West* published a statement in February of 1868 which argued that, although "there is at present much of evil and abuse in the popular observance of the Carnival," nevertheless, "reformation is better than destruction, and that to elevate and refine the amusements of the people is better than to forbid them altogether."[60]

The police were not inclined to listen to this middle-class sentiment, however; so long as they had the support of the ruling class, they aimed to crack down on Carnival with full force.

Particularly unsettling to officers was the popular activity of ritualized stick fighting: large groups of aggressive black men roaming the streets armed with sharp sticks (these groups were called "stickbands") piqued fears of revolt among Trinidadian authorities, leading officers to ban (and confiscate) any item which could be construed as a weapon.[61]

Despite the official ban, the stickbands were still going strong when Arthur Wybrow Baker was appointed Captain of the police. Captain Baker took it upon himself to rid Trinidad of stickbands altogether, often resorting to overtly violent tactics to achieve this goal. The resulting resentment among those dwelling below the "diamètre" culminated in the so-called "Canboulay Riots" of 1881. On the night of February 27, Baker and his men ambushed the bands as they began their traditional torchlight Canboulay procession.[62] Having had advanced warning of this attack, the stickmen had scattered sharp rocks along the streets, which they proceeded to hurl at Baker and his officers. The free fight which ensued between police and stickmen went on for nearly three hours, resulting in multiple and severe injuries on both sides.[63]

Although Baker did not succeed in stopping stickfighting altogether—the practice continued underground until its official unbanning in 1951—he did succeed in making it much less visible.[64] As a result, fighting sticks were (publicly) replaced with musical instruments, and calypso songs or stylized insults substituted for physical combat.[65]

Thus, in a roundabout way, we have the Canboulay riots to thank for the subsequent development of Calypso music.

In the wake of the violent events of 1881, R.G. Hamilton, a Colonial Office representative from London, was asked to write up a report recommending changes to the way Carnival is policed.[66] Many of his recommendations were subsequently adopted and, even more significantly, the attitude of the Colonial Office regarding the best means of tempering the revelers' rowdiness took a significant turn. As evidenced by a public statement issued from the office of the Colonial Secretary in 1882 offering "advice" to potential revelers, the authorities had at last concluded that Carnival could not simply be shut down, and that they were more likely to achieve positive results with respectful requests for cooperation than with threats.

"Let not any riotous or indecent behaviour on your parts stop to mar the pleasure of your sports, and by any uncalled for fight cast a stain on the Carnival of 1882," the Colonial Secretary appealed.[67]

The long-suggested *laissez faire* tactic appears to have been successful: the 1882 Carnival ranks among the most peaceful on record.

Large-scale violence has resurfaced only twice since that time, both in the 19th century: in 1884, this time in October rather than February, during the Muslim festival of Hosien,[68] and at the 1891 Carnival, when police forcibly shut down a lively dance party, resulting in a confrontation known as the "Arouca Riot."[69] Although this appears to have been the last of the official clashes between officers and revelers at Carnival, the mutual animosity and ambient tension between the two parties continued, and to some degree continues to this day. Carnival provides an annual opportunity for those tensions to be ritually played out on a public stage. As cultural critic Gerard Aching notes:

> "...amidst the annual revelry in which different classes and sectors of Caribbean society simultaneously took to the streets, the festivities also became events through which colonial authorities exercised, measured, and reaffirmed their power employing exhibited techniques of crowd control."[70]

In other words, the police officers in attendance at Carnival were giving (and still give today) their own performance, displaying their power over the revelers, and at the same time their ultimate powerlessness should the public fail to recognize the legitimacy of their authority.[71]

In the decades that followed the Arouca Riot, Carnival was slowly but steadily transformed by the increasingly powerful colored population into a reflection of middle-class values, and subsequently adopted as a respectable example of official "Trinidadian" culture. Although the act of masquerading continued from the early, upper-middle class Carnival, through the Jamette Carnival of the mid-late 19th century, to the 20th century colored middle-class Carnival, the purpose of donning a disguise and taking to the street clearly shifted from era to era. Scher suggests that:

The working class masquerade is very different from the middle-class masquerade in that the working-class masquerade is marked by a desire for freedom to act with authority, with a sense of power, while the middle-class masquerade is marked by disguise or freedom from the constraints of their own moral codes or a desire to forget the responsibilities that result from having power.[72]

Both of these types of masquerading have survived, and can be seen in the contemporary celebration of Trinidad Carnival.

The major innovations introduced by the middle class in the 20th century were not so much focused on what was and was not done during Carnival, but on *how* and *why* those activities were ostensibly to be undertaken. Whereas the Jamette Carnival was seen as a celebration of wanton idleness and anti-authoritarian spirit (both viewed as primary enemies of middle-class morality), the new Carnival was to be a shining example of enterprise and creativity. Competitions were instituted so that those activities previously seen as idle amusement could be redefined as legitimate enterprise. Notes Scher:

"Competitions function as a rationalization of artistic endeavor, herding it from display to enterprise. In the competition, one has to work for a prize, the process of which teaches diligence, dedication, and discipline."[73]

I would add that competition also teaches competitors to conform to standards and values imposed upon them by those empowered to judge. Hence, the introduction of competition to Carnival was a multi-layered victory for the pro-Carnival middle class: not only had they redeemed a reprehensible, reputation-besmirching activity (that is, participation in Carnival) into a relatively socially-acceptable pursuit, they had created a means not only of publicly glorifying middle-class values, but of actively *imposing* them upon Trinidadian society as a whole.

Along with competitions came commercial sponsorship, hierarchy, and the creation of a new cultural elite. The cultural product known as "Carnival," aggressively advertised on the global market, is the direct result of the middle-class push toward structure and competition. Writes Scher:

> "The organization of Carnival into competitions, each with a distinctive focus (i.e. calypso, steelband, masquerade) and oriented toward a capital reward, lay the foundations for the commodified cultural products that are part of Carnival today."[74]

So although the middle-class succeeded in saving Carnival from extinction at the hands of the authorities, they are equally responsible for transforming it into an immanently marketable cultural commodity. Ironically, this has created what Scher terms "a kind of terminal nostalgia" for a spontaneous, non-commercial Carnival that most likely only ever existed in the Trinidadian collective imagination.[75]

Such nostalgia is certainly not unique to Trinidadians: in fact is seems to be one of the defining qualities of carnivalesque festivals the world over. Pining for the "good old days" when the celebration was purer, more innocent, less structured, less touristy (etc.) is an outright epidemic among participants in every event event discussed in this book.

As longtime burner James G. notes of Burning Man in the "Burning Man Re-Embered" chapter of my conclusion:

> "Every year, people complain that it's not as good as it used to be. But they were saying the same thing even back in '97! 'Oh it's terrible this year, it was so much better ten years ago.' I think there's always that sense of nostalgia, that it was better in the old days."

In many ways this is perfectly understandable: such longing for a mythic moment of innocence and purity echoes the Societal nostalgia (discussed in my introduction) for Childhood, as well as the underlying individual nostalgia for an impossible Jouissant wholeness of the self. However, in terms of performed rituals such as carnival, nostalgia for long-dead traditions is rather misguided.

This is because ritual is not, and in fact can never be static and unchanging, as performance theorist Margaret Thompson Drewal argued in *Yoruba Ritual*. The act of repetition or *mimesis* necessarily creates difference, even as it provides a comforting sense of stability, familiarity, and predictability. "Repetition," writes Drewal, "is the common denominator for differentiation."[76]

Within the larger structure of a ritual that is repeated (though never *duplicated*) at some predictable interval, there is a good deal of "repetition with revision," a formulation Drewal credits to African American literature theorist Henry Louis Gates Jr., or "repetition with critical difference," which she borrows from parody theorist Linda Hutcheon.

The idea is that, in terms of live performance, repetition necessarily implies revision: no matter how faithfully the actors follow the script, there is always some degree of spontaneity or *improvisation* in play. Just as Butler has argued of "subversive/disruptive repetition," Drewal's formulation of repetition within ritual practice describes it as a creative act, one capable of engendering change. "Improvisation is transformational," writes Drewal.[77]

This is true not only in terms of the ability of improvisational performance to transform the structure, meaning, and content of the ritual itself, but in terms of the ritual's ability to transform the performers and observers. As Drewal notes, "Practitioners of Yoruba religion are aware that when ritual becomes static, when it ceases to adjust and adapt, it becomes obsolete, empty of meaning, and eventually dies out."[78]

In other words, rituals that cease to transform will lose the power to transform participants, and will therefore have outlived their usefulness as rituals.

My interest here is not in discovering some static U.S. carnival tradition that can be neatly summed up, captured on film, shuffled into a museum, and pointed to as a proud example of "our" carnivalesque. Rather, I am on the trail of a living carnivalesque ritual that changes and adapts to suit the transformative needs of a specific group of U.S. residents: college students.

. . .

5. "New World" carnival scholarship

As this brief history demonstrates, the Trinidad Carnival is a complex and contradictory event, and one in which both the Jouissant and Oedipal fathers feature prominently. Since the United States shares Trinidad's complex relationship to authority, it would seem a more fruitful exercise to examine the theoretical frameworks that have been created in response to the Trinidad Carnival itself, rather than relying on the Bakhtinian and post-Bakhtinian viewpoints, which are largely based on the European carnivalesque.

For, while these two ostensibly opposing camps disagree about the social *function* of carnival (i.e. whether it is ultimately a liberating or a conservative force), they do appear to be in accord in regards to its *structure* as a ritual reversal of the social norms, rules, and hierarchies accepted during the remainder of the year. This structural account, however, simply does not appear to hold true in what Peter Burke has termed the "New World carnival."[79]

In addition to embracing complexity and paradox, the new generation of Caribbean carnival scholars has largely rejected the idea of carnival as an exceptional moment of social opposition, a temporary reversal of quotidian existence.

As Richard D. E. Burton argues in *Afro-Creole: Power, Opposition and Play in the Caribbean*, "What happens during the four days of carnival in Trinidad is not *fundamentally* at variance with what happens during the remaining 360-plus days of the year."[80] Rather, he views carnival as an *intensification* of everyday life in the Caribbean. "During carnival time," Burton argues, "various strands of 'normal' Trinidadian social and cultural life [...] knit together to form a nexus of particular intensity."[81] Burton is thus arguing that carnival is precisely *not* a temporary reversal of the social order, but is rather an isolation, and an exaggeration, of the status quo.

Gerard Aching takes this idea even further in his exploration of the political potential of masquerade, *Masking and Power*. Writes Aching,

"…Styles and modes of public visibility during carnival have historically described and embodied fundamental aspects of both the organization and contestation of social hierarchies. Hence, it is not that surprising that these styles and modes also provide important information about social conduct in Caribbean societies *during the rest of the year*."[82]

Again, Aching recognizes the contradictory functions of Caribbean carnival, and his insistence that it is, hence, "not that surprising" that similar modes and styles of public visibility would prove useful in deciphering social life in the Caribbean year-round suggests that quotidian Caribbean life is marked by similar contradictions, and a similarly ambiguous attitude toward authority.

However, Aching does not conclude (as Burton does) that because Caribbean carnival—and therefore Caribbean culture more generally —is not overtly nor exclusively aimed at overturning the status quo, that it is therefore apolitical and lacking in long-term revolutionary potential. Rather, Aching describes "the repeated… and partly hidden manifestations" of carnival in the Caribbean as a kind of "lower-frequency" politics. Aching has borrowed the notion of "politics on a lower frequency" from Paul Gilroy's *The Black Atlantic* (1993), and uses it to defend masquerade as a viable form of activism. Writes Aching:

"Popular revolts, it is often argued, fail because they are chaotic, carnivalesque, or improvised, and, subsequently, because they supposedly fall short of achieving the status of those famous, occidental narratives of revolution that emerged at the end of the eighteenth and beginning of the nineteenth centuries."[83]

Citing the theories of Karl Marx and Slavoj Žižek, Aching argues that the process of revolution must necessarily include numerous small-scale revolts and rebellions, including multiple failed attempts and false starts, most of which will be carnivalesque (in the sense of spontaneous and chaotic), and many of which will not be recognized as revolutionary at the time.

His aim is to correct the "limited view that Caribbean masking practices and other manifestations of popular urban culture are *merely* symbolic sites of subversive activities and, by implication, *failed* attempts at transforming the social order."[84]

This is a view which, as we have seen, has enjoyed a certain vogue, particularly among Marxist scholars, in the latter 20th century. Yet carnivalesque revelers rarely, if ever, consciously set out to create permanent social upheaval, so to call their manifestations "failed attempts" at doing so is both unjust and inaccurate.

Rather, Aching proposes that Caribbean carnivals should "be valorized as instances of *lower-frequency politics* that do not always aim to achieve social upheaval but seek to gain and maintain visible representation within the region's democracies" (emphasis mine).[85] That representation, he argues, is ultimately more useful and, over the long-term, more likely to yield permanent and sustainable social change, than the kind of dramatic, sudden upheavals which have come to be defined as "revolutionary" since the 18th and 19th centuries.

Aching names the act of masquerading in particular as being fraught with incremental revolutionary potential. "Masking and mimicry in specific instances," insists Aching, are tactical activities[86] that "constitute effective lower-frequency politics."[87]

As an example, Aching describes certain "disguises" adopted during Carnival that are not so much intended to conceal identity as to induce *recognition* of the social reality in which the masqueraders exist year-round. When black Caribbean revelers smear their face with molasses and soot in order to enact the traditional characters of the *negue jadin* ("garden" negro or domesticated servant) and the *jab molassi* (from the French *diable molassié*, literally the "molasses devil," or parody of an off-the boat African "heathen"), they are not disguising their marginalized condition, but rather exaggerating it.

These examples are excellent reminders that a disguise is not necessarily intended to distort or conceal identity, but rather to manipulate identity to achieve a desired effect. As Aching insists, scholars must transcend the romantic notion of a mask as concealing a "true" identity if they are to understand the political function of masquerade.

Ironically, Aching describes the effect of coming into contact with a masked subject as one of "an unexpected and undesirable *self*-recognition," which he labels "demasking."[88] This demasking effect subtly cajoles the community into confronting those people, and those realities, it would prefer to ignore. Carnivalesque festivals, in other words, are not necessarily intended to reverse the existing social order, or to reaffirm the authority of those already in power. Instead, they are meant to draw attention to that which is marginalized within a given community, opening up a space of visibility and empowerment for the normally-invisible.

This kind of participant empowerment places carnivalesque street theatre squarely within Baz Kershaw's definition of "radical performance." Kershaw argues that radical performance—which he carefully distinguishes from "political theatre," a genre he sees as inextricably bound up in dominant ideologies—has the potential "to create various kinds of freedom that are not only resistant to dominant ideologies, but that also are sometimes transgressive, even transcendent, of ideology itself."

He describes the "freedom" invoked by radical performance as functioning on two conceptual levels of "the radical": not only as a force of *resistance*, to "oppression, repression, exploitation," but as a force of *transcendence*, offering "freedom *to reach beyond* existing systems of formalised power, freedom to create currently unimaginable forms of association and action."

Kershaw, like Aching, is less concerned with the question of how radical performance "might *represent* such freedoms, but rather how radical performance can actually *produce* such freedoms, or at least a sense of them, for both performers and spectators, as it is happening."[89]

The answer, it seems to me, is via the simultaneous empowerment of both performer and audience to creatively act, react, interact, and even act up.

In short, by empowering the participants to present and re-present themselves to each other, to re-cognize and creatively mis-recognize one another, carnival indeed offers the kind of radical freedom described by Kershaw, while flying under the political radar of the Trinidad police and other powers-that-be.

Thus while Caribbean carnival practice cannot be said to ultimately undermine nor reinforce existing power dynamics, it can and does provide visibility for marginalized groups, lifestyles, and ideas, as well as a means of empowering participants to re-present and re-cognize themselves and each other both as individuals and as a group.

In this sense, carnivalesque street theatre can be considered a form of radical performance, producing freedoms and empowering participants, even as it publicly plays out standard middle-class narratives of consumption, commercialism, and reification.

THE U.S. CARNIVALESQUE

According to the theoretical framework I have been constructing in the course of this section, the United States carnivalesque should display a complex, contradictory relationship to authority, in reflection of a larger ambiguity surrounding the very concept of authority within discourses of postmodernity. A carnivalesque event in the U.S. is thus likely to be marked by continual opposition to, and/or attempts at co-option by, those in power. In terms of form, it should include the act of masquerading which, as I have argued, is a form of radical performance that destabilizes essentialist notions of identity and empowers participants to re-conceptualize themselves and each other, and should rely heavily on the arts of mimicry, parody, and repetition with revision. Furthermore, it is likely to be found in a marginalized space, and to be celebrated by a population that is disenfranchised in some sense.

As I will demonstrate in subsequent sections, all of these requirements are present in the celebration of Halloween in Isla Vista, and may well be present in many (adult- or probient-centered) Halloween celebrations, as well as many large-scale street parties staged on or near college campuses, in the United States. In this section, I will give some background on how these celebrations evolved, and why I have chosen to focus on this phenomenon as a representative example of the U.S. carnivalesque.

1. Tricks and treats: Halloween in the U.S.

Although the Celtic festival of Samhain (pronounced SOW-in) is often cited as its most direct ancestor, the United States tradition of Halloween is a curious cultural amalgam of Celtic, Roman, English, American, and other assorted traditions.[1]

In addition to boisterous pranking and mischief-making, some form of masquerading has been present since the earliest recorded U.S. celebrations.[2] It was largely an adult holiday in the late nineteenth and early twentieth centuries, revolving around courtship rituals and conspicuous consumption in the form of feasting and, in the 1920's, wild, themed costume parties.

During the Great Depression, however, the feasting died out, and bands of destitute, desolate youth began to use Halloween as an excuse for particularly destructive pranking. In self defense, some households began offering treats as a kind of bribe to keep their property safe from harm; thus the invention of modern-day trick-or-treating.[3] Over the next three decades, Halloween evolved into the child-centered ritual of going house to house in search of treats that is now most popularly associated with October 31st.

Since the mid-1970's, however, purists have begun to complain that Halloween has become the occasion of adult masquerading and general carnivalesque revelry. As journalist Michael Demarest declared in the October 31, 1983 issue of *Time*:

"It used to be a children's romp [...] and now it has been taken back by the grownups—masks, costumes, witches, jack-o'-lanterns and all. Increasingly in the '80's, Halloween has become an escapist extravaganza for adults, a trickless treat more closely resembling Mardi Gras than the candy-and-apple surfeits of yesteryear."[4]

It is appropriate that Demarest labels Halloween as being "taken back" by the grown-ups, since these Mard Gras-like celebrations are in many ways a return to the masquerade balls so popular among adults in the first two decades of the 20th century. Historian Nicholas Rogers also compares contemporary Halloween celebrations to Mardi Gras:

"Like Mardi Gras, Halloween emphasizes appetite, desire, and feeling rather than duty, obligation, or formal allegiance. [...] People act out on Halloween in ways that they normally do not."[5]

Although he highlights the spontaneous, "infectious, playful quality" of Halloween and claims that "at its most critical, it has approximated what the French philosopher Michel Foucault would call a heterotopia," Rogers also insists that Halloween has a strong mainstreaming function.

For example, commercialism is heavily present, as Russell Belk argues in "Carnival, Control, and Corporate Culture in Halloween Celebrations." Belk argues that Halloween, which "has long remained an essentially uncommercialized folk holiday," has begun to be co-opted by corporate, consumerist culture—both in terms of an increase in marketable "Halloween" themed products such as costumes and candy, and in terms of businesses using Halloween as "a vehicle for enhancing corporate culture."[6] Thus the subversive function of Halloween is tempered by the normalizing function of the holiday.

Cultural historian David J. Skal similarly emphasizes the contradictory nature of the Halloween holiday:

"The cultural collisions, controversies, and occasional catastrophes attending Halloween may simply be hardwired into a holiday forged from the tug of war between glitter and grave dust, the sacred and the profane, order and lawlessness, the mainstream and the marginalized. [...] Halloween is a holiday that refuses to play by anyone's rules."[7]

In other words, contemporary American Halloween is marked by an ambivalent relationship to authority, and paradoxically resists and reinforces dominant ideologies. So that even as Halloween is increasingly adopted into and adapted by corporate culture, the holiday remains an occasion of rebellion, reversal, and resistance.

To be explicit: there is an apparent link between Halloween and rioting in the United States.

Since the mid-1980's, Halloween has been the occasion for numerous public clashes between would-be revelers and police officers in various locations across the country. On the evening of October 31, 1988, for example, the L.A.P.D. broke up a group of around 100,000 (mostly costumed) revelers gathered on Hollywood Boulevard. The L.A. Times described the situation as a rowdy crowd of "vandals and looters," forcibly (though not necessarily effectively) broken up by "170 police officers in riot gear."[8] However, Mike Davis claims that eyewitnesses described quite a different scene: peaceful revelers, suddenly charged by a mass of officers on horseback and in squad cars; terrorized onlookers and incensed revelers retaliating with bottle-throwing, window smashing, and very specific looting (for example, baseball caps emblazoned with "L.A.P.D.").[9]

Another well-known example is that of Boulder, Colorado, where the once-flourishing "Mall Crawl," (later renamed the "Boulder Boo" in an attempt to attract a more family-oriented crowd) a loosely-organized street party on the pedestrian Pearl St. Mall, was forcibly quashed in 1990 by city police, who felt the annual event had gotten out of hand. Since that time, there have been at least two Halloween riots in Boulder (in 1997, and again in 2000), resulting in considerable property damage and numerous injuries.[10] In both cases, the rioters were largely college students from the University of Colorado, Boulder, and the locus of the skirmishes were in the student-heavy neighborhood adjacent from campus, locally known as "The Hill."[11]

2. College carnival

Indeed, rioting appears to have become somewhat of a traditional activity on—or very near—college campuses in particular at

Halloween time. Violence, vandalism, and looting has marred the annual "Killer (Halloween) Party" at the University of Wisconsin, Madison several years running (2002-2005), inciting the Mayor to consider instituting Martial Law in 2006 to quash the festivities for good.[12]

Rioting has also broken out during Halloween celebrations at Southern Illinois University, Carbondale, the University of Oregon, Eugene, Chico State University, and Ohio University, Athens.

Carnival-related rioting in college towns is not restricted to Halloween, however. For example, rioting broke out in Austin when women began exposing their breasts during the 2001 "Sixth Street Mardi Gras" festivities near the University of Texas.[13] In 2003, an annual off-campus party at the University of Massachusetts, Amherst, also resulted in rioting,[14] and a private party turned riotous at Iowa State University in 2004.[15] Also in 2004, large-scale rioting broke out after and at Cal Poly, San Luis Obispo's Mardi Gras festival, prompting administrators to take drastic measures toward outlawing the festivities in 2005.[16]

It would thus appear that the American college campus has become a primary site of tension between chaos and control, and that this tension is frequently played out in the form of carnivalesque cele-bration-turned-riot.

This makes sense in terms of the cultural lore of college students as instigators of change (as in the much-glorified role of students during the political unrest of the 1960's), or simply as discontented rebels-without-a-cause. Within Lacanian psychoanalysis, the desire to rebel against the Oedipal father (fed by an unconscious desire for an impossible jouissance) is directly connected to the pre-Oedipal drives (Anal/Oral/Aural/Scopic), all of which ultimately translate to the death drive. Rejecting the Oedipal father and following any of these drives to repetitive excess, warns Jagodzinski (following Lacan), can only result in self-destruction. Jagodzinski sees this as equally true for subjects of any age, but notes that anxieties about self-destruction are often projected by the older generation onto the younger generation. Cultural critic Mike Davis simultaneously makes note of and demonstrates this anxiety when he writes in *City of Quartz*:

> "Across the spectrum of runaway youth consumerism and the impossible fantasies of personal potency and immunity, youth of all classes and colors are grasping at undeferred gratification – even if it paves the way to assured self-destruction."[17]

In a similar vein, Sarlo warns that the global market "courts the youth it has instituted as protagonist of most of its myths," leaving them simultaneously vulnerable to exploitation and deluded by the "impossible fantasies" described by Davis.

I agree with Jagodzinski that probients are often unfairly cast as more likely than their adult counterparts to succumb to the self-destructive lure of the Pre-Oedipal drives. However, I also feel that probients *are* particularly vulnerable to the myths of the market, since their fear of disempowerment makes them prone to believe that which promises them potency, security, agency—in short, all those things they are relentlessly reminded that they lack. Thus their fear of, and rebellion against, one kind of power (the "castrating" law of the Oedipal father) leaves them at the mercy of another (the pre-Oedipal drives of the Jouissant father). It therefore stands to reason that probients should be simultaneously associated with self-destructive "hard-partying," with rebellion and rioting, and with mindless conformity to market-driven commercialism and posturing.

Probients are understood to inhabit spaces of "controlled disorder," to use Sarlo's phrase,[18] where it is difficult to tell whether there is an underlying structure designed to create the illusion of disorder, or whether chaos reigns and the superficial "order" imposed upon it is the illusion. As I have argued, it is within these marginalized spaces of "controlled disorder"—or perhaps of "disordered control"—that the carnivalesque most often appears within contemporary United States society. The American college campus is one such space, and the frequency and the vehemence with which the carnivalesque surfaces there, coupled with the strong reaction it receives from those who are highly invested in keeping accepted classifications well defined, make this particular space one that is worth exploring further.

This study of Halloween in Isla Vista is intended to be an initial step toward such an exploration. Many of the assertions I will make regarding Halloween in Isla Vista could just as easily be applied to any number of carnivalesque events on college campuses throughout the country, a handful of which I have already mentioned.

However, I have chosen to focus on Halloween in Isla Vista as a representative example because I felt strongly that this initial study should remain grounded in terms of its historical and geographical background. During my time at UCSB, I have had ample access to valuable primary sources which thus far had gone untapped, and I saw in this project an opportunity to reach beyond the immediate, rediscovering forgotten histories and shedding much-needed light on a hot-button issue within the community.

This study is not intended to make a conclusive statement on the relationship between the American college campus and the carnivalesque; rather, it is an open invitation to scholars from all disciplines to further investigate the interplay between college, carnival, and the double edges of adolescence and adulthood.

PART III
HALLOWEEN IN ISLA VISTA

MORE THAN JUST A PARTY

"Halloween in Isla Vista is part Mardi Gras, part riot and part police state, with wholesome family fun lurking on the edges, trying to look brave."

- Brendan Buhler (Staff writer, *Daily Nexus*)[1]

A mystified colleague of mine once asked his students to explain the attraction of Halloween in Isla Vista. At first, he got a lot of vague responses along the lines of "because it's fun," "because my friends are there," "because everyone is so drunk," and so forth. So he probed further, "but don't you get those things at other parties? Why is Halloween so much better?" One of his quieter students spoke up then: "Because Dude, there's just so fuckin' many of us." A chorus of agreement from the other students followed. And finally, my colleague understood.

Crowd density alone confirms the importance of this annual street party, which has at times attracted as many as 40,000 revelers.[2]

Despite relentless opposition from local authorities, University officials, and Isla Vista residents, the annual Halloween celebration in the
student-heavy seaside village adjacent to UCSB has become a significant gathering for college students, mainly from campuses in California and Arizona. In the October 2004 issue of Maxim magazine,
Isla Vista's Halloween party was hailed as one of the top four "Monster Bashes" in the country.[3] Worth highlighting here is not simply the
fact of the event's popularity, but its remarkable persistence in the
face of continual contestation, a trait it shares with the Trinidad
Carnival, the history of which I have laid out in condensed form in
chapter one.

I first stumbled across Halloween in Isla Vista by accident.
Although I had been told that there would be a good deal of "partying"
in my neighborhood over the weekend, I was surprised when, on the
evening of October 31, 2001, as I walked through Isla Vista's
Anisq'Oyo Park, I heard a sound like the roar of a stadium crowd
coming from the direction of the ocean. My curiosity got the better of
me, and I wandered over to take a peek. When I reached Del Playa, I
stood at the edge of the crowd, frozen in awe at the swirling mass of
costumed students stretching out far beyond the reach of my vision.
How, I wondered, could this be considered anything less than a major
event? Why had no one told me about it? Where were the amenities,
the vendors, etc.? And why were there so many police officers in
attendance? What, in short, was going on out there?

The answer, as I argue in this and in subsequent sections, is a
uniquely United States carnivalesque event. According to the theoretical framework I've outlined, carnivalesque events in the United
States, like their Caribbean cousins, will display a complex, contradictory relationship to authority, simultaneously resisting and reinforcing the status quo. In this section, I describe Halloween in Isla
Vista's ambiguous relationship to authority, illustrating its genealogy
as traceable to two ostensibly opposing impetuses: social conformity,
and staged resistance to the establishment.

I argue that the current Isla Vistan Halloween event grew out of
the commingled ashes of the defunct Homecoming festivities (which

fizzled after the UCSB football team was disbanded in 1971), and the political unrest of the late 1960's and 1970's in Isla Vista (see section three), creating an event that is indeed "part Mardi Gras, part riot, part police state"—in short, much more than merely the out-of-control college party it is popularly painted to be.

ORIGINS: 1962-1970

1. **From Homecoming to Halloween**

To discover the origins of the annual Del Playa block party, we must reach all the way back to the opening of the current UCSB campus site. Despite aspirations of a reputation for intellectual rigor and high behavioral as well as academic standards, UCSB was considered a "party school" from its earliest days. According to Robert Kelley, author of *Transformations: UC Santa Barbara 1909-1979*, the remote situation of the UCSB campus on the Goleta bluff necessitated a certain spirit of self-amusement among the students residing there. Kelley writes that by 1960, "Santa Barbara, in consequence, had the reputation of being a party school, languid by its beaches."[1] In the late 1950's and early 1960's, social activities at UCSB were never in short supply. Kelley cites numerous examples:

- Frosh Camp
- The Gaucho Grand Prix
- Playboy and Sadie Hawkins dances
- The Residential Hall Association formal
- The Galloping Gaucho Revue
- Spring Sing

72

- The Drill Team
- A Homecoming Parade down Santa Barbara's main street complete with a queen and her princesses, yell leaders, and song girls
- A Residential Hall Association King and Queen
- An Easter Relays Queen
- A Military Ball Queen
- The King and Queen of Diamonds
- A L'il Abner.[2]

The common element in many these activities is the opportunity for members of the opposite sex to court one another in a socially acceptable, appropriately supervised setting. In addition, the election of a Homecoming "queen," and occasionally an accompanying "king" and/or court of "princesses," emphasizes the importance of physical beauty, particularly for coeds.

More specifically, such events foregrounded the importance of being considered attractive to the opposite sex. This is especially true for women: once the finalists had been chosen, only men were allowed to cast votes to elect a Homecoming Queen, for example. In that era, an annual Homecoming parade was held along Santa Barbara's State Street, and an accompanying bonfire rally was held on the beach near campus. There had also been, from the earliest years of UC Santa Barbara's existence, an "All Cal" Halloween party (also of Homecoming origins) at UC Berkeley, to which students would flock by bus and by train, and which featured a large bonfire.[3] Thus, in these early years, Homecoming and Halloween were celebrated in similar fashion, at the same point in the school year, offering a back-to-school opportunity for socializing, stylized flirtation, and sanctioned self-display.

Eventually, both of these events died out. References to the All Cal Halloween party had all but disappeared from the *El Gaucho* by the mid-1960's, and the UCSB Homecoming parade lasted but a few years after its transfer from downtown Santa Barbara to Isla Vista in 1968. The parade, the bonfire rally, and all the associated Homecoming festivities were already on the wane when the political events of the late 1960's, and the 1971 dissolution of the UCSB football team, did them in entirely. The disappearance of these two important social events left a palpable void in the UCSB calendar, a void which, I will argue, was eventually filled by the spontaneous, localized celebration of Halloween in Isla Vista. As I will argue, the rituals of social conformity and courtship that were in evidence at the UCSB home-coming festivities have far from disappeared: they are alive and well and clearly manifest in the contemporary Halloween event.

2. HALLOWEEN "HIGH JINKS"

The lack of an autumnal event aimed at socializing and particu-larly courtship is only half of the equation, however. The Halloween celebration in Isla Vista has also displayed, from its earliest manifesta-tions, a markedly anti-social, anti-establishment energy.

Disruptive behavior such as rioting, vandalism, and general rowdi-ness has been, and continues to be, as much a part of the Isla Vista Halloween scene as the socializing and the stylized courtship rituals. The first recorded mention of "Halloween high jinks" in Isla Vista came in the form of a November 1, 1963 article in the *Santa Barbara News Press* entitled "Near Riot, Broken Windows, Vandalism Mark Halloween."

The editorial staff of the *News Press* stated its collective opinion on the matter in the aptly named, "Not University Conduct," an editorial reprinted, and subsequently rebutted by a handful of UCSB students, in the UCSB *El Gaucho* (renamed *The Daily Nexus* in 1970). The 1963 articles refer to a Halloween "ruckus" in Isla Vista, perpetrated by what English major Denis Green called "a bunch of guys standing around on street corners throwing fire crackers, insults, and language more appropriate to the men's room wall." The *News Press* staff argues that while such "raffish exuberance is explainable in young teenagers from rowdy homes and neighborhoods," it should not be tolerated "in a student housing area serving a major campus of the University of California."[4] Although Green does not defend the actions of these "hoodlums," he insists that the "near-riot" on Halloween must be understood as "a conscious objection to a society which is no longer tolerant of humor in education."[5] And so the debate begins.

Although 1963 does not mark the beginning of the Isla Vista Halloween high jinks, it certainly marks a tone shift in the response to such activities. A 1965 article in the *El Gaucho* points out that in 1962 a fight broke out between two dormitory living groups, involving "waterballoon and mud-clot throwing."[6] The campus police were indeed called in to break up the fight, but did so "jovially," and left in good spirits, according to Gayle Clark Olson who wrote her Master's thesis on the history of law enforcement at UCSB.[7]

When the same groups indulged in similar activities a year later, however, one student was arrested, and a ten p.m. curfew was enforced by the Campus Police and the Sheriff's Office. This incited UCSB police captain Willis A. Lowe to launch a publicity campaign to keep the campus quiet on Halloween 1964. The result was an "even quieter than normal weekend night."[8] The merrymakers were back in force, however, the following year. In fact, Malcolm Gault-Williams points out that certain, long-time Isla Vista residents will insist that the first I.V. riot took place, not in February of 1970, but on Halloween in 1965. Although Gault-Williams makes a point of distinguishing that ("non-political") riot from the later, more overtly politically motivated protests, the Halloween disturbance certainly suggests that many of the domestic elements which led to the unrest of 1970 (i.e. a desperate sense of helplessness in the face of institutional power) were already reaching a boiling point.

In the next section, I discuss the infamous Isla Vista unrest of the late 1960's-early 1970's, and the remarkable spirit of community that emerged in its wake. For now, let me say that I do not believe it to be a coincidence that the Halloween celebration in Isla Vista appeared at the same time that the political unrest was beginning to gain momentum, nor that the Del Playa block party gained its own momentum in the 1970's, at a time of unprecedented experimentation and a heightened awareness of community. Isla Vista activist Carmen Lodise has described the community-building efforts post-1970 as an attempt to create "a viable and semi-independent community whose new institutions would reflect the new values of the youth culture."[9]

The question of whether or not Halloween has served as one of these "new institutions" remains up for debate: although it does appear to "reflect the new values" of the current youth culture, many long-time Isla Vista residents and activists have ultimately come to look upon Halloween as antithetical to their vision of a sustainable, ethically enlightened community. What is clear, however, is that alongside its apparent socializing aspects, a certain spirit of anti-authoritarianism has been, and continues to be viscerally present in the celebration of Halloween in Isla Vista.

THE EARLY YEARS: 1971-1977

Although the event must have expanded considerably during the 1970's, Halloween happenings are conspicuously absent from both the UCSB paper and the community press until 1978, when a so-called "mini-riot" broke out, an event to which I will return in a moment. Despite the lack of press coverage, I have been able to piece together, through discussions with participants and long-time residents, a sense of Halloween in Isla Vista's development between the political riots of 1970 and the Halloween riot of 1978.

In these early years, Halloween is described by participants as a small, casual, decentralized, community-based celebration that emphasized creativity and social interaction. Eye-witnesses describe a friendly, jovial scene where no one would dare be caught without a costume. Long-time resident Alison Zuber stated in an interview that, in the 1970's and early '80's, she would bring her young children to Del Playa to go trick-or-treating and never feared for her safety or theirs. In later years, however, the enormous crowds and epidemic use of alcohol and hard drugs changed the dynamic so significantly that she would not dream of bringing a child there. Although she acknowledges that marijuana and hallucinogens were fairly ubiquitous in Isla Vista in the 1970's, Zuber insists that people in that earlier era drugs were used to fuel creativity and interaction, not to replace or evade these things.

At a certain point (of alcohol or drug use), people get so wrapped up in their own internal sensations that they're not interested—or able—to interact with others. So rather than a scene you get a street full of monologues. [...] (when) individual sensory experiences take over [...] community celebration is forgotten.[1]

The attraction of Halloween, for Zuber and many other long-standing Isla Vista residents, lay not in a chemical high but in the creative interactions that once characterized the holiday.

However, another long term resident, Stan Hoffman, insists that there was also an element of civil disobedience in these ostensibly harmless spontaneous Halloween parades.

Noted Hoffman in a March, 2005 interview, "People were out there to have fun, of course, but they were also, in a sense, marking territory [...] sending a message [to the police] that this is the kind of community we are, and they had better get used to it."[2]

This is unsurprising, given the anti-establishment (and particularly anti-police) sentiment which, in the wake of the political riots and the ensuing fallout, was still marked in Isla Vista. The events of 1978 and 1979 would seem to confirm this anti-police element to the festivities, though, as I will argue, even a "riot" is open to multiple, conflicting readings.

THE MINI-RIOTS: 1978-1979

1. **Twin Transgressions**

On Halloween night in 1978, and again in 1979, two so-called "mini-riots" broke out on Del Playa.[1] These twin transgressions are frequently cited as setting a historical precedent for violence between police officers and participants, one that has found contemporary reflection in recent rioting at similar events on other college campuses.[2] They are also, however, considered to mark the commencement of Halloween as Isla Vista knows it, the moment at which the Del Playa block party became a recognized annual event, rather than an informal gathering.

Within a decade of the "mini-riots," Isla Vista had developed a reputation among California college students and a widening circle of other probient populations as one of the most exciting spots to spend the Halloween holiday. I cannot say for sure whether or not there is a direct causal relationship between the mini-riots and the popularity of the event.

Nonetheless, it is apparent that the mini-riots were formative moments in the evolution of the Halloween event. An understanding of how these occurrences were viewed by participants, by police, and by the local press, can therefore offer considerable insight regarding the event's ambiguous relationship to authority, as well as the community's ambiguous relationship to the event.

A campus riot, by definition, is an unauthorized transgression. In fact, the first example of revolutionary activity listed by Umberto Eco is "campus confrontations," followed by "ghetto riots."[3] As I will argue in the next section, Isla Vista's political demonstrations of the late 1960's and early 1970's, notably the burning of the Bank of America, have earned the community a reputation for unauthorized transgression not soon forgotten, nor forgiven, by local authorities.[4]

Furthermore, the heavily student-populated community of Isla Vista suffers from overcrowding, low median income, chronic neglect, and rampant petty crime and sexual assault. Students complain of substandard construction quality in rental units, inflated rents, termites, unfairly seized deposits, and unbearable noise pollution. In short, despite the fact that many of the temporary residents are from upper-middle class families, the "ghetto" label does in fact fit.[5]

To clarify: I fully recognize that the majority of UCSB students living in Isla Vista are only temporarily, and only partially marginalized. Furthermore, many of them use the substandard conditions of their surroundings as an excuse to treat their community, and often each other, with blatant disrespect. However, the fact remains that without a governing body, without even a permanent group of resident adults to represent them, Isla Vistans know that they have no advocacy, no official recourse against the absolute power of the police within their neighborhood. Add to this the increasingly strict regulations on activities traditionally associated with university life (alcohol consumption among them), it comes as little surprise that students tend to view uniformed officers with suspicion, and no small amount of fear.

While these students may not be fully conscious of the ways in which they are exploited and/or excluded within the local political and economic arenas, they do carry a collective sense of abandonment which perennially resurfaces in the form of anti-police sentiment.[6] Likewise, local officers have come to view Isla Vista as a hotspot for troublemakers, particularly during Halloween weekend, and with good reason. Due to the lingering, and frankly understandable threat of unauthorized rebellion, all "authorized" transgressions in Isla Vista are only grudgingly granted, with considerable effort focused on containing and controlling the festivities.

The events of the 1978 and 1979 Halloween festivals have been labeled "mini-riots" – itself an ambiguous term which, despite the suggestion of subversive intent, does leave some room for interpretation. Certainly, "riot" is a term not to be used lightly in a community once torn apart by violent unrest; its tempered usage in regards to the '78-'79 Halloween celebrations suggests both a desire to invoke that violent past, and to allay fears of an encore of similar proportions. The *Daily Nexus* described the following sequence of events, beginning on Saturday, October 28, 1978, when the four officers on duty in Isla Vista were called in on a routine complaint of loud music. When the officers asked to speak to those responsible for the music in question, someone from the crowd threw a bottle at one of the officers, grazing his head. More bottles followed, and additional police were called in, decked out in riot gear. The crowd was ordered to disperse around eleven p.m., and students appear to have voluntarily, if begrudgingly (and rather bewilderedly) complied. Although eyewitness reports vary, the following events do appear to have been corroborated: one officer was injured by a bottle thrown from the crowd, and many officers were threatened with physical violence; an officer pulled a young woman out of her car by the hair and threw her up against the side of said vehicle; two officers broke the window of a house and dragged out a young man suspected of throwing bottles at the officers; and two young women were pulled from another house in "a very brutal manner."[7]

2. Riot vs. revelry: competing readings

The issue of the *Daily Nexus* immediately following the riot (Monday, Oct. 30) offered diverse, and often conflicting, readings of the event, roughly divisible into two major camps: those that framed the riot as a form of political protest (unauthorized transgression), and those that emphasized its theatricality, preferring to read the event as yet another moment of exciting but ultimately benign Halloween mayhem (authorized transgression).

"It was the old story of US against THEM," wrote *Nexus* contributor Marnie Webster, "the innocently idealistic college students against the regimented, law abiding cop. What sixties fanatic could ask for anything more?" Whether or not Webster actually considers herself to be a "sixties fanatic," she does appear to equate the '78 Halloween riot with Isla Vista's infamous political protests of the previous decade.

In fact, Webster claims to have heard rioters shouting "why not burn the bank?" as the crowd advanced and retreated, alternately chasing, and being chased by, the police. Noteworthy also is her depiction of the event as a clash of dichotomous forces: that of innocent idealism versus law-abiding regimentation. Other descriptions feature similar dichotomous framing, liberally sprinkled with direct comparisons between the Halloween riots and political protests at UC Berkeley and elsewhere.[8]

The political readings take Halloween rioting to be what James C. Scott referred to as "a privileged peek backstage... a rupture in the performance" of the *public transcript* that is daily played out between police officers and Isla Vista residents. Scott defines a public transcript as "a shorthand way of describing the open interaction between subordinates and those who dominate."[9] In other words, the daily routine of displaying and submitting to power, so ingrained within the social fabric as to go largely unnoticed—that is, until a rupture occurs, allowing the *hidden transcript* of inequality to show through.

This reading paints the student population not as willing conspirators in their own oppression, but as clever performers who are well aware of their situation, but who choose to wait for the opportune moment—for example, Halloween night—to express their normally-disguised indignation and rage. The implication, then, is that the "masquerade" of Halloween is in fact *less* of a masquerade than the everyday social reality of these students, the endless stream of requisite prostrations and subjugations to this often archaically hierarchical system of academia.

I would argue that the temptation to view the Halloween rioting as a hidden transcript made public is one that should be resisted. There are two main reasons for this. First, such a reading reduces the complex motivations of the officers and the students to an inappropriately dichotomous framework.

As Henry Giroux explains, to pit "youth" against "authority" is to refuse probients the power that is their due as citizens, and to cast them instead as symbols and metaphors rather than active subjects. He writes:

"Increasingly denied opportunities for self-definition and political interaction, youth are transfigured by discourses and practices that subordinate and contain the language of individual freedom, social power, and critical agency. *Symbols* of a declining democracy, youth are located within a range of signifiers that largely deny their representational status as active citizens. Associated with *coming-of-age rebellion*, youth becomes a *metaphor* for trivializing resistance."[10] (Emphases mine)

While a conception of the Halloween enactments as resistance to authority may at first appear to grant agency to the revelers, it ultimately relegates their acts to the realm of the symbolic rather than the actual. Here we see again the "limited view that [carnivalesque manifestations] are *merely* symbolic sites of subversive activities and, by implication, *failed* attempts at transforming the social order" which Gerard Aching argues against in regards to Caribbean carnival (see section two).[11] In other words, within the theoretical framework of the hidden transcript, the rioting of the revelers is read as an unsuccessful attempt at social transformation, rather than an opportunity for empowerment—both for students and officers alike.

As Aching points out, this framework is based on a very narrow definition of social change as sudden, often violent revolution. Although the "mini-riots" included violence, and were clearly intended to send a message of discontent, to view them as attempts at social transformation would be an apparent overstatement. Furthermore, to consider rioting at Halloween as a bubbling up of probient discontent devalues such acts by linking them to that vague, and ultimately impotent anti-authoritarianism commonly associated with "coming-of-age rebellion." This notion is based on the myth (which I aimed to debunk in my introduction) of adolescence as a social disease characterized by aimless discontent and misguided revolt. By this logic, any resistance offered by the revelers can be quickly and easily dismissed as an unfortunate (albeit perfectly "natural") byproduct of their age, and either punished, or simply ignored.

Second, such a reading fails to take into account the interdependence of the two oppositional camps. Whether or not they care to admit it, the police officers, particularly those from the Isla Vista Foot Patrol, need the revelers to recognize, and to validate their authority. Like the colonial police force at Carnival in Trinidad (see section two), the assortment of officers at Halloween in Isla Vista (which includes officers from throughout Santa Barbara county and the larger UC system), are giving their own performance, displaying techniques of crowd control and providing a spectacle of order, control, and authority. As G.W. Hegel argues in *Phenomenology of Spirit*, power exists only when it is acknowledged by another: the Master is only Master so long as there is a slave that recognizes him as such.[12]

In the same way, police officers are only authority figures so long as they have someone over whom they might publicly exercise their authority. By the same token, the revelers need the officers, not only to keep them safe from outsiders, each other, and even themselves, but as representatives of the authority they must ritually resist in order to feel empowered. The Halloween high would not, *could* not exist if every transgression were to go unpunished; rather, it is the ever-present threat of reprimand that makes these otherwise banal activities so irresistibly exhilarating.

The mutual dependence and complicity between the two camps, however unconscious, becomes legible in moments when officers and students forget to play their respective roles and begin to enjoy themselves, or to be genuinely terrified, in unison.

One memorable example was recounted to me by a UCSB student who called herself "Supertramp." On Halloween 2003, she and a group of her friends were attempting to make their way down Del Playa when the crowd became so thick that she found herself unable to move. "It was crazy; I got stuck there like this," she told me, demonstrating the awkward pose she had been forced to strike, her arms stretched up above her head. Luckily, her costume included a metal bra which protected her breasts from the multiple elbows and shoulders with which she subsequently collided. Then, as the crowd began to move again, she found herself pulled in opposite directions. "They spun me around, like a top, only a lot slower. It felt like I was in a kind of whirlpool almost." It was at that point that Supertramp noticed that she was not alone in her "whirlpool":

"So I look over and here is this *cop*—an officer, in uniform and everything—and he's getting spun around and around just like me, in the center of this enormous mass of people. And he sees me […] there and we look at each other, right? And I can see that he's as freaked out as I am. Probably that was a bad sign but like, I […] took comfort in it […]. I guess I must have been smiling because he started smiling back, and then […] we both totally busted up laughing. 'Cause like, there was nothing else to do, you know?"[13]

This unison reaction to the danger, and the absurdity, of the situation, suggests that Supertramp and the pinned police officer had a good deal more in common than either one would normally care to admit. That the fears and desires of those in a position to dominate are perhaps not so far from the desires of the subjugated is, I would argue, a far more subversive notion than the rather trite diametrical opposition of youthful libertinism to law-bound conservatism.

An alternative, ultimately more radical reading of the Del Playa street party, views it as capable of subsuming even the "real" opposition between the authorities and the marginalized revelers into the sweeping scope of its pervasive pretense. *Nexus* staffer Meg McCandless' observation that, during the Halloween riot, the confusion had been compounded by "a lot of party goers dressed as policemen," suggests that the theatricality of the Halloween setting made it difficult to distinguish where play ended and conflict began. "It was hard to tell the real police from the costumed police," said McCandless.[14] Mitchell M. Gaswirth's editorial, "Night on the Town," goes even further, arguing that the riot was quickly and easily re-contextualized by the revelers as an exciting, and not altogether undesirable part of the festivities.

> "People were out there for fun before the cops arrived; but they were out there for excitement afterwards. People were truly bummed when the cops high-tailed it down Camino Del Sur. A few bottles followed the retreating cars, but people were hoping they'd return, maybe with tear gas so we could have *a real riot*. As the crowd at the corner of Sabado Tarde and Camino Del Sur sipped and smoked their separate ways, *one could tell that the whole arrangement was just a joke.* 'Hey, somebody hired those guys to dress as cops for a Halloween party, right?' 'Later man, it was great rioting with you.' 'Right, see ya in history.'"[15] (Emphases mine)

By calling into question the "reality" of the riot, Gaswirth is able to reframe it as an eruption of spontaneous drama which, although unprecedented, was hardly incompatible with the spirit of the celebration itself—a block party characterized by improvisational street-theatre. In doing so, he is not only subverting the official reading of this event as a genuine conflict between the authorities and the revelers, but actually re-contextualizing it as a successful Halloween prank, perpetrated and enjoyed by the revelers themselves. The authorities are thus written out of the equation altogether, their presence having already been consumed and digested by the voracious imagination of the party-going public.

As if the '78 riot's theatricality were not already sufficiently apparent, the following Halloween, it was given a repeat performance. In contrast to the spontaneous eruption of the '78 disturbance, the '79 re-enactment appears to have been an intentionally staged, and much-anticipated event: flyers were actually printed up and distributed at SBCC and local high schools inviting students to "come to a mini-riot on Halloween."

Revelers did in fact throw rocks and bottles at police, but, given the advanced warning offered to police via the flyers, they were met with more organized resistance than the year before, and were quickly shut down. Twenty people, including five juveniles, were arrested during the 1979 Halloween weekend, and the trouble was later blamed on "drunk high school students," who were apparently trying to mimic the UCSB rioters from the year before.[16]

The 1979 "mini-riot" was therefore not so much a second event as a deliberate re-enactment in commemoration of the first, itself a sort of reconstruction of what contemporary students understood of their predecessors' rioting nearly a decade earlier.

THE GOLDEN ERA: 1980-1986

*T*he years 1980-1986 are often considered the "glory days" of Halloween in Isla Vista.[1] In that era, the issue of *The Daily Nexus* that follows each Halloween weekend is resplendent with photographs of blissful revelers in clever costumes, and even the occasional amused officer, posing merrily alongside participants.

Robert Bernstein, who lived in Isla Vista from 1982 to 1989, and now lives in nearby Goleta, describes his early Halloween experiences as being very similar to the nouveau-bohemian Santa Barbara Solstice parade, "except that it was at night."

Said Bernstein in an October, 2005 interview, "There were extremely elaborate costumes and large groups of people who had coordinated to create theatrical presentations. People were very creative and resourceful, using unusual materials and pushing the envelope in unexpected ways."[2]

Thus, in the Golden Era, Halloween appears to have been focused on creativity, free expression, and social interaction.

In the early-mid 1980's, Halloween was widely accepted as "a part of life" by Del Playa residents, police officers, and university officials.

Although alcohol was ubiquitous, until the 1986 "open container" law was put into effect, revelers happily wandered the streets, drinks in hand, and even shared their beverages with the attending officers. Sam Gross, senior deputy of the Sheriff's Department was quoted as saying that "much of the trouble is caused by juveniles who start fights," rather than by UCSB students. [3] Indeed, there appears to have been an overall friendlier relationship among revelers and officers than at any time before, or since the Golden Era.

Highlighted in the *Daily Nexus* coverage for these years were such things as creative costume sightings, camaraderie among groups of celebrating friends, and the liberating aspects of masquerading. "People's personalities changed," noted freshman Valerie Pang, who had dressed up as Robin Gibb of the Bee Gees. "Because you were in costume, you could be crazier, more obnoxious."[4]

A similar sentiment was expressed by alumnus Andrew Spangler, who called Halloween in Isla Vista "a momentous occasion for assholes in polyester." He encouraged readers to enjoy Halloween while they can, as they will not get another occasion to "act like assholes once [they] graduate into the real world."[5] Spangler's comments suggest that, in that era at least, Halloween was regarded not only as an exceptional moment during the school year, but as a representation of an exceptional moment in the life of the participants.

Halloween, in other words, was at that time viewed by participants as a symbol of the social experimentalism exceptionally allowed during attendance at an American university.

Many alumni and long-time locals who experienced the Golden Era of Halloween in Isla Vista are critical of the strict regulations now placed on the festivities, and express an acute nostalgia for Halloween "before the fall," as Alison Zuber put it.[6]

Long-term Isla Vista resident Erika Thost opined, "Once upon a time, Halloween in I.V. was a beautiful thing. I feel sorry for these kids who think this [i.e. the contemporary Halloween event] is as good as it gets."[7]

Although Robert Bernstein agrees that the prolonged "police crackdown" to which the event and the neighborhood have been subjected is misguided and unfortunate, he sees a lot of the elements that were present in the early eighties returning in the contemporary Halloween event. He said of the 2005 celebration that there seemed to be "a lot more creativity" in evidence than in years past. He also added that, contrary to popular belief, "it's all really very innocent: there isn't much actual sexual activity going on in the streets, it's mainly these stylized, parodic encounters that may or may not lead to sexual activity later on."

UCSB Physics Professor Harry Nelson concurred that, excepting the large amounts of bared skin, the scene was in fact more reminiscent of a 1950's school dance than the wild bacchanals he experienced back in the 1970's. "The sexuality is all very theatrical," he noted.[8] Although the Golden Era is long gone, this return to theatricality and creative interaction is certainly an encouraging development.

Of course, not all was golden in the Golden Era: it appears that sexual assault was already a problem by the mid-'80's, judging by the counter-measures taken by concerned Isla Vistans such as Michael Katz and Charlie Jones. Katz described the group as older residents, mostly "hippies" in their 30's, who decided to attend the festivities in order to "observe and intervene if they saw incidents of women being abused."[9] A student group, "Red Alert," was also formed in 1986, in an effort to keep Halloween in Isla Vista safe. Bernstein compared this group to the "Volunteer Marshalls" that used to patrol the mass protests in Washington D.C. during the Vietnam War, whom he described as "volunteers who were with the movement, patrolling around making sure people were safe."

It made for a much more sensible atmosphere where you knew these were people you could trust, they were on your side, and you knew they were there to take care of people and to get rid of folks who were looking to cause trouble.

Unfortunately, Red Alert was eventually disbanded due to concerns about legal liability, and no similar group has ever been reformed.

AFTER THE FALL: 1987-1992

Despite the efforts of concerned citizens to make Halloween safer and saner, things quickly got much farther out of hand than anyone could have imagined. Robert Bernstein described the new Halloween scene as follows:

> "Somewhere around 1986-87, there was an abrupt turn and suddenly half the people weren't in any costume at all, and you had these roving groups of people just looking to grope women and do nasty things. That was when they first overturned the toilet with people in it and just nasty vicious things. That was the end of that really creative culture, and then the cops started doing really vicious nasty things also. I can remember seeing some guy just walking along and these cops tackling him and beating the crap out of him..."[1]

As attendance numbers soared, the mutual animosity that had always existed between officers and revelers became markedly exacerbated, resulting in violent and destructive behavior on both sides.

In 1986, an estimated 30,000 revelers jammed the streets of Isla Vista. One man was stabbed that year, and two more were seriously injured after falling from the nearby cliffs. As a result, local authorities began taking the idea of crowd control seriously, barricading streets in Isla Vista and stepping up police presence to 20 California Highway Patrol officers, and virtually the entire UCSB campus police force.[2]

Intensive planning preceded the 1987 and 1988 celebrations, including (in 1988) an expensive University-sponsored "nice costume, bad attitude" campaign aimed at discouraging partiers from other universities from attending.[3]

After a relative respite between 1989 and 1990, Halloween once again fell on a weekend, resulting in yet another attendance record in 1991, estimated at 14,000 on Friday night and 16,000 on Saturday.[4] That weekend, one-hundred police officers made eight hundred and fifty three arrests (two-thirds of which were out-of-towners), resulting in two hundred and fifty incarcerations; an additional five hundred and eighty two citations were handed out, mostly for alcohol-related offenses. [5] A fight on Sunday morning resulted in two arrests and assorted injuries, and two more "cliff divers," as those who stumble off the Isla Vista bluffs had come to be known, were rushed off to the hospital.[6] All told, twenty revelers received Emergency Room treatment that year.[7] Illegal drugs, particularly cocaine and MDMA (more commonly known as "ecstasy" or "X"), were heavily in evidence, much to the disgust of many long-time locals.

> "If people smoked as much ganja as they drank alcohol," one resident suggested, "it would be a much more mellow scene and the costumes would be a lot better."[8]

A number of UCSB students also expressed distaste for the dangerous Halloween scene that year, such as Angie Eng, who called Halloween in Isla Vista "overrated." "You outgrow things like that," said Eng.[9]

The 1992 Halloween celebration, which featured numerous live bands at private parties along Del Playa, Sabado Tarde, and Trigo roads, is reported to have attracted an estimated 40,000 revelers. Yet it appears to have been viewed as somewhat of a let-down to those who were expecting an unprecedented blowout, the holiday falling as it did on a Saturday that year. The cover page of the *Daily Nexus* on Monday, November 2, pretty well sums up the general consensus:

"Halloween 1992: Sure, It Was Huge, But Some Were Left Unsatisfied by the Anticlimax."

Kimberly Epler describes a similar sense of let-down, or perhaps simply relief, in her article from that same issue, "Condoms, Cows, and Cretins":

"Despite advance horror stories of mass invasions and unprecedented violence, this weekend appears to be just another in a long line of wild and drunken abandon known as Halloween in Isla Vista."

Indeed, Tim Gracey of the Santa Barbara Sherrif's Department called 1992 "a success from a law enforcement standpoint." Over one thousand arrests were made that year, and only two critical injuries reported.[10]

NO TOLERANCE: 1993-2002

*D*espite their positive statements to the press, the police were already busy planning for Halloween 1993 before the 1992 Jack O' Lanterns had begun to rot.

In the wake of the destruction wreaked during the enormous 1992 bacchanal, local police, under the leadership of Sheriff Jim Thomas, drafted a "Five Year" plan to reel in the rowdiness.

The first order of business was to create a "Festival Ordinance" that was to forbid the playing of live or pre-recorded music out-of-doors from six p.m. onward during Halloween weekend. This ordinance, which also prohibited any "unlicensed live performances with the capacity of attracting 500 people or more,"[1] is eerily similar to the "Anti-Masquerader Ordinance" passed in Trinidad in 1868 (see section two). In addition to the Festival Ordinance, a "No Tolerance" policy was adopted, asserting that anyone caught breaking the law must be arrested. Custody arrests were to be made whenever possible, and citation fines were to be raised, particularly for alcohol-related offenses.

Also in that era, police instituted a policy of confiscating any costume piece or hand-held prop that could conceivably be used as a weapon.

Like the anti-stickband ordinances passed under Captain Baker in Trinidad, the confiscation of any weapon-like object at Halloween in Isla Vista has affected the revelers' costuming and interactions. Now rather than carrying either real or representative arms, revelers who wish to look "tough" have resorted to adopting physical characteristics (clothing and behavior) associated with street gangs, and/or to carrying concealed weapons (knives, handguns, etc.). Much like the Trinidad calypsonians who battle in song, these Isla Vista gangsters often engage one another in verbal skirmishes, some of which erupt into fist fights or beyond.

In order to warn potential partygoers from out-of-town of the stricter policies in place, the University inducted the help of the local (Central Coast) media.[2]

The No Tolerance policy and Festival Ordinance were still in place on Halloween, 2005, though police ceased to refer to this strategy as the "Five Year plan" after its seventh year of successfully curbing attendance. In fact, the new policies did such an excellent job of deterring visitors that students began to lament the death of their signature event. In 1993, an estimated 25,000 revelers cycled through Isla Vista. The following year, approximately half that number (13,000) attended, and in 1995, a paltry 2,000 revelers showed up for the party, a crowd hardly worthy of the eighty-five police officers sent to control it.

To combat the accompanying sense of despair, lagging school spirit, and bitterness towards police and University officials, and to attempt to bridge the student and (largely Hispanic) working-class family communities of Isla Vista, a sober "alternative" celebration was organized in by Associated Students and the Isla Vista Parks and Recreation District. The first annual Halloween/Dia de Los Muertos Festival was held in Anisq'Oyo park on October 31, 1996. Although the festival continues, in 2002 its titled was shortened to the "Dia de Los Muertos Festival," and unlike in 1996, the festivities now cease at sundown. Activities have include live bands (performing before 6 p.m. so as to avoid running afoul of the Festival Ordinance), a costume contest, various carnival games, a traditional Mexican candlelight procession to honor the dead, and a showing of *The Rocky Horror Picture Show* at the I.V. Theater.

Meanwhile, the Del Playa street party waxed and waned, but never died out entirely. In 1994, Chancellor Henry Yang attended for the first time, a ritual he was to repeat each year from then on, and noted that it seemed quite crowded to him. Sheriff Thomas said of the celebration that year: "It's been perfect—nobody's dead."[3] The relatively miniscule turnout in 1995—smaller, even, than the usual weekend average in Isla Vista—prompted police and some community members to celebrate the event's return to its roots as a small, local gathering, while others, mostly students, insisted that Halloween had been snuffed out by Sheriff Jim Thomas and his Five Year Plan. The *Daily Nexus* advised readers in 1996 to "Get Out of Town!" in search of a less restrictive environment, and many students appear to have taken his advice, migrating to downtown Santa Barbara or elsewhere for the weekend.[4]

When, in 1997, the Five Year Plan reached its sixth year, students began to cry foul. An opinion piece entitled "Five Year Plan? Halloween Is No Longer the Huge Party It Once Was, So It's Time for a Smaller Police Presence," argued that

The purpose of increased protection is to return the holiday to the community, which is a commendable goal. However, students are a large part of the community, and denying them the chance to have a good time, legal or not, seems wrong.[5]

Although it could certainly be argued that an illegal good time should not be allowed to anyone, the matter of who decides which activities are legal and illegal, and for whom, is worth considering. Another opinion piece, this one from the previous year, sums up the problem quite succinctly:

What it comes down to is that, because we are students, we frighten people, and are denied our own party-safe zones when we want to raise hell. So when a bunch of fat, old, rich Santa Barbarans want to dress up in cheap "Mexican" costumes, close down a street and get ripped, it's Fiesta, but if we do the same, it's a potential riot.[6]

Although officers certainly cannot be faulted for recognizing the potential for riot at Halloween in Isla Vista, the accusation of a double standard set up between Santa Barbara festivals such as Fiesta and Solstice, and Isla Vista's only notable event, Halloween, deserves consideration.

Fiesta, formerly known as "Old Spanish Days" is a week-long festival that takes place in downtown Santa Barbara each summer. The festival is intended to celebrate Santa Barbara's Spanish heritage and includes two parades, and numerous performances of Flamenco, Mariachi, etc. Part of De La Guerra plaza is transformed into a beer garden for the occasion, thus the reference to closing down a street for the purpose of "get[ting] ripped." There are certain carnivalesque aspects to Fiesta, such as the tradition of breaking confetti-filled eggs on the head (or other body part) of fellow participants. Masking, however, is usually confined to those performing in one of the many official, staged spectacles of Spanish and Mexican culture; themed costuming on the part of the general public (aside from the occasional hat or blouse) is relatively rare.

The Solstice parade began as a private birthday party and has grown into an annual event in which hand-made, non-motorized floats, performing groups, and other artistic creations parade down State Street in downtown Santa Barbara. The parade route leads to a public park where vendors, a beer garden, and live music stages are set up for an all-day event. This event is more overtly carnivalesque than Fiesta: outrageous costuming and theatrical behavior is common and encouraged among the general public. However, as it has become more structured and family-oriented, it has lost much of its original spirit of chaotic revelry and counter-cultural ferocity.

Admittedly, a certain amount of the discrepancy between the way Santa Barbara and Isla Vista's signature parties are treated is a simple question of economics. Fiesta in particular brings in considerable revenue for the city; downtown restaurants, bars, hotels, shops, (etc.), all benefit from the influx of out-of-town visitors and celebrating locals. In Isla Vista, however, there are *no* hotels, few shops and restaurants, and of those only a small percentage risk remaining open during Halloween for fear of vandalism and looting. The only business owners who have historically supported Halloween are, predictably, those that sell (or serve) alcohol. In short, Halloween's major problem thus far is that no one has cashed in on the event, and therefore it has no one to lobby in its favor. Furthermore, the transience of Isla Vista's student population undermines any attempt at continuity and organizational infrastructure.

Yet the fact that Halloween in Isla Vista remains a free, spontaneous, un-sponsored event is also its strongest selling point among the college crowd. To legitimize the event, to make it a profitable, sensible celebration regulated by the county and backed by the business community would surely spell its death as a specifically probient event. Nevertheless, although the vehemence with which the county has tried to shut Halloween down is understandable—as it only serves the interests of an inconsistent minority group with little or no lobbying power—it is ultimately lamentable, since that group also deserves an opportunity to commune, and to collectively create, celebrate, and publicly perform its identity.

1. The (new) Isla Vista problem

For many longtime residents, the late 1980's mayhem was anathema to the kind of community they had worked so hard to create.

Genesis Lodise, who lived in Isla Vista from 1974-1993, wrote in an email communication that Halloween "degrade(d) what the community had previously stood for."[7]

Alison Zuber expressed a similar sentiment, but rather than blaming the political disintegration of the community on Halloween, she sees Halloween as the most apparent symptom of a larger social trend in Isla Vista. Following the riots, she explained, Isla Vista began to fill up with "partiers" and to empty of "politicos." "In other words," clarified Zuber, "more boozers and less pot-heads." Her theory is that this trend was not accidental, but rather the result of decisions made by administrators regarding who they would and would not admit to the University.[8] The wild, decadent, drug-and-alcohol heavy binge that had come to be Halloween seemed to Zuber nothing more than a reflection of the new inhabitants' values and priorities.[9]

I find Zuber's explanation of the shift in Halloween energy more convincing than Lodise's. It seems highly unlikely that one annual event could single-handedly dismantle the cultural structure that was apparently thriving in Isla Vista following the riots; it is rather more likely that, as Zuber suggests, the event transformed in response to the changing needs, desires, and values of its probient participants.

Although the cultural shift between the early '70's and the mid-1980's in the Isla Vista community must be understood within the larger context of a shifting political and ideological climate in the United States, the role of the University in hastening cultural change in Isla Vista should certainly be taken into consideration: as an institution with the right to admit, or to refuse admission to students based on its own criteria, the University unquestionably carries a good deal of the responsibility regarding what sort of students are attending UCSB, and consequently, living in Isla Vista.

In this I find a kind of poetic irony: in attempting to solve the "Isla Vista problem," the University's efforts to attract a less problematic (read: politically active) student body, may have unwittingly helped to create a new problem, one that would haunt UCSB administrators for many, many years to come.

It should be noted, however, that not everyone has unhappy memories of the wilder years of Halloween in Isla Vista. Some participants admit to having thoroughly enjoyed the enormous, chaotic benders of the 1980's and early 1990's, and even express a certain amount of nostalgia for the wild days gone by. Bill Singer, driver of "Bill's Bus," a private operation that connects Isla Vista to the downtown scene after hours, told *Nexus* writer Ted Andersen in 1999, "It's not as much fun out here as it used to be. The days when thousands of people would come to town are gone."[10] Likewise, alumna Tiye Baldwin displays a marked nostalgia for the Del Playa scene of the late-80's Halloween scene in Isla Vista when she writes,

"I might be getting old, but ahhh, the memories. Halloween Night
1989, sophomore year for me, and I was there, riding along the
massive wave of out of control youth on D.P. - pure chaos, our own
little pocket of inebriation, full of inhabitants and visitors simply
ecstatic to be participating in Bourbon Street West.[11] [...] I hold back a
tear when I think that no one will ever again know the unadulterated
joy of the party that was Halloween in I.V."[12]

Both Singer and Baldwin seem to feel that the dense, chaotic
crowd, "united," as Baldwin puts it, "in the spirit of intoxication," was
the best part of Halloween in Isla Vista, and that the misbehavior of
the revelers in that era has been exaggerated.

"I never knew anyone who got in trouble," claims Baldwin, "When I
read about how many people got arrested and did bad stuff back then,
I don't remember that part. Either I got lucky and missed it, or was
having too much fun to notice."[13]

For these and similar-minded locals, the Five Year Plan effectively
cut the heart out of Halloween, turning it into a small, tightly-
controlled "community celebration" rather than a wild, vibrant,
uncontrollable gathering of probient peers.

Halloween veterans have shared with me some truly phenomenal
tales about their participation in these relatively unregulated festivities. In the interest of space, and multiple requests that I keep the
juiciest bits "off the record," I will repeat only one, a story that seems
to me to epitomize the euphoric element of such gargantuan
bacchanals.

Former Santa Barbara resident Michael Andrews, who played in a
band during the late 1980's, shared this story with me in a March 27,
2005 telephone interview. He and his band-mates, who changed the
name of their band at every performance in defiance of traditional
marketing schemes, frequently played the Cold Springs Tavern, a
venue located in the foothills behind Santa Barbara, and became

popular among the UCSB students who would come there on weekends to dance.

In October 1987, a small group of these students asked Andrews' band to play at their Sabado Tarde home on Halloween weekend. Andrews was hesitant, having heard stories of the wild happenings in Isla Vista on Halloween—the violence, the couch burnings, the angry police officers. Eventually, however, his band-mates talked him into participating, saying that Sabado Tarde, although only one street away, was not Del Playa, and that they would be in a private home, not out on the street. They decided on the name "The National Gardenias," and adopted a military motif for their outfits on the evening of the performance.

Upon arrival in Isla Vista, they realized that the police had (for the first time) barricaded the streets, and that they would not be able to drive in with their equipment. Consequently, they were reduced to parking over at the University and "smuggling" their gear across Isla Vista piece by piece. Their military garb only added to the feeling that this was some kind of covert operation, and by the time they had set up to play, they were, as Andrews put it, "high on" the spirit of resistance to authority.

The scene that Andrews witnessed was not nearly so wild as that which had been described to him, in fact he described it as having "a kind of innocence" to it. They played in the back yard of these students, between their patio and a brick wall described as being "about twenty feet high," until around ten p.m., to a small, invite-only crowd. By ten, however, the masses had clearly discovered them since, as Andrews described it:

You could *feel* the crowd building up on the other side of that wall. You could hear them clapping and you just knew they were listening, that we were the best band out there that night and they had figured that out.

Energized by their growing audience, the National Gardenias went on playing, even louder than before.

At that point bodies started to appear at the top and around the sides of the wall. "They were like ants," said Andrews, "crawling all over this wall." Suddenly, bricks began to disappear, and the wall began to give way. "It was the most incredible feeling," Andrews averred, "watching that wall crumble and seeing this ocean of people stretching out as far as the eye could see. I can't even begin to estimate how many people." Suddenly, the National Gardenias were the focal point of an enormous crowd, and they eagerly soaked up the spotlight.

We were the center of this chaotic swirling mass of people—the eye of the I.V. storm. It was amazing—the T.V. crews came—it was the most exhilarating moment of my musical career.

When asked to describe the mood of the crowd, Andrews said there was a sense of "reckless abandon" that was both liberating and terrifying. Although he didn't see anything particularly dangerous occur, he admits that the potential was certainly there, and that it was, in part, that potential for disaster that made the whole thing so exciting.

Though Andrews did concede that there seemed to be "rogue groups of young men looking for women to victimize," he noted that there was by that time a growing attitude of intolerance for that kind of behavior. "Most people were just out there to have a good time," Andrews summed up, "and when you have that many people out to have a good time, there's a good time to be had."

"I.V. is the place your parents warned you about," noted Santa Barbara native Emily McCoy, now living in Seattle. "When I was a teenager, my Mom would say to me, 'Whatever you do, DON'T GO TO ISLA VISTA! You never know what might happen there.' So of course, as soon as I was old enough to get there, I started going to I.V. for Halloween."[14]

When asked what, exactly, *did* happen, McCoy described her first Halloween experience as "eye-opening," and confessed that she had so much fun wandering from party to party dressed as a sexy black cat,[15] "trick or treating" for alcohol and attention, that she came back the next year, and the next.

When asked if she thought her mother's opinion of I.V. influenced her decision to return year after year, McCoy flashed an impish grin, green eyes narrowed, and asked, "What do *you* think?"

2. The bunny tale

As we have seen, the enormous crowds which characterized the Halloween celebrations of the late 1980's and early 1990's have been both deplored and celebrated by participants. Some alumni are nostalgic for the more low-key, community-based celebrations of the 1970's and early 1980's, while others insist that the true "glory" of the event was its very enormity, and cite the crowded celebrations of the late 1980's – early 1990's as examples of "great" Halloweens past.

But regardless of whether the presence of out-of-towners is viewed as a positive or a negative, the remarkable attendance records at various points along the way do beg the question: how did a water-fight between two residence halls balloon into an internationally-recognized event?

I am inclined to agree with a statement made by alumnus Vikki Bowles in the 1990 (UCSB) LaCumbre Yearbook: "How I.V. became the center of the world for Halloween is still unknown."[16] Yet most people who are conversant with the event – students, professors, police officers, and journalists alike – will confidently, and rather dismissively, provide the following explanation for its remarkable reputation: sometime in the late 1980's, Isla Vista was hailed "the best party in America," by *Playboy* magazine, and this unexpected bit of publicity ostensibly instigated a dramatic rise in out-of-town visitors.

This account, however convincing, appears to be a myth. Despite varied reports in *The Daily Nexus*, LaCumbre yearbooks, *The Santa Barbara News Press* and elsewhere of a nod from *Playboy* made some-time between 1985 and 1992,[17] the rumor is apparently unfounded. After carefully combing through each and every issue of *Playboy* within this range (you're welcome!), I can safely say that if ever such a pronouncement was made, it was certainly not featured prominently enough to have attracted much attention, even from those who do indeed read *Playboy* for the articles. In fact, not one of the *Playboy*s I perused offered any advice about where to spend October 31, let alone an annual list of Halloween hotspots.

Furthermore, UCSB did *not* appear – even as an honorable mention – in *Playboy's* January 1987 listing of the top forty party schools in the nation. It would certainly be an odd choice on the part of the *Playboy* editorial staff to omit even a cursory nod to the school that hosts "the best party in America."

Contrary to popular belief, the next *Playboy* party schools listing, this time numbering twenty-five, was not to be compiled until 2002, when UCSB ranked in at number twenty-two, with nary a mention made of the infamous Halloween bash.[18]

Even in the "Girls of the Top Ten Party Schools" spread from the May, 2006 issue of *Playboy*, where UCSB is featured as the number two party school in the nation (just behind the University of Wisconsin, Madison), the brief paragraph accompanying the spread of UCSB coeds in various states of undress makes *no* mention of Halloween in Isla Vista, whereas Madison's Halloween bash is listed at the top of the page under the heading "best annual party."[19]

Perhaps most suspicious is the presence of nearly identical assertions made about other college parties within a similar time frame. For example, the University of Virginia's "Easter's Weekend" is claimed by various online sources to have been named "the best party in America" by *Playboy* in either the early '70's, the late '70's, or the early '80's.[20]

In Isla Vista, the *Playboy* urban legend has been circulating since around 1986 (if not earlier), and occasionally includes an equally fictitious reference to a *USA Today* list of top Halloween haunts, in which Isla Vista supposedly comes in third, just after New York and New Orleans.[21] Some of the individuals I interviewed who were living in Isla Vista at that time also claim to have seen the list as published (they assumed in *Playboy*) but, when pressed, confess that what they saw was a Xerox copy of a list which could have been created by a student in order to perpetuate the rumor.

The *only* national publicity I have been able to verify came quite recently: the October 2004 issue of *Maxim* includes an article entitled "Fright Night" in which four "Monster Bashes" are listed, all of them directly linked to college campuses: Isla Vista first, followed by Madison Wisconsin, Athens Ohio, and Carbondale Illinois.[22]

Though apparently unfounded, the *Playboy* rumor deserves closer consideration. Up to this point it has been assumed that a commercial and – not insignificantly – pornographic publication was responsible for transforming what was once a laid-back, local gathering into a major hub of subversive activity among West-coast college students. The image is one of invasion, of a media-created monster devouring the naïve hamlet of Isla Vista.

And yet, if there never was such an article, then the credit – and the blame – for the event's frightening popularity must be returned to its rightful owners: the probient participants themselves. In that case, the image of an invading media-monster necessarily metamorphoses into one of a home-grown creation, fashioned and aggressively publicized by college students acting alone.

In the absence of an actual crowd-producing publication, the media conspiracy theory crumbles, and Halloween in Isla Vista is revealed as something much rarer and more remarkable: a wholly probient-generated and -perpetuated event.

"THE PARTY IS (NOT) OVER"

Although its causes remain mysterious, the (negative) effects of this enormous, bacchanalian bash are infamous. Halloween weekend is popularly associated with an increase in crime, particularly property damage, physical and sexual assault, and a host of alcohol- and drug-related offenses. Although statistics do not necessarily bear out this assumption (the number of reports and arrests on Halloween weekend 2003, for example, do not look appreciably different from those of other weekends from that year chosen at random),[1] Lt. Sol Linver is quick to point out that the sheer size of the crowd makes it impossible for police to catch every offense, and that the number of actual laws broken—particularly alcohol-related laws—is in fact significantly higher than what is shown by the statistics.[2]

Furthermore, Carol Mosely, Director of the UCSB Women Center's Rape Prevention Education Program, notes that most of the sexual assaults that occur over Halloween weekend, and year round in Isla Vista for that matter, go unreported; police numbers are therefore unreliable.[3] And as I discovered (see below), unless a perpetrator is found and arrested, an incident cannot be considered an assault, significantly reducing the number of "assaults" that make it into the crime statistics.

During the four Halloween weekends I have observed in Isla Vista (2002-2005), I have witnessed a number of fights, several alcohol-related injuries, and one theft, and was myself the victim of an unprovoked physical assault.

On the night of Saturday, October 29, 2005, I dropped a friend off at her car, which was parked on campus. I was dressed as Pebbles Flintstone that evening, though at that point I was wearing a full-length coat which obscured most of my costume. As I walked back toward Del Playa unaccompanied, I noticed a man in a green-and-white striped football jersey walking quickly toward me. I moved away from him slightly, leaving plenty of room for him to pass. Instead, he lunged toward me, his arm straight out, and knocked me hard in the throat.

I was thrown to the pavement by the blow, and I screamed, anticipating some further violation. He simply walked on, however, just as if nothing out of the ordinary had occurred.

No one stopped or turned; I can only assume they couldn't differentiate my scream from all the other screaming on nearby Del Playa. Once I realized that no one was coming to my aid, I simply got up and continued on to Del Playa, looking for a police officer to whom I might report the incident.

As I walked, I recorded the following phrase in a strained and shaken voice, not realizing my tape recorder had slipped into half-speed: "I am convinced that I am not safe walking by myself out here."

I walked for several blocks before finding any police. When I did find an officer, he was accompanied by about five more officers. I told them I had been assaulted and described the incident. I got the feeling they didn't know quite what to make of me: an apparently sober woman, in costume though wearing a coat, explaining in a relatively calm and collected manner, though through an apparently constricted throat, that I had just been attacked for no apparent reason. They asked me for a description of the guy and said they'd go look for him, though without asking me exactly where it had happened or in which direction he was headed.

I thought there was very little chance they would find him at that point and was disturbed that they hadn't bothered to get more information from me. I was also disturbed that they hadn't gotten my name or any way to get a hold of me should they happen to find the perpetrator. How would they make an arrest without me there to identify him? I stopped by the IVFP office the following morning, only to discover that no official report of the incident had been filed, and that even filing such a report would not mean that the incident would be counted as an assault, as no arrest was made.

In light of that experience, I can state with absolute certainty that the crime statistics collected during Halloween weekend are not reflective of the actual number of crimes being committed.

It seems likely, however, that this is the case year-round in Isla Vista. As I argued in the previous section, the U.S. carnivalesque, like the Caribbean carnivalesque, is not a reversal of quotidian culture, but rather an intensification of what goes on in a given community year round. The major identifying features of the Halloween celebration—i.e. conspicuous consumption of alcohol, skimpy costumes, exaggerated sexual overtures, etc.—are also recognizable components of Isla Vista's year-round culture. Indeed, Carol Mosely is convinced that, aside from the ubiquitous practice of "ass grabbing" (see section five), the number of sexual assaults that occur on Halloween are not significantly different from those that occur on any given weekend in Isla Vista.[4] As California Polytechnic State University ("Cal Poly") student Nick Hopping wrote in an editorial (the point of which, interestingly, was that Cal Poly, located in nearby San Luis Obispo, ought to be working harder to maintain its Party School image):

"At UC Santa Barbara, or the University of Casual Sex and Beer, one can cruise down to Isla Vista on virtually any night and find something to do (usually including a keg and scantily-clad ladies). It's impossible to even drive on Del Playa past 9 p.m. because the strip is packed with college students. That's why they're ranked No. 22 on [Playboy's] list [of the Top 25 Party Schools in the Nation]."[5]

Much to the chagrin of University officials, this is a fairly typical description of the so-called "University of Casual Sex and Beer," and particularly Isla Vista.[6] Even the Los Angeles Times described UCSB as having "the image of a college where anything goes, a school of hard partying, heavy drinking and easy sex."[7] As we have seen, this reputation is not new—the "party school" image can be traced back to the earliest days of the Goleta bluff campus. But the Halloween event has provided a blatant, physical manifestation of that image that has more or less permanently solidified UCSB's party school reputation.

The university has worked tirelessly, and largely in vain, to rid itself of the party school image.[8] In a general appeal to students to party "responsibly" (particularly on Halloween), Chancellor Henry T. Yang told Daily Nexus reporter Daniel Haier in October of 2003, "If our students are portrayed or perceived as behaving in irresponsible ways, it harms the reputation of our campus community." The Chancellor went on to say that he believes the majority of students are "disturbed" about the media coverage of the Isla Vista party scene, because "they know we are a serious academic institution, and they know they are working hard to achieve their academic goals and to ensure future success in their chosen careers."[9]

The coverage in question was almost certainly related to the fall 2003 "reality porn" scandal, [10] covered in the September 2003 issue of Rolling Stone magazine (and, two days after Yang's interview was printed in the Nexus, on NBC's Dateline).[11] However, Chancellor Yang's comments, made in the context of pre-Halloween precautions, were quickly interpreted as connecting this kind of negative national spotlighting of the community to the annual Halloween mayhem. Isla Vista community members and business owners are similarly quick to blame Halloween for the booze-and-sex-soaked reputation of their neighborhood.

Riccardo Fundament, owner of Dublin's Restaurant on Pardall Road agreed that "Isla Vista gets a bum rap. Halloween gives it a stigma for the rest of the year that it doesn't deserve."[12]

There are, however, some community members and institutions that do appear to recognize Halloween merely as a symptom of a larger problem. The Isla Vista Teen Center, for example, has to deal with the alcohol-soaked, party-oriented ethos of its neighbors on a daily basis. Case manager Yesenia Curiel cited an incident in which a large Heineken banner was hung from a residence on the 6700 block of Sueno, in clear view of the teens when they are at the center. Though she asked the residents to remove the banner, explaining that it glamorized alcohol and undermined the teen center's aim "to motivate these kids to stay away from alcohol," the students refused, and the banner remained.[13]

Health Educator Jacob Sandoval lamented that although the center's proximity to UCSB should be a positive influence on the attending teens, the irresponsible behavior of many of the college-aged residents turns it into a negative one. "The kids see college students getting drunk and having a good time," Sandoval told *Nexus* reporter Daniel Haier. "They're given this false image of how things should be."[14]

Lieutenant Sol Linver of the IVFP agrees that Halloween cannot be separated from the larger Isla Vista party scene. Said Linver in an October interview:

I think you can't say "Okay, we're just going to deal with Halloween during Halloween" and not deal with the rest of the year. The [problem is with the] entire culture of I.V. [...] So if you try to deal with Halloween during those three or four days or however long it is, it's going to be an impossible task.[15]

Indeed, taming the Halloween scene has certainly proved an unwieldy, if not impossible task for police, who continue to ask for more funding, more officers, and more resources in order to combat the unruly October crowds. Meanwhile, Linver continues to advocate for taking a harder line against the Isla Vista party scene year round, introducing such controversial measures as the "fall offensive," a kind of back-to-school crackdown intended to curb illegal activity (largely alcohol- and drug-related offenses) from the first week of school.[16]

Meanwhile, the community and administration anxieties over the Halloween celebration, and the accompanying party-school reputation, do not appear to be shared by current UCSB students and alumni. According to Francis Burns, a political science major residing on Del Playa in 2003, "Halloween is part of our culture here... [it's] just part of I.V."[17] In fact, Halloween is frequently held up with pride as an example of UCSB's partying prowess. As Baldwin declared:

> "It's hard to explain, but Halloween was more than just a party; it was our flagship event. I.V. was ground zero for fun and everybody in the world seemed to know it. It was a thing of pride - not just your average partiers, we tore the roof off. As my friend Dan Umana put it, 'UCSB reveled in its reputation as a party school; we were in the top three party schools.' That's competitiveness on a national level."[18]

Current students may be quick to complain that "wandering up and down Del Playa... [gets] old super fast,"[19] yet they are equally quick to defend their party from accusations that it is no longer the raucous romp it once was. Current UCSB student Tyler Whalen protested, "I hate how everyone older is like, 'it's bad,' 'the party's over'... I don't see what's wrong with it. Everyone is there to party and have a good time. That's all it is."[20]

Though Halloween parties thrown in the bars and night clubs of downtown Santa Barbara's State Street have begun to offer viable competition to the Del Playa street scene, the relative crowd density at the 2003-2005 Isla Vista celebrations suggests that the open-air festival is still the preferred way to spend the holiday (particularly for those who are not yet twenty-one and are therefore barred from entering the downtown clubs).[21] Furthermore, the students I interviewed, regardless of how they feel about Halloween as an event, were uniformly opposed to intervention by the University. In short, the concerns of University policy makers, and those of the students, do not appear to mesh on this matter.

Perhaps due to this widely-recognized discrepancy, the university's official stance regarding Halloween remained, until quite recently, patently ambiguous. When asked for an opinion about Halloween in Isla Vista, most University officials have proclaimed themselves to be in favor of a "responsible" celebration. Associate Dean of Students Carolyn Buford told *Nexus* reporters that while no one was trying to keep anyone from enjoying the festivities, "the bottom line is that we are concerned for the safety of our students," Chancellor Yang concurred:

We do not wish to dictate our students' behavior or to prevent the people of Isla Vista from having a good time on Halloween; We do want to protect our students by promoting a safe and law-abiding environment where everyone can be free to enjoy themselves responsibly.[22]

Yang, who ventures into Isla Vista each Halloween with his wife, Dilling, and takes regular strolls along Del Playa year round, told *L.A. Times* reporter William Overend, "Our goal for Isla Vista and Del Playa is not to eradicate parties. We have no problem with low-risk drinking. The problem," said Yang, "is that there is very little that can be done to control the whole thing."[23]

Up until recently, the University has tried to maintain a hands-off approach when it comes to Halloween, allowing the police to handle the tricky matter of controlling "the whole thing."

Still, local police also paint a generally rosy picture of their relationship with UCSB students when addressing the press. "Well over half of our contacts and interaction with groups are positive," Isla Vista Foot Patrol (IVFP) Sergeant Tom Walton told *The Daily Nexus*. Officers, too, profess as their major concern the safety of the revelers, aiming not to shut down the party altogether, but merely to make it smaller, less dangerous, and more controlled. Stated UC Police Department Corporal Molitor in regards to the 2003 Halloween party: "There were a lot more people who we could have cited or arrested, but because of the crowds, safety came first."[24] Linver has expressed a similar preoccupation with safety, insisting that although he is a "firm believer" in having a good time, he cannot stand back and allow students to get hurt, or even to die, on his watch.

"I am very hurt that we had a young man fall off the cliff [in 2004, and that in 2003] we had a young girl fall of the cliff [who] survived although very, very seriously injured. We continually get people—emails, small groups—saying hey you shouldn't enforce alcohol laws, you know just let 'em have a good time. But they fall off cliffs. Their behaviors change under the influence of alcohol. They punch people, they get in fights, they assault people, sexual assault, all kinds of things. They become victims sometimes. But to me, loss of life, that's the ultimate."[25]

Linver insists that he feels a certain sense of responsibility to keep the students safe, even from themselves, and that his policing tactics stem directly from that sense of responsibility. He insists, however, that his aim is not to eradicate the Halloween event.

"The community enjoys it, I'm sure the business community enjoys it, and the students enjoy it. [...] There's some very creative students out here, and I've seen some really good costumes [...] I'd love to see a parade."

Although he hastened to add that he would prefer a sober, family oriented event, he nonetheless recognize that total sobriety is an unrealistic expectation for a college-aged crowd. "Party," advised Linver, "but do it safely and responsibly."[26]

In contrast to this ubiquitous, laissez faire rhetoric, however, apparent steps *have* been taken by local police, and ultimately the University, toward shutting down or at least severely restricting the Halloween festivities. The majority of policies instituted have been intended to control the influx of out-of-town visitors, who are, according to police statistics, largely responsible for the increased crime rate during Halloween.[27]

In 1988, for example, the Office of Residential Life instated a policy limiting the number of guests allowed during Halloween weekend to one hundred per residence hall, as opposed to the previous policy of one guest per resident.[28] Other interventions include: parking restrictions, warning letters sent to one hundred and fifteen colleges throughout California and Arizona, barricades around Del Playa and nearby Sabado Tarde that can only be crossed by providing proof of residency, and of course, the infamous Five Year Plan and all that accompanied it.[29]

> As one IVFP officer put it in an inspired statement that could easily pass for the opening lines of a rap song; "Safe and sane, you know, keep it home-grown that's the name of the game; keep the out-of-towners away and let's just have a lot of fun, that's all I have to say."[30]

Though the majority of the University and the police's efforts have been focused on reducing the number of out-of-town visitors, in 2003 direct action was taken to discourage UCSB students themselves from attending. Larger crowds were anticipated that year due to Halloween falling on a Friday in 2003, and to the unexpected, wholly undesirable publicity of the aforementioned *Rolling Stone* detailing UCSB students' exploitation by reality porn companies such as "Shane's World."[31] Media reports soon followed, including an October 23 article in the *Los Angeles Times* characterizing Halloween in Isla Vista as a wild, booze-soaked "Mardi Gras of the West."[32]

Hoping to inhibit participation in the dangerous and destructive Del Playa street party, the Office of Student Life sent out a university-wide email, whose subject line read "The party is over." The email sought "to inform [students] about possible fines, penalties and county ordinances and laws that [students] may very well face if [they] are in Isla Vista for Halloween this year." In the second paragraph was written, "There is NO party."[33]

Ironically, this ostensible "cancellation" of the Halloween party appears to have fueled the determination of the revelers. Current UCSB student Christina Ossa noted that, prior to receiving the e-mail, which she described as "threatening" in tone, she hadn't yet decided whether or not she wanted to go to Del Playa for Halloween. After reading the email, however, she became determined not only to go, but to talk her friends into joining her.[34]

Sophomore Carrie Awalt echoed this sentiment during a recent interview, saying that the email brought out her inner "warrior." Her apartment lease, along with the leases of many of her friends and neighbors, has what has come to be known as a "Halloween Clause," an increasingly popular method utilized by landlords to minimize property damage by explicitly disallowing out-of-town visitors during Halloween weekend. Yet, after having read the email, Awalt decided to take the risk of inviting friends to stay for the weekend regardless. When asked how she thought most students reacted, she replied, "I think pretty much everybody deletes it."[35] Judging from informal discussions with other students, I would have to agree with Awalt's assessment that the warning was largely ignored, if not taken as an outright dare.

The university's administrators were soon forced to confront this realization, as their 2003 attempt to shut down the Halloween party backfired spectacularly. As professors Catherine Cole, Harry Nelson, and Walter Yuen wrote in the final report of the Isla Vista Action Group,

"The various countermeasures derived from years of previous experience [...] appeared to be insufficient [...] the strength of the attraction of young people to see and be seen on Halloween was [...] underestimated."[36]

Indeed, the attraction of the event for probients had been underestimated, just as the effectiveness of the crowd-reducing measures had been overestimated, in 2003 as in other years. The result was extreme crowding, creating highly dangerous conditions that frequently bordered on stampeding.

One UCSB student, whom I shall call "Cindy," related a harrowing experience during the 2003 Del Playa street party: while wading through the enormous crowds with some friends, she became pinned against the side of a parked car when the flow of pedestrian traffic bottlenecked due to an impromptu strip-tease performed atop another parked vehicle. "A panic followed as people realized they were trapped. People began to push and even hit," Cindy writes. As more people attempted to force their way into the area, Cindy was repeatedly thrown against the car, kicked, and elbowed.

I felt several bodies land on top of me, crushing me against the car so that I couldn't breathe. I screamed. Finally someone on the other side of the car helped me to get over it and onto the sidewalk. [...] I saw some police officers standing together [...]. I told them that people were getting hurt and panicking nearby. [...] They shrugged at me and said, "We can't do anything about that."[37]

As Cindy's story illustrates, the police officers in attendance found themselves equally endangered under the extremely crowded conditions, and therefore unable to reach problem areas or to effectively help those who had been injured or violated. Cindy blames the police for failing to protect the revelers, stating "I ended up going home [...] very angry at the people who said they were there to protect us."[38] And yet, ironically enough, her tale provides compelling support for the need to reduce crowd density, which has long been the justification for the steady increase of officers patrolling the streets of Isla Vista on Halloween.[39]

1. Wrestling vs. rioting: new competing readings

Nearly three decades after the "mini-riots," violent theatrics, and theatricalized violence, continue to hold a prominent place in contemporary Halloween celebrations in Isla Vista. And just as it was in the late seventies, the difference between the two is largely a matter of perspective. I offer two examples from Halloween, 2004: first, a series of consciously staged "fights" by a group of revelers in Mexican wrestling regalia, resulting in the near-arrest of the performers, and second, an altercation between two revelers and subsequent arrest. Revelers read both events as forms of entertainment, while police officers interpreted both as threats to public safety, and to their authority.

On Halloween night, 2004, just as the crowd density was reaching its peak, my companions and I noticed a large circle of revelers forming around some kind of activity at a nearby intersection. Was it a performance? Was it a fight? As it turns out, it was a performance *of* a fight: three revelers dressed as Mexican wrestlers had staged a theatrical match in the middle of the intersection. Later, I discovered that one of the wrestlers was in fact an acquaintance of mine, Ethan Roberts, and I was able to fill in the details of the creation process, the performance, and its aftermath, in a March 2005 interview. "Two of my buddies and I rented some tights and bought Speedos and Mexican wrestler masks on e-bay, and we were Mexican wrestlers," explained Roberts. In order to ensure the attention of their peers, Roberts and his cohorts "staged these little fights."[40]

Those "little fights," as it turns out, were considerably more involved than I had first imagined. Not only had the performers rehearsed choreographed wrestling moves, they had gone to great lengths to set the stage and attract a crowd:

> "Two of my friends were in drag, they had water balloons for boobs and they were our sort of like 'rounds bearers' or whatever you call that. So we made signs that said 'round one' and we actually went to SOS and got some Budweiser posters, and we cut 'em up so it says Budweiser at the top, just like [at] a real wrestling match. And so [our two friends in drag] went around and they'd [...] walk around in a big circle, and hold up the signs, and people would just stop, and look, and say 'What's going on, there's two people holding up signs' you know, and then one of [the round-bearers] would go 'ding ding ding,' and we'd start the match. And we had these like, little choreographed moves worked out, and I had done some acting and so I knew how to take a stage dive, and how to sort of get hit without getting hit. So we had these really big wrestling matches, you know."

The performers' efforts to attract an audience most definitely paid off: I would estimate that the crowd gathered around the performance near where we were stationed counted between three and four hundred revelers, and Ethan described that crowd as being of "average" size for one of their impromptu performances.

Ethan went on to explain that, in addition to the choreographed fight moves, the performers had worked out a simple, good-versus-evil storyline, much like those presented in performances of professional wrestling.[41] He described the scene:

> "I was all in black, and my buddies were in green and purple. So they were the good guys and I was the bad guy, and they'd like tag-team me, and I just got like, mutilated and just like thrown on the ground and just like beat up all the time, but it was just so much fun, 'cause [...] people were like, 'Yeah, go black, go evil, go!' Everyone loved it, it was so funny."

Like the "devil bands" of Caribbean carnival, Ethan's "evil" character was embraced as a carnivalesque (anti-)hero, winning the crowd's support and thus triumphing despite being continually "mutilated" by his opponents.

The police, however, failed to see the humor in these presentations, which they read as incitements to violence among an already-volatile crowd. Officers continually warned Ethan and his friends to cease and desist, under threat of arrest.

> "The cops would come in every time and they'd say, like, 'Break this up! If you do this again, we're gonna arrest you for inciting a riot' you know like, 'rararar.' So, we'd just like walk down the block and do it again. And again and again, like, all night. 'Cause fuck the police, they can't do that shit; we're allowed to do what we want. So, anyway, we did. And we almost got arrested—Man, that was awful. And then we stopped. So, that kind of sucked. But yeah, it was really fun."

Although Ethan admits that coming so close to getting arrested was "awful," the joy with which he recounts the wrestlers' persistent, and rather flagrant violation of police orders, suggests that he felt it to be worth the trouble. In fact, it seems clear by his defiant, mocking tone ("rararar") that part of their motivation in persisting with the performance was to send the police, as well as the audience, a message. In fact, he states that message quite clearly in the above passage: "...fuck the police, they can't do that shit; we're allowed to do what we want." The persistent performance is thus intended to remind the police of their ultimate powerlessness over the activities of the revelers, and to encourage the revelers to "fight for [their] right to party."

Lt. Sol Linver explained the reason police were instructed to break up any potential crowd-drawing activities in an October 18, 2005 interview, saying,

"We can't afford to support a Mardi Gras mentality out there. We just don't have the room, or the resources, to deal with dense crowding. [...] It's fine for people to be walking up and down Del Playa, but we want them to keep moving."[42]

The Mexican Wrestling demonstrations presented a direct threat to public safety, in the opinion of the attending officers, by stopping the flow of traffic. In addition, the demonstrations, while clearly undergone in a spirit of playful theatrics, would seem to glorify hand-to-hand combat as entertainment.

Indeed, when a fight broke out later that same night, just two blocks from the spot where the wrestlers had begun their performance series, it was difficult to differentiate the two events based on crowd reaction. Just as with the faux fight, this actual altercation quickly drew a sizable following, and, as with the earlier, staged version, prompted much yelling and cheering on the part of those gathered. After a few moments, the police penetrated the crowd and handcuffed one of the combatants. Loud booing then erupted from the crowd, followed by a discernible chant: "Let him go! Let him go!" The police, however, did not release their suspect, and eventually the crowd dispersed.

Although one event was intended to amuse, the other to inflict bodily harm, both displays were read in nearly identical ways by the crowd (as entertainment) and by the police (as dangerous, riot-inciting behavior).

The revelers' reading of the fight as entertainment explains their resentment when the police, who read it simply as violence, arrest one of the "performers". Still viewing the event as an opportunity for amusement, the revelers once again transform the genre of the performance, this time from a sporting event to a political protest. Their collective chant of "let him go!" recasts the gathered revelers as protestors, the police as oppressors. This, however, simply strengthens the conviction of the arresting officers that they are dealing with potential rioters and are therefore charged to maintain order, whatever the cost.

These competing readings suggest that the revelers and attendant officers are still not in agreement regarding the place of violence, and yes, of theatre, at Halloween. They further suggest that the very purpose of the event is still up for debate, and that neither the police nor the revelers are likely to adopt the other's point of view when such grandiose concepts as public safety and personal liberty are viewed as hanging in the balance.

2. Taking action: the IVAG

Given this ongoing disagreement about the function of Halloween in Isla Vista, it should come as little surprise that attempts to address its dysfunctional aspects have been largely unsuccessful. There are, however, a few exceptions to this rule, and I would like to examine what I believe to be one such an exception: the planned intervention in the 2004 Halloween carnival by the Isla Vista Action Group.

Partly in reaction to the near-disaster of the overcrowding in 2003, and partly in reaction to the fall 2003 "reality porn" scandal, a group of UCSB faculty members, staff, and students, in addition to members of the larger Isla Vista community joined forced to create the Isla Vista Action Group (IVAG). The IVAG produced a final report that was similar to the review carried out by the Trinidadian Colonial Secretary in 1882, and which resulted in comparable changes in policy.[43]

Rather than resorting to the kind of threatening language used prior to the 2003 celebration (which ironically resulted in one of the largest, most volatile crowds to hit Del Playa since the early '90's),

Halloween planners took a more complicit approach in 2004, asking revelers to take responsibility for their own party by keeping the festivities "safe" and "local." As in Trinidad, this yielded a much more positive result for all involved.

Like the wild weekends of the 1980's, the 2003 influx of out-of-town visitors was blamed on a perceived link to pornography, and to unsolicited publicity in a national magazine. Also, as in past years, discussion focused on how to curb attendance and increase law enforcement's ability to control the crowd.

But unlike in preceding years, the planning for Halloween 2004 *did* take into account the attraction of that which has been banned, and rather than attempting to keep UCSB students away from Del Playa on Halloween, efforts focused on circulating a "keep Halloween local" sentiment among the UCSB student population. As various IVAG members pointed out during the numerous planning meetings leading up to the weekend of October 31st, 2004,[44] students were more likely to respond positively to a campaign that encouraged them to reclaim their party from potentially destructive outsiders than to one that characterized the students themselves as destructive outsiders invading, and most likely trashing, the University-enclosed enclave of Isla Vista.

In order to enforce the "keep Halloween local" attitude adopted by the IVAG and the Major Events Committee, several specific actions were taken, all of them aimed at curbing outsider attendance.

First, a highly restrictive parking plan was put into effect for the weekend of October 29-31: no one unaffiliated with the University would be permitted to park on campus after 5 p.m. UCSB students, on the other hand, were offered a free parking pass for that weekend in order to protect their vehicles from the mayhem and rampant vandalism which traditionally accompany the holiday. Furthermore, any cars parked on Del Playa drive would have to be moved prior to 5 p.m.: no street parking, and no traffic circulation would be permitted during the festivities.

Concomitantly, a strict no-visitor policy was adopted for all those living in on-campus housing, and parking at off-campus university-owned facilities, as well as a number of commercial and residential areas surrounding Isla Vista, was highly restricted.

Despite trepidation on the part of several IVAG members (including me) the plan was put into effect, and was by most accounts highly successful. The absence of parked cars on Del Playa freed up a remarkable amount of space for pedestrians, so that even at its largest, the crowd never appeared to be teetering on the edge of a stampede, and participants did not report feeling the same sense of panic or potential disaster as in 2003.

Likewise, police felt considerably more in control of the situation than they had the previous year. In an interview with *Daily Nexus* reporter Matt Dozier, Lt. Sol Linver of the Isla Vista Foot Patrol said:

"The restrictions forbidding parking on DP during this year's Halloween weekend have helped tremendously in keeping the celebrations safe and manageable for police and residents. I think it was one of the best things we've ever done."[45]

Police were certainly able to make more arrests than in previous years: more than 300 people were booked over the course of the weekend. While many UCSB students felt the police had been unnecessarily aggressive, police defended their tactics by pointing out that almost no violent crime was reported during the course of the weekend.[46] As Linver put it, "One of the goals with the arrests is to stop incidents before they occur."[47]

This trend continued at the 2005 Halloween event, which saw slightly fewer arrests and which, according to Linver, also boasted "No stabbings, no serious injuries, no serious assaults, or assaults with a deadly weapon."[48]

The question remains, however: was the relative lack of reported violent crime and serious injury in 2004 and 2005 due to law enforcement's increased ability to identify and arrest potentially violent revelers (thanks to a higher police-to-reveler ratio than in previous years), or was it indeed out-of-towners who had been injecting unwanted violence into an otherwise-innocent and fun-loving crowd?

My observations, and those of interviewees and fellow graduate students taking field notes, do indicate a correlation between large numbers of out-of-towners and an increase in incidences of violence, harassment, vandalism, and general hostility, as well as a decline in the creativity and quality of the costumes.

In 2005, for example, there was a drastic contrast in atmosphere between the Saturday night crowd, which was heavy on out-of-town visitors, and the Friday, Sunday, and Monday (October 31) crowds, which were comprised almost entirely of UCSB students and their guests, and even a few local families. The following description of the Saturday night crowd is excerpted directly from my field notes:

"Saturday had a markedly different feel to it than the rest of the weekend. The crowd began peaking much later – around 11:30 rather than 10, as was the case Friday – and I would estimate that more than 50% of those late arrivals were out-of-towners (OOTs). The OOTs marked themselves not only via behavioral signifiers—i.e. asking for directions, complaining about the lack of amenities, (etc.)—but also by their costumes, which seemed relatively thrown-together and less group-oriented than the other nights. There were also large groups *not* in costume at all, and nearly all of these groups were comprised of young men.[49] There was a good deal of discontent and aggression palpable by midnight. Those who had not found a party were disappointed and increasingly desperate, and began harassing women rather than offering clever come-ons as they had earlier in the evening. One could hear a number of OOTs complaining that the event had not lived up to its reputation as a place to get trashed and laid, and were beginning to head back to their cars, angry and disillusioned."[50]

As I was escorted home that night by a concerned friend (an hour or so after having been assaulted), I recorded a rant by one such an angry out-of-town visitor, walking with his companions in the direction of Goleta where, presumably, they had been forced to park. Here I offer a partial transcript as an example of the kind of vehement, anti-Isla Vistan (not to mention misogynistic) sentiment that was rapidly circulating by the end of the night:

> "Fuck this fucking place. I'm never coming back to fucking I.V. The only time I end up here is on Halloween cuz everybody says 'it's off the hook, you gotta come down,' but then I get here and the chicks are all gone, there's no fucking beer and all the girls think they're hot shit. Fucking sluts."

This probient fellow's anger and disappointment at having come all the way "down" to Isla Vista (likely from San Luis Obispo or perhaps Santa Cruz) on the (apparently false) promise of free beer and easy women is quite telling. He disregarded the warnings, drove many miles, and walked a few more in the expectation of achieving gratification, empowerment, and social advancement. Instead, he found himself in the decidedly disempowering position of being blocked from entry to the parties that might provide the kind of gratification he was seeking.

On a personal level, this rant offered me some insight as to what kind of inner monologue might have been running through the mind of my attacker earlier that night. Perhaps I represented to him this place that he believed to have made a fool of him in some sense—worse still, I was a *woman*, yet another "slut" who would likely refuse him the satisfaction and social advancement implied in sexual conquest. And honestly, he wasn't wrong about that.

Or perhaps he simply wanted to victimize someone—*anyone*—in order to feel more empowered, and as a woman walking alone, I was an easy target. In either case, hearing that young man's angry words after experiencing a random act of violence did seem to lend support to the theory that the kind of aggressive, destructive behavior that has led locals to view Halloween in Isla Vista as a scourge upon their community can be largely attributed to out-of-town visitors.

More generally, it left me with a sense that there may be more to this behavior than a simple equation of rampant hormones plus lack of parental supervision equals violence and destruction. Rather, it may be that the attending probients who have been frustrated in their attempt to gain social advancement and personal satisfaction via culturally-defined gratification (in this case, free beer and easy sex), victimize others as a means of reducing their own feelings of disempowerment.

The ingredients feeding into this volatile solution are: the event's reputation as a place of empowerment and gratification for probients (which, as we have seen, is largely the work of the probients themselves), and the contrasting reality of a space in which such empowerment and gratification is severely limited, largely due to restrictions placed by law enforcement in conjunction with the University (i.e. the Festival Ordinance and the No Tolerance policy).

Although the "Keep Halloween Local" policy appears to have been successful in reducing some of the most heinous side-effects of the annual bash in 2004 and 2005, I would argue that out-of-towners will continue to seek entry, and will continue to become angry and disillusioned, so long as law enforcement continues to outlaw any kind of activity that might be deemed satisfying and/or empowering to those who cannot gain entrance to a private party. Lt. Linver spoke to this issue when he said in an October, 2005 interview that he is considering adding in new elements over the next few years that may act as alternatives to the private party scene on Del Playa, for example, a parade:

> "If you want to do the costume thing on Halloween night, fine, let's have a parade around the loop, [or] around town where you show off your costumes. [...] I mean, I think that'd be great if on Halloween the fraternities and sororities made floats to compete. And their floats are judged, the costumes are judged [...]. Get some competition involved, that sort of thing. I'd love to see that."[51]

Linver also expressed a desire to make Halloween a more community-oriented event by involving local families. He said that although the IVRPD's annual Halloween / Dia de los Muertos event in Anisq'Oyo Park is a good start, there is much more that could be done to transform Halloween in Isla Vista into "a more family-oriented event."

> "We keep a giant bowl of candy here at the foot patrol so when kids come by we'll give them stickers and candy and things along those lines. But I would love to be able to see more trick-or-treaters, deputies handing out candy and such things. And for the older kids, if you will, a parade. [...] I'd love to see a parade, and involve the kids. You know how at Fiesta they have a parade, and on the following day they do a children's parade? Why not something like that out here?"[52]

Given the historical failure of policies aimed at stifling the carnivalesque—not only in Isla Vista but in communities world-wide—I would argue that ideas such as those offered by Linver, aimed at transforming rather than trampling Halloween in Isla Vista, are much more likely to be successful in combating its ills. A grass-roots parade run by student and community organizations, could indeed do much to emphasize the creative, expressive, theatrical, and transformative elements already present, as well as to engender cooperation across the lines of age, race, and class along which Isla Vista is currently segregated. It could also provide out-of-town visitors with free entertainment (i.e. gratification), and an opportunity for participation in a more recognizable public spectacle (i.e. empowerment).

However, I would warn against anything too institutionalized or rigidly structured: if the students do not feel they are in control of the event, and particularly if they see it as a paltry substitute for the Del Playa scene, rather than a welcome addition to their self-styled event, it is not likely to take root and flourish.

THE BEGINNING OF THE "PARTY AT THE END..."

*I*n the course of its relatively protracted history, Halloween in Isla Vista has managed to garner a number of remarkable parallels to Trinidad's epic tale of regulation and resistance.

From its inception, it has been the subject of heated debate in the local press; complaints and quips about the overtly sexual costumes, and the raunchy, disrespectful behavior of the revelers have become so commonplace as to be practically traditional. Like its Caribbean cousin, Halloween in Isla Vista has seen multiple attempts by local authorities to regulate or outright annihilate the festivities associated with it, some more successful than others.

And, like their Trinidadian counterparts, the Isla Vista Halloween revelers have met these setbacks with various strategies of resistance, also with varying degrees of success. The No Tolerance policy adopted by county police has altered, though not necessarily ameliorated, the Halloween revelers' behavioral patterns, particularly in regards to alcohol consumption.

Like the Trinidadians, Isla Vistans have evolved complex strategies for avoiding arrest, without actually abstaining from the outlawed activities. And just as the Trinidadian authorities eventually concluded that the Carnival cannot be quashed, that their only hope of regulation lies in securing the help of the revelers themselves, County police and University officials appear to have come to a similar realization in regards to Halloween in Isla Vista.

In the previous section, I set up a theoretical framework for recognizing carnivalesque phenomena in the United States, stating that events in this category should display an ambiguous relationship to authority, and will likely face continual opposition to, and/or attempts at co-option by, those in power. I trust I have made it apparent in the course of this section that this is patently the case for Halloween in Isla Vista.

While Chancellor Yang publicly denounces Halloween as the primary culprit in terms of perpetuation UCSB's party school reputation, he hasn't missed his annual October 31 stroll down Del Playa in over a decade. And while local police continue to rail against the dangers of Halloween in Isla Vista, it is apparent that the event has come to be an important annual public performance, and even celebration, for law enforcement as well. For attending officers, the Halloween weekend begins with a mass debriefing which I think I will be forgiven for comparing to an opening-night gala: everyone arrives decked out in uniform, and the press is exceptionally allowed in to snap a few photos and to record the official statement of welcome.[1]

Next, Embarcadero Hall (ironically enough, the former site of the Bank of America, burned by rioters in 1970—see section four) is transformed into the aptly named "staging area," an impromptu headquarters for police operations during the Halloween weekend. In addition to housing police equipment and serving as a sort of "home base" for officers, the staging area also serves as a public spectacle of police presence.

Yet even that spectacle is ambiguous. On one side of the building, a field booking station acts as a sort of living cautionary tale, a constant visual reminder of where revelers might end up if they step out of line. On the other side of the building, off-duty officers enjoy roast chicken hot off the rotisserie grill, feasting and socializing in full view of revelers on their way to and from Del Playa. This is their party, too

—or at any rate, they have created their own party in reaction to, and coincident with, that of the revelers.

Meanwhile, the spectacle of the revelers continues to adapt and evolve in reaction to, and coincident with, the police performance. Though each event defines itself in opposition to the other, the two performances overlap, feed into and refract off of one another; they are codependent, amorphous, inextricable. The one cannot exist without the other, and I predict that each will continue—albeit perhaps unwittingly—to serve as antidote for its shadow-event for many years to come.

I believe this is only the beginning for the "Party at the End of the World," as the Del Playa Halloween scene is affectionately known among the initiated. What it becomes and what becomes of it will depend not only on the conscious actions of participants, police, and University administrators, but on the collective unconscious of the community of Isla Vista.

In fact, cultural climate may well play a larger role than any kind of calculated planning, which is part of what makes Halloween such a rich resource in term of reading contemporary probient culture. In the next section, I provide a selected history and description of the place of Isla Vista, so that readers might better understand the specific cultural-geographical context of this, my chosen representative example of the contemporary United States Carnivalesque.

PART IV
MASKING AT THE MARGINS

CONFINING THE CARNIVALESQUE

ISLA VISTA: ON THE EDGE

"If the ancient, religious carnival was limited in time, the modern, mass-carnival is limited in space: it is reserved for certain places, certain streets, or framed by the television screen."

- Umberto Eco[1]

1. **Pilgrimage to the party place**

Strolling down Del Playa one early August morning of the year 2005, a companion and I were surprised to see a sizable procession of bicycles headed towards us. The sight of so many casually-dressed cyclists, many of them holding six-packs of beer and whooping loudly, would not normally have been so surprising within the Isla Vista milieu. Yet the wide age range of the participants, along with the baffled responses to our inquiries from Del Playa residents, suggested that this was not, in fact, a traditional Isla Vistan event.

We followed this strange procession of rowdy revelers, which included such unusual sights (within the Del Playa milieu, that is) as pre-teen children, middle-aged and gray-haired adults, and even a pregnant woman, out to Devereux Point, just behind West Campus Family Student Housing. There, some four-hundred cyclists were gathered, spreading out across the access road and into a field normally populated by rabbits, lizards, and the occasional errant jogger.

The roar from the crowd was so overwhelming that we didn't dare approach the revelers directly. Instead, we asked an officer stationed in his vehicle, "What event is this?"

With a weary sigh, he explained that, for the last four years, on the final day of Fiesta, a group of revelers has been riding from Stearn's Wharf in downtown Santa Barbara, all the way out to Isla Vista and back. "Most of them are smashed out of their minds," he said, shaking his head, "already had a pretty nasty crash, whole slough of them in the hospital."

Turning the corner, we noticed an ambulance, patiently awaiting the next batch of casualties. The revelers, however, seemed entirely undaunted by the specter of a police citation, or even a trip to the Emergency Room. As we watched them whooping it up, drinking and carrying on mid-street, my companion and I agreed that it was not difficult to see why they had chosen Isla Vista as their destination of choice. Where else but Isla Vista could one take over this much public space in the name of drunken revelry?

2. The graffiti wall

Whenever I try to conjure a comparison to describe the function of Isla Vista within the surrounding community, I come up against the same image: a small, graffiti-covered brick wall on the outskirts of Geneva, Switzerland.

When I first arrived in that immaculate, cosmopolitan city, I was stunned by how clean and orderly it all seemed. *"How do they do it?"* I wondered, strolling past wall after pristine wall. It wasn't until I had lived there several months that I discovered the answer to my question: there is a wall, approximately ten feet high and twenty feet long, poised on the threshold of downtown Geneva, which is incessantly covered—every inch of it covered—with graffiti. Although it has not been officially designated as a "graffiti wall" by the city, those in charge of painting over graffiti have clearly given up on that one brick bastion, and unofficially allow the city's spray-can artists to reign there. The graffiti wall signifies a sort of tacit agreement between a city obsessed with unsullied structures and those citizens who long to deface them.

I posit that this is Isla Vista's function within the well-to-do communities of the University of California and Santa Barbara: it is the graffiti wall, the unofficially designated marginal space for the unruly impulses which those in power would prefer not to have to confront on a daily basis.

So as not to besmirch the carefully-guarded public spaces of Santa Barbara, would-be revelers are forced either to crowd into commercial spaces downtown—bars, clubs, and (during Fiesta) beer gardens—or to relocate to the streets of that designated party place, Isla Vista. It is a vibrant space, just as the graffiti wall is more colorful and exciting to look at than the unmolested but uninspired solid-colored walls surrounding it. But it is also an exploited space, viewed by outsiders as abandoned and forlorn, and used as a dumping ground for the rejected behaviors of polite society.

Like the probient revelers who converge on Isla Vista during Halloween, these Santa Barbarians and assorted tourists cycle across the marshlands to take advantage of what has come to be recognized as Isla Vista's only natural resource: space; an open area large enough to accommodate this kind of carnivalesque social abandon.

Isla Vista, like the graffiti wall, is an intriguing mess, as attractive as it is repugnant, and both provide an unspoken explanation for the surreal orderliness of the surrounding communities. In this section, I will argue that Isla Vista's geographical layout, combined with its unusual cultural history, have created a space that is uniquely suited to hosting such an infamous annual event.

RADICAL FREEDOM AND THE MARGINALIZATION OF MASQUERADE

"Whereas before, prohibition relied upon discourse and could therefore be confronted, now it seems that only the police remain."

Beatriz Sarlo[1]

*D*espite the ubiquity of notions of individual sovereignty in the contemporary U.S., "freedom" is still a tricky question. Even as postmodern Americans are pressured to express and exploit to the logical limit their unprecedented freedom of choice, other freedoms are being increasingly limited in the name of public safety.

Indeed, "Public safety" itself has come to mean something quite different than it once did, and thus the role of those charged with defending it (read: the United States police force) has shifted significantly. Because individual happiness, defined, as I have argued, by culturally-driven consumption, is the goal of postmodern existence, the task with which the contemporary police are charged has necessarily changed. Whereas in the 19th and early 20th centuries, police represented the central authority of the nation-state, and were charged with defending public safety and order, in the late 20th and early 21st centuries, police are expected to protect the interests of individuals by ensuring that private space remains private, and public space remains safe and comfortable for consumers. The result is that those who are unwilling or unable to maintain a private space, or to correctly perform the rituals of production and consumption, are recast as the enemy against which upper- and middle-class citizens must be protected.

Nowhere is this more true than in Los Angeles, where the technologically sophisticated police force is charged with defending private space (and, increasingly, so-called "public" spaces such as parks and shopping centers) from unwanted intruders—in other words, to keep the have-nots away from the haves. This has prompted Los Angeles historian Mike Davis to nickname the L.A.P.D. the "space police": not only are they space (age) police in terms of their weaponry and equipment, their primary role is to enforce divisions of space: who is authorized to be where and for what purpose.[2]

While public faith in authority (government in particular) continues to decline, the police and the U.S. military, understood as the public's only defense against imminent disaster, are ironically offered the power to deny individual freedoms in the interest of the greater good.[3] Sarlo illuminates this paradox when she writes that "authority has lost its terrible and intimidating aspect (which stirred rebellion) and is now only authority when it exercises (as it does with increasing frequency) repressive force."[4] In the context of the United States, I take this to mean that authority (in the form of government, police, or military) no longer inspires awe or fear until it is clear that one's rights/freedoms are being blatantly denied.

One of the most popularly rescinded freedoms within the current political climate is the right to public assembly, particularly for the purpose of carnivalesque celebration. As public space shrinks and behavior within it becomes increasingly regulated, the place of the carnivalesque is pushed even further toward the margins of society, and increasingly quarantined within spatially limited, relatively controllable areas.

As Umberto Eco notes, contemporary carnival is no longer limited to certain times of the year; the carnivalesque can now be found year round, but only in "certain places, certain streets, or framed by the television screen."[5] In the postmodern world, the carnivalesque arts of rule-reversal and outrageous behavior are generally experienced vicariously through film and television, and the act of masquerading mostly takes place over the internet, in "chat rooms" where identity is obscured and interactions otherwise deemed socially inappropriate are safely allowable.[6] In a sense, it comes as no great surprise that carnivalesque energy would now be spatially rather than temporally limited, since contemporary carnival has become ideologically separated from the cyclical rites upon which ancient carnival was based. Yet the fervor with which the carnivalesque is suppressed in the public spaces of the United States, and the violence with which it resurfaces in certain marginalized spaces suggests an underlying cultural anxiety that deserves further investigation.

My theory is that the need in the U.S. to limit the spaces in which carnivalesque performance is permissible is rooted in a collective cultural anxiety about the perceived encroachment of the virtual into the realm of the "real," the impossibility of accurately distinguishing "between a meaning-packed world, in which every sign breathes significance, and a world in which signs have become 'self-sufficient' – a society of 'hyperreality' in Jean Baudrillard's terms."[7] Timothy Bewes names this late-capitalist anxiety *Reification*, or the "thingly" quality of human experience: the ease with which the world as we encounter it, including our selves and the products of our labour, is transformed into a serious of objects that are removed from us, and towards which we may feel a sense of reverence, or loss, or revulsion.[8]

To use a pop cultural analogy: the "reality T.V." craze in the United States ("reality porn" included), along with popular films like the *Matrix* series[9], would certainly seem to suggest an American preoccupation with authenticity, a collective longing for some "reality" on which simulation is based.

Yet these mediatized attempts to capture "the real" succeed only in further reifying experience, solidifying people into recognizable "types" and alienating viewers from lived experience via a process which Jagodzinski names "interpassivity." According to Jagodzinski, interpassivity is the point at which "passivity itself simply vanishes" so that "the program itself is paradoxically enjoying all of your affective states as it manipulates you into doing its bidding." Jagodzinski's claim is that as you (i.e. the viewer) allow the characters on a reality T.V. show (for example) to emote for you, to experience and take action in your stead,

You simply 'vanish' into its symbolic universe as 'it' does it all for you. Although you think you are being active in it, you are being duped of your jouissance.[10]

Thus the anxiety over the loss of "reality," the perceived dearth of immediacy and authenticity in contemporary American life, has ironically resulted in an art form that relies on reification, interpassivity, and distance.

"The very idea of reification," argues Bewes, "implies a society in a state of degeneration, and a prevailing sense of nostalgia for what has vanished: pathos, joy, immediacy, beauty."[11]

Again, the term "nostalgia" implies that the vanished objects (pathos, joy, immediacy, beauty) need not have actually existed in a more tangible form at some previous state, only that their perceived loss induces a collective anxiety which, ironically, reproduces the experience of reification itself. Feelings of anxiety and nostalgia over this perceived loss of "the real" are, according to Bewes, "constitutive of the experience of reification." In short, "the anxiety towards reification is *itself reifying.*"[12]

The street theatre of carnivalesque masquerade produces a great deal of anxiety over the perceived loss of the mythical dividing line between the real and the virtual, reality and representation. This nostalgia for authenticity is manifest in the collective desire for a clearly delineated separation between the stage/screen as a place of pretense, and the public street as the domain of the real. The carnivalesque inverts this rule of separation, brazenly demonstrating that art and life, the possible and the real, imitation and innovation, are in fact indistinguishable. Not only does it deliberately defy convention and contradict cherished classifications, it actively calls into question the legitimacy of those classifications, their assumed primacy as the "natural" order of things.

Iteration, imitation, and exaggeration are not only constructive tools, solidifying reality through repetition, they are also deconstructive: by exposing the arbitrary and mechanical process of reality-construction, they can ultimately undermine our faith in the primacy of the reigning schema.

Judith Butler refers to "subversive" or "disruptive repetition" as a strategy for destabilizing compulsory social tropes. The desiring self, argues Butler, is continually constituted, and reconstituted, through repetitive play (i.e. performance). And yet, "it is precisely the *repetition* of that play that establishes as well the *instability* of the very category that it constitutes."[13] Via disruptive repetition, the ostensible "copy" of some supposed "original" exposes that "original" as equally constructed, derivative, and reliant on continual reiteration.

In other words, the entire framework of copy and origin proves radically unstable. [...] *imitation* does not copy that which is prior, but produces and *inverts* the very terms of priority and derivativeness.[14]

The notion of imitation as an agent of destabilization is particularly relevant to carnivalesque play. Masquerade exposes identity—both individual and collective—as an unstable construct in need of continual reinforcement via performance. As Butler argued in *Gender Trouble*, "there need not be a 'doer behind the deed,' [rather,] the 'doer' is invariably constructed in and through the deed."[15]

I argue that the "deed" of carnivalesque masquerade illustrates the constructedness of the masquerader, and indeed of anyone with whom the masquerader comes into contact.

The cherished classifications of "art" (mimesis) and "[real] life" (existence), are dependent upon the notion of an underlying subject that precedes performance, a primary, "natural" self that can "pretend" to be other than itself through the act of mimicry. By exposing the self as actually constituted by the act of mimicry, rather than prior and opposed to it, Carnival constitutes a viable threat to the dominant paradigm. For this reason, U.S. carnival traditions tend to thrive within already-marginalized spaces—for example, the Castro District in San Francisco and Greenwich Village in New York (both bohemian, predominantly gay neighborhoods; both home to well-known Halloween parades and other carnivalesque events), and Brooklyn's Crown Heights (a volatile neighborhood of mixed Hasidic, African-American, and Caribbean-American inhabitants; home to the New York Carnival in September). And although Mardi Gras parades once took place in many different New Orleans neighborhoods, after the September 11, 2001 terrorist attacks, the routes were considerably shortened and confined to easily monitored areas such as St. Charles Avenue. Furthermore, the majority of the recognizably carnivalesque behavior—i.e. masking, suspension of social hierarchy, intoxication, and generally raunchy and outrageous behavior—has always been confined to the French Quarter, an isolated "theme park" of old French culture.

There are some notable exceptions to the rule of marginalization, but on closer inspection these would seem to prove that rule rather than undermine it. Caribana, the Toronto Carnival celebration, parades through a main, harbor-front section of the city. However, it should be noted that this tradition, rather than beginning in the usual way—that is, as a repeated, semi-spontaneous outburst of celebratory energy among a large group of people that is eventually solidified into an official event—Caribana was consciously created by ten individuals of West Indian heritage living in Toronto, in conjunction with the Canadian government.

As Pat Shepard of the Multicultural History Society of Toronto notes, the "dream" of Caribana "was forged in the heady days of 1967, when Canada was celebrating its Centennial and the West Indian community was asked to make a contribution which would enhance the celebrations of Expo '67. It took the form of a colourful parade down Yonge Street."[16] It seems clear from the tone of this official description of the event's creation that the commissioning of the first Caribana parade was a calculated move on the part of the Canadian government to project an official image of Canada as a nation that celebrates diversity and subsidizes "colourful" multicultural projects like the Caribana parade. The subsequent adoption of Caribana as an annual celebration can be seen as a continuation of that original, politically-motivated and exoticism-fueled impulse, as well as an impressive victory for Canada's West Indian population in terms of political visibility and economic return.

Similarly, the Philadelphia Mummer's Parade, easily one of the most overlooked Carnival celebrations the world over, takes place in the heart of downtown Philadelphia. The parade takes over the central thoroughfare of Broad Street (ending at City Hall) for the whole of New Year's Day, with Mummer-related activities stretching well into December and January, and preparations taking place throughout the year. However, as Medieval performance scholar Claire Sponsler argues in *Ritual Imports*, the New Year's festivities that preceded the creation of an official parade were hardly embraced by Philadelphia's ruling classes. The mainstreaming of the Mummer's Parade must be understood as part of a calculated political effort on the part of the city's elite to reify the city's imagined link to "the real and imagined festive rituals of medieval England." Once known as "*belsnickles*, callithumpians, fanatasticals, or shooters," the rowdy New Year's revelers began to be called "mummers" in Philadelphia's news-papers around the end of the nineteenth century. Argues Sponsler,

> "It is no coincidence that this semantic shift occurred during the years of the great wave of immigration to the United States from eastern and southern Europe that created an anxious search for ways of 'Americanizing' new immigrants whose cultural traditions were not those of Protestant northern Europe."[17]

Much in the same way that middle class Trinidadians sought to transform the rowdy "Jamette" Carnival into a celebration of official (read: middle class) Trinidadian culture, Philadelphia's civic authorities aimed at redeeming what they viewed as a chronic headache into an organized event that would encourage "assimilation into a nationalism that was increasingly defined as Anglo-Saxon."[18] Thus, just as the Trinidadian "stickfighters" were transformed into "mas players," the Philadelphian "shooters," an epithet that bespeaks violence and unrest, became the "mummers," a term intended to conjure visions of lighthearted dancing and merriment.

As in the case of Trinidad, the transformation has been largely successful, although the Mummer's Parade "still manages to provoke controversy, and disruption still lurks beneath its surface." Writes Sponsler: "despite the efforts of reformers, it seems that at least some features of the parade's earlier incarnations have survived to challenge the official spectacle."[19]

This ongoing threat of disruption, controversy, and general rowdiness may serve to explain why the Mummer's Parade remains so pointedly overlooked. Despite its popularity within the greater Philadelphia metropolitan area, it is not televised nationally and remains virtually unheard of outside the Northeastern United States. So although this New Year's carnival has been exceptionally allowed to overtake a major Downtown section of its city of origin, it remains patently marginalized within the popular U.S. imagination.

THE END OF THE WORLD

ISLA VISTA'S SPATIAL SYSTEM

"Of course Isla Vista was a Ghetto [...] with the highest population density in California. Two-thirds of the residents were under twenty-one years old, making Isla Vista a sociologist's dream for pure research in a 'youth community,' a revolutionary's ideal of a potential 'liberated zone.'"

John Stickney, late 1960's Isla Vista observer[1]

One could not possibly wish for a more marginalized space than that of Isla Vista, California.

Isla Vista is not in fact a city, but rather a geographical-cultural space that requires a good deal of explanation/orientation to those not familiar with its layout and the history that forged it.

In keeping with Una Chaudhuri's notion of "spatial intelligibility"—the idea that *where* an action unfolds goes a long way toward explaining it—I think it useful to offer a description of the geographical space in which this unique place exists, and the unusual ways in which that space is utilized by its inhabitants, before exploring Isla Vista's rich and complex history.[2]

Isla Vista is, quite literally, in a rather awkward position, caught between extremes of isolation and over-exposure. Surrounded on all sides by physical, social, and psychological barriers, yet offered little protection from natural and man-made forces of destruction, Isla Vista is both marginalized and continually scrutinized by the surrounding communities of Goleta, the University, and Santa Barbara. All of these factors have earned it the affectionate appellation "the End of the World."

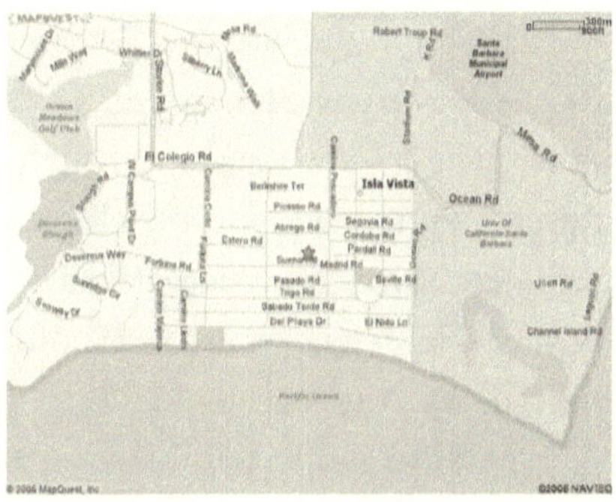

To the South lies the ocean: a seductive and occasionally destructive neighbor; to the East the so-called "Eucalyptus curtain" demarcates the barrier between I.V. and the U.C.S.B. campus; to the North lies more University-owned land, the Santa Barbara municipal airport, Highway 101, and beyond that, the mountains; and to the West, along with yet more University-owned land, there remains an endangered swath of open-space, a reminder of the kind of rugged, inhospitable landscape in which Isla Vista first took root.

Although working-class families are beginning to populate the outer edges of Isla Vista, the central core of the place, Del Playa in particular, is remarkably homogenous in terms of age.

Largely considered a "slum" or "ghetto" by residents and non-residents alike, the area is continually maligned in local lore as a kind of holding-tank for out-of-control students: an unattractive, shoddily constructed cesspool of iniquity only a boozy undergraduate could love.

1. A cityless center?

Although I have been walking or bicycling across its length twice a day for four years now, after reading Michel de Certeau's *The Practice of Everyday Life*, I have become hyper-aware of the nontraditional layout of Isla Vista, and the ways in which pedestrians like me make use of it.[3] Just as de Certeau predicts, in privileging progress/process —i.e. the time it takes me to travel from University-owned Family Student Housing (which hugs the Western perimeter of Isla Vista, bumping up against the Devereux Slough and Ocean Meadows Golf Club) to the campus proper—the space through which my body moves becomes my conceptual blind spot.[4] My physical proximity and quotidian engagement with the space of Isla Vista, as foretold in the philosophy of Martin Heidegger, has correspondingly reduced my conceptual awareness of it. And yet, as Heidegger warns, I cannot consider my being, separate from my being *here*, in this spatial container of Isla Vista.[5] In other words, what I do is inextricably tied to the space in which I do it, and the same is true for everyone around me. Thus, if I hope to illuminate *what* happens at Halloween—the *behavior* of the revelers—I must first become aware of *where* it happens—the space-place of Isla Vista.

Isla Vista, like all localities, presents a particular spatial system. This system, according to de Certeau, "organizes an ensemble of possibilities [...] and interdictions," ways in which I can and cannot choose to move.[6] The choices I make, along with those of all the other bodies I encounter, compose the "urban text" of Isla Vista, one that we are collectively writing and which none of us is fully able to read. In fact, few of us bother to try: if we are at all aware of this text, we are solely focused on our own particular role in it, the lines of our individual movements; rarely do we even attempt to imagine what this performance might resemble or convey when taken as a whole. The layered patterns of our walking, cycling, skating, and driving compose "a manifold story that has neither author nor spectator," only myriad actors moving across a common stage.[7]

If de Certeau is to be believed when he states that "spatial practices in fact secretly structure the determining conditions of social life," then the key to understanding Isla Vistan society lies somewhere between its physical layout and the navigational patterns of those who move through it.[8]

2. What happens in Isla Vista, stays in Isla Vista

Despite an apparent lack of casinos, neon signs, strip clubs, drive-in wedding chapels, Elvis impersonators, etc., there are ways in which Isla Vista evokes Las Vegas. Its decentralized, fragmented layout resembles the mitigated chaos of the inside of a casino, although, unlike casinos and their more prolific cousins, shopping malls, the effect is apparently incidental. Though the neighborhood is isolated, cut off from the surrounding cityscape by geographical and ideological barriers, this was not a calculated design principal, but simply an accident of location. And unlike in a casino or a mall, time passes in Isla Vista: the sun rises and sets, the tides come in and out; and there is no protection from changes in the weather.[9] But just as in a casino, the overarching principle for the structures within Isla Vista is that of spectacle, a fair façade to cover consistently hasty workmanship.

Sarlo argues that, taking their cue from the diffuse suburban sprawl of present-day Los Angeles and the casino culture of Las Vegas, many cities worldwide are beginning to cluster around space capsule-like shopping centers rather than a culturally and historically defined "downtown" or "city center."

"Today Los Angeles, that immense decentered city, is not as incomprehensible as it was in the sixties. Many Latin American cities, including Buenos Aires, have embarked upon a process of 'Los Angelization.'"[10]

This process of "Los Angelization" described by Sarlo is the process of Suburbia taking over urban spaces, of a proliferation of centerless cities.

Although Isla Vista, too, is in some ways a centerless city, it could more accurately be described as a cityless center: a chaotic cluster of people and apartments and cars and bikes and skateboards with a few shops and a sprinkling of hard-won park space, but with no real urban identity, and no discernible planning. Despite multiple attempts, Isla Vista has never achieved self-sovereignty, nor has it managed to ally itself with one of the surrounding urban conglomerates. Thus its existence as a "city" is entirely conceptual, willed through the collective imagination of those who surround it, those who cycle through it, and the vocal minority that has made of it a permanent home.

Visitors are often surprised to discover that this infamous spot is so glaringly lacking in the usual markings of a city. For example, on October 31, 2004, I and the three graduate students accompanying me that evening were approached by an older couple with a strong Germanic accent. The couple asked where they could find the "city center." When we explained that they were already there, they looked positively alarmed: the only operating businesses in sight were a pizzeria, a coffee shop, a Mexican restaurant, and several liquor stores. They asked us where they might find a hotel, and we explained that they would have to go into Goleta for such accommodations. Utterly bewildered by this point, they asked us when the "festivities" would begin. Laughing, we explained that they had begun three days earlier, and pointed the visitors toward the steady background stadium roar emanating from Del Playa. In a daze, they thanked us and wandered off in the direction we had indicated.

Though it may lack a city, Isla Vista does have a center. In this infamous party-place, all roads lead to Del Playa, if they can be said to lead anywhere at all. This cliff-hanging strip where the sidewalks end, is understood as a kind of theme park of partying, home to no one and open to all.

In reality, there most certainly are those who have made Del Playa their permanent home, particularly on the west end of Isla Vista, the area farthest from campus. But the revelers generally ignore these homeowners, just as the homeowners do their best to ignore the revelers; it is not, after all, the reality of Isla Vista that these revelers are seeking, but the myth: that hope-giving fiction that simply to have one's feet on this legendary street is to be a part of the perpetual party at the end of the world.

In the course of my research, I have come to recognize the validity of this perspective. Like any place of pilgrimage, Del Playa has become a sacred space for probient partiers, and as such, it carries a certain magic for believers.

3. Spectator sports

On any given weekend year-round, the Del Playa scene is a people-watcher's dream come true: scantily-clad coeds and spontaneous eruptions of dramatic interaction are hardly confined to Halloween weekend. In fact, I argue that spectatorship and performance (or at the least, conscious self-display) are the very backbone of the Isla Vista social scene, as evidenced by the proliferation of furnishings and contraptions designed to facilitate spectatorship along Del Playa and other Isla Vista streets.

In addition to standard patio and balcony furnishings, Isla Vista residents have built platforms, scaffolding, tree-houses, and even raised couches up on stilts, all for the purpose of securing a better view of the street/stage. Since Del Playa, like much of Isla Vista, lacks a contiguous sidewalk system, walking in the street is the norm.[11] This makes for a much wider catwalk for self-display, and a more widely visible playing area for impromptu scenes of dramatic interaction.

Adam de Boer, a UCSB College of Creative Studies student, has created a series of paintings based on life in Isla Vista which amply illustrate the central role of spectatorship in Isla Vista. His recent show, "All is Well," dubbed "an anthropology of college life," by Arts Fund Executive Director Cody Hartley, featured numerous tableaus depicting students watching other students engaged in various activities, including drinking, dancing, fighting, vomiting, and masturbating.[12]

At Halloween time, the unofficial street-spectacle is further solidified via the addition of flood-lights (provided by the IVFP as a crime deterrent since 2003), attention-attracting costumes and behavior, and a temporary increase in the kind of elevated seating described earlier.[13] Also, spectators often take a more active role at Halloween time, frequently offering commentary on, or interacting with, those who have marked themselves as performers through their positioning and/or behavior. This phenomenon is discussed more thoroughly in part five, particularly the second subsection of chapter 22, "Defining We; Defining Me," called "The judgers and the judged."

The Isla Vistan emphasis on performance and spectatorship has some very positive indications for the community. Indeed, the environment on Del Playa in particular is in some ways one of remarkably open and unfettered social interaction: it is not unusual for doors to be kept unlocked, and for students to knock on strange doors or even walk into open apartments in order to offer invitations, make requests, or simply to strike up conversation. In public meetings regarding Isla Vista, students have fervently defended their neighborhood, even describing it as superior to the surrounding community by virtue of its friendly, open, laid back atmosphere. Young women in particular have described feeling safer in the public streets of Isla Vista than in private homes, where they might easily be sequestered and taken advantage of. Many of the adults in attendance at these meetings have expressed surprise at this preference, clearly unable to fathom a community like the one which Isla Vistans have created.

The open atmosphere in Isla Vista is certainly unusual, particularly within the larger environment of Southern California, where public space is an increasingly rare commodity, and where interaction with strangers is whittled down to the barest possible minimum. Mike Davis has written perhaps the most thorough exploration to date of this phenomenon in *City of Quartz*, a fascinating study of Los Angeles, the city where there is no there:

"The universal and ineluctable consequence of [Los Angeles homeowners'] crusade to secure the city is *the destruction of accessible public space.* [...] The American city, as many critics have recognized, is being systematically turned inside out – or, rather, outside in. The valorized spaces of the new megastructures and super-malls are concentrated in the center, street frontage is denuded, public activity is sorted into strictly functional compartments, and circulation is internalized in corridors under the gaze of private police." [14]

As Davis points out, the phenomenon of shrinking public space is no longer limited to Los Angeles or even to Southern California: it is increasingly the case all over the United States. More disturbing still, it is becoming a global phenomenon, as evidenced in the writings of Beatriz Sarlo and other cultural critics. Thus the fact that much of the private space in Isla Vista is made (relatively) public marks the community as a significant deviation from the norm.

Unfortunately, the Isla Vistan cult of spectatorship also has markedly negative implications. Spectacles of violence, such as fighting, wrestling, assault, and destruction of property, inevitably draw the largest and most vociferous crowds. For example, de Boer's painting "For You, For Life," depicts two boys wrestling in a typical Isla Vista backyard, surrounded by a crowd of onlookers whose expressions range from rapt to attention to feigned disinterest. Also, a double-panel painting by de Boer, "But Do Not Touch," features two girls fighting on one panel, and a group of five watching the action on the other. As in "For You, For Life," the spectators in "But Do Not Touch" are presented as detached and impassive, calmly watching the spectacle of violence without any apparent intention of intervening.

Furthermore, the dynamics of spectatorship are decidedly split along gendered lines: for the most part, men cast themselves as spectators, while women understand that they are there to be looked at. This unequal dynamic of male as gazing subject and female as looked-at object recalls Laura Mulvey's now-famous formulation of the gender dynamics of spectatorship in her 1975 essay, "Visual Pleasure and Narrative Cinema."[15] Mulvey argues that "In a world ordered by sexual imbalance, pleasure in looking has been split between active/male and passive/female."[16]

Although the absolutist binarism of Mulvey's argument is problematic, the idea that males generally understand their role to be that of the active gazer, and females understand theirs to be passive, gazed-at object, certainly holds true in the spectatorial dynamics of Isla Vistan street performance.

The skewed power dynamics of the Isla Vista scene are clearly illustrated in a deeply disturbing April 2006 occurrence at a Del Playa residence. According to the Isla Vista Foot Patrol's report on the incident, a young woman who had consumed too much alcohol fell unconscious at the suspect's residence. The suspect then propped the unconscious woman up against a plate-glass window and sexually assaulted her in full view of the street. A crowd of between 100-150 people gathered below to watch, many of them hollering and cheering the assailant on.[17]

It is unclear whether or not those watching from the street were aware that the woman was unconscious, and that what was occurring was therefore a rape, rather than a consensual act of crowd-pleasing exhibitionism. What we do know is that at some point, two women became concerned for the safety of the woman in the window, and gained entry to the apartment, where they found the victim partly clothed and hysterical. The suspect had fled by that time, and was later apprehended by the IVFP.[18]

Regardless of whether or not the gathered crowd was aware that they were cheering on a rapist, the assailant's decision to frame his act as a public performance provides ample evidence of a dangerously unequal gender dynamic. His use of an unconscious woman as a prop in a performance clearly designed to gain the attention and admiration of his peers, coupled with the overwhelmingly positive response he received, suggests that women are still primarily viewed by Isla Vistan males as sexual objects rather than active subjects. Yet it should be noted that the two women who intervened on behalf of the victim provide equally ample evidence that there is also active resistance to that masculinist dynamic in Isla Vista.

There is also an unsettling racial and class-based dynamic at work, in that the largely white, middle class student population of Isla Vista is often described not as a truly marginalized group, but one that is *playing at*—in other words, *performing*—marginalization. As long-time Isla Vista resident Alison Zuber notes, it seems that many of the students living in Isla Vista are simply adopting the *styles* associated with marginalization, rather than truly living, and learning from, the experience of being marginalized.

"They're slumming it," explained Zuber, "you know, the way that rich people go 'slumming' in poor neighborhoods. It's a game to them because they can always go home if it gets to be too much."[19]

Professor Catherine Cole concurs that white students tend to adopt exaggerated, theatricalized "ghetto rat" personas, which minority students frequently deem offensive.[20] This kind of perpetual masquerading as a racial or economic Other can be understood as a means of highlighting privilege while still making a public display of denouncing it. In other words, to dress as a "gangsta" is to tell one's peers, "I am *not* a gangsta, but I have learned how to pass for one, and that makes me not only privileged but street-wise."

This is similar to the process of style appropriation described by Hebdige: white working-class "mods" who adopted Reggae slang, symbols, and mannerisms, may well have been expressing "an emotional affinity with black people." At the same time, however, they failed to engage with that community on a level beyond the symbolic. "The black man," states Hebdige, served the mods "symbolically as a dark passage down into an imagined underworld."[21] In other words, it was above all the fantastical Otherness of the black community that fascinated the mods, a magical difference that allowed them to transcend ordinary life and escape the "straight" world. By adopting faux "ghetto" personas, the Euro-American probients living in the predominantly white space of Isla Vista are making use of transcendent Otherness as a means of evading, and inverting, mainstream society.

These performances of marginalization must furthermore be

understood as part of a larger cultural phenomenon of using style as a means of simultaneously advertising, and solidifying, one's class standing. Isla Vista, as a place of temporary student residence, offers probients a unique opportunity to advance (or reiterate) their place within the larger class-hierarchy of society, a commonly-understood goal for many contemporary college students.

As we have seen, the University of California—Santa Barbara is currently separated into two distinct spaces, divided by the "Eucalyptus Curtain." On the one side, there is campus, an intellectualized space intended to provide educational-vocational capital that can later be transformed into economic and social capital in the form of a higher-paying job and/or more respectful and deferential treatment. On the other side, there is Isla Vista, an experiential space which offers two contrasting forms of social capital. The first of these is leisure capital, which could also be conceptualized in terms of "coolness" or desirability points, accrued via the public performance of hardcore partying, violence, and sexual conquest. The second is exilic hardship or perspective-through-suffering points, accrued via separation from the comforts of home and communal endurance of ghetto-like conditions.

As a number of pedagogical theorists have pointed out, higher education is increasingly understood as a tit-for-tat exchange of tuition money for marketable skills and intellectual-cultural capital.[22] Yet in this, the Post-Oedipal era, which, as Jagodzinski argues in *Youth Fantasies*, is defined by the displacement of authority by the demand for *jouissance* (see section two), the vocational-educational capital provided by attendance at a University is no longer enough to assure one's class standing. In addition to the marketable enlightenment purchased through attendance at the university, contemporary college students are also expected to gain a certain amount of social and leisure capital. In other words, in order to be desirable citizens of the contemporary United States, Southern California in particular, residents must not only work hard, but play hard as well.

Contemporary probients are acutely aware of this additional expectation, so that gratification itself has become a competitive pursuit; students feel pressured to spend their free time racking up "pleasure points" via the public performance of activities deemed sufficiently stimulating, deviant, dangerous, or otherwise enjoyable by popular opinion (as circulated in the mainstream media). As performers within Isla Vista's hardcore partying scene, participating probients can rack up a significant amount of these pleasure points, which can later be transformed into social capital that will help assure class standing (access to leisure being a tell-tale mark of class distinction), as well as social standing within one's peer group, (sexual) desirability, and so on.

Meanwhile, Isla Vista's reputation as a ghetto—a marginalized, segregated space—provides students with another, equally valuable form of experiential capital: that of (temporary) exile. In *Staging Place,* Una Chaudhuri describes the function of exile within the popular imagination:

"On the one hand, exile is branded by the negatives of loss and separation; on the other, it is distinguished by distance, detachment perspective. [...] the poetics of exile offers a mechanism whereby suffering is exchanged for a certain moral authority, personal rupture for aesthetic rapture."[23]

With increasing numbers of students living away from home during their studies at American universities, some degree of exile is becoming an assumed part of the college experience. The suffering induced through separation from the home and forcible acclimation to an unfamiliar environment is thus exchanged for perspective, a certain authority regarding who one is, where one comes from, and where one is headed in life. Particularly for students from wealthy backgrounds, voluntary exposure to the slum-like conditions of Isla Vista may offer a rare opportunity to reap the benefits of exilic suffering without actually abandoning their privileged status.

Potter and Sullivan provide a clear illustration of how experiential capital is accrued through temporary suffering in a popular anecdote, in circulation as of fall 1970:

> "A girl [...] was approached by an elderly black man in a discount store in Santa Barbara, during 'Isla Vista III.' He demanded to know if she lived in Isla Vista. She admitted that she did, and he asked pointedly if things were really as bad as reported in the papers. When she answered that they were, he replied, 'Good. Now you know.'"[24]

Two important things are revealed by this exchange: first, the (rather common) attitude that it is "good" for students to know what it is to experience marginalization, even if only temporarily, and second, the fact that the experiential capital this young woman had gained via exposure to the Isla Vista riots provided access to a community that may otherwise have been off-limits to her. Although the events of 1970 have, thankfully, not been repeated (at least not with consequences of such sweeping scope), living in an area still described in the popular press as a "student ghetto" continues to provide students with experiential capital that may win them a certain degree of respect, thanks to the attitude exemplified in the now-legendary discount store dialogue.

Clearly, this kind of temporary relegation to a beachside pseudo-ghetto cannot be compared to the life-long marginalization experienced by many minorities and other disadvantaged groups. Indeed, these probients are no more experiencing true exile than weekend warriors on a three-day backpacking trip are experiencing true homelessness or wilderness survival. Yet the fact that Isla Vistan probients are only "playing at" marginalization works in their favor in terms of accruing class capital: the exchange of these experiences into advanced class standing depends on their having been *voluntary*. One who is born in a ghetto, on a street corner, or in a third-world country, is deemed simply unfortunate and to be pitied. But one who voluntarily sacrifices her/his comfortable, privileged existence in order to experience the suffering of these misfortunate Others is lauded, his/her temporary suffering transformed into crucial socio-economic capital.

This is similar to the way in which contemporary middle class probients use travel, as described by I. Munt. He argues that travel, as opposed to the much-maligned activity of *tourism*, is used to "stoke up on cultural capital," which can later be converted to economic capital.[25] This idea is expanded upon by Luke Desforges, who describes this kind of travel as a means of "collecting places."[26] Through this intellectualized act of gathering knowledge and experience of the Other, the traveler, like the colonist before him (or her), is in fact accruing power to be wielded back home—the "planetary consciousness" described by M.L. Pratt.[27] I argue that this same colonial logic is at work in the act of voluntary student exile: by temporarily allowing themselves to be marginalized, middle-class college students can accrue cultural capital to be used upon their re-introduction into mainstream society (read: graduation). Its function as a space of temporary, voluntary exile, combined with its conduciveness to socializing on a massive scale may serve to explain why the apparently dysfunctional community of Isla Vista is so oddly beloved, and so vehemently defended by its probient residents.

4. Where logic ended: why the streets don't meet

Even Isla Vista's most vocal proponents, however, readily admit that its spatial system can be rather bewildering, particularly to the uninitiated. Another graduate student doing research on Isla Vista, Jennifer Strand, neatly summed up the community's remarkably chaotic layout in her 1994 dissertation. In the following citation, Strand described the spatial situation she encountered in Isla Vista in the mid-1980's:

> "The street layout puzzled and frustrated me [...]. Three roads ran parallel along the ocean bluff. Five streets ran perpendicular between these roads and the access road out of Isla Vista. [...] This was where logic ended in the Isla Vista Street arrangement. Tiny streets lay all over Isla Vista, ending suddenly or meeting one of the bigger streets in a T and seemingly being reborn on the other side of the street, a few yards down and stretching on in the same direction under another name."[28]

To understand how this layout came to be as it is, it will be necessary to delve into the history of the land now known as "Isla Vista."

In exploring the evolution of this bluff-top community, I turned to longtime local historian-activists Carmen A. Lodise, who has compiled an impressive website detailing Isla Vista's evolution "from Chumash times to the present." I also relied heavily on Malcolm Gault Williams' impressive compilation of Isla Vista Oral Histories and archival data. To supplement these highly useful sources, I explored the other Dissertations, Masters Theses, and committee reports which have been written about the community of Isla Vista, and spoke with a number of longtime Isla Vista residents. Like any historical narrative, it is only part of the story. [29] This first portion is focused on the shaping of Isla Vista's physical landscape; later in the section that focus will shift to the cultural and socio-economic history of the community.

5. From Anisq'Oyo to Isla Vista

Prior to the arrival of Spanish explorers in the 16th century, the land that is now home to UCSB, Isla Vista, and the Santa Barbara municipal airport, was a major settlement for the Chumash people. At that time the landscape was dominated by a large lagoon (later filled in by heavy rains), in the midst of which sat an island that was itself home to around 800 Chumash inhabitants (later leveled by the Army Corps of Engineers in 1941 to provide fill for a Navy airport). There were also many Chumash villages around the edge of the lagoon, and although the Chumash did not build their homes on the oak-covered coastal mesa known to them as "Anisq'Oyo," they made good use of its abundant resources, including the natural tar still found on its beaches, which they used to caulk their ocean-going canoes. Archeological excavations on the UCSB campus suggest that the Isla Vista area may have been reserved for religious purposes. [30]

Isla Vista today has preserved this portion of the mesa's history by naming the area's largest and most centrally located park "Anisq'Oyo". Despite the fact that the Chumash are considered to have been one of the largest and most advanced populations on the Pacific coast, very few survived the Spanish Period (1567-1822). The introduction of European diseases, as well as the failure of Mexican authorities to live up to their promise to distribute land among the surviving Chumash families in the early-mid nineteenth century, spelled the end of this once-thriving community.[31]

During the Mexican Territory Period (1822-46), the area was owned by cattle rancher Nicholas Augustus Henry Den, who died during a period of extraordinarily heavy rains (1862-63). Following his death, a terrible drought killed off most of Den's cattle, and his family was forced to sell off all the land save the coastal mesa, which was divided between Den's two sons. The sons planted a row of Eucalyptus trees to mark the boundary between their two portions, a line that now marks the separation between UCSB and Isla Vista. Known to the UCSB community as the "Eucalyptus Curtain," this largely impenetrable boundary has been the target of much criticism throughout the years from community activists, who argue that the "curtain," like the proverbial "tracks," serves as a kind of psychological moat, protecting the Ivory Towers of academia from the socio-economic realities of Isla Vista.

In the 1870's, the Den brothers rented their ranch to the More brothers, who cut down the oak trees in a failed attempt to sell them to a burgeoning whaling industry, which had set up camp on what is now Goleta Beach County Park. In consequence, the topsoil was lost and the mesa was left with nothing but blow sand. Thus the only economically viable ventures remaining in the area were the whaling industry and asphalt mining.

During the 1920's the still-unnamed, largely uninhabited mesa was subdivided as a resort community by three sets of entrepreneurs: a pair of attorneys, a single professional woman, and a couple. One of the subdivisions was named "Isla Vista," ungrammatical Spanish for "Island View," and the name soon came to be applied to the whole area. The resort project was never particularly successful, quite possibly due to the heavy deposits of tar on the beaches, and to the lack of potable water and salable resources. The subplots remained, however, slicing the landscape into not-quite-uniform, never neatly matched-up parcels.

Indeed, remarkably little has changed since Strand's first encounter with Isla Vista; her description is as valid today as it was in 1984. Not only have the original, awkwardly divided parcels and mismatched streets remained in place all these years, overcrowding and chronic neglect by the county has further compounded the problem of safe circulation in Isla Vista. Again, to understand the root cause of these conditions, we will need to continue our exploration of Isla Vista's history.

6. Isla Vista: Birth of a student ghetto

During World War II, the land that is now the airport and the UCSB campus were home to a U.S. Marine Air Base. After the war, the portion of the mesa owned by the Marine Corps was sold to the University of California regents for the bargain price of ten dollars. In 1953, UC Santa Barbara, which had been residing on the Riviera mesa overlooking the downtown area since its inception as a teacher's college in 1909,[32] moved to its present location.

There were a number of reasons for this move, but in terms of the history and development of Isla Vista, one particular reason comes to the fore: two men on the UC Board of Regents, Samuel Mosher, president of Signal Oil, and Thomas Storke, owner of the Santa Barbara News Press, owned significant parcels of property near the Marine base site. The land had by that time proven itself barren of any profitable natural resource: stripped of its oak forest, lacking in oil or any mine-worthy mineral, lacking even a reliable source of fresh drinking water, "Isla Vista" was essentially useless to these two investors in its present state. They knew, however, that the arrival of the university would make the property valuable simply by virtue of its proximity to campus.

Indeed, thanks to a decision by the Regents to leave the half-square mile area beyond the Eucalyptus line open to private development, Mosher's property became even more valuable than he had anticipated. As to Mr. Storke, much of his property was purchased by the university to the tune of $1.15 million; when he gifted half of these profits back to the university, they named the property, a building, a bell-tower, and a major academic achievement award in his honor. Just as Mosher and Storke had predicted, the arrival of the university created an immediate, and nearly insatiable need for the one thing that Isla Vista had to offer: space.

In 1954, when UCSB first opened its doors in its current location, it had a projected enrollment of 2500 students. Four years later, UCSB announced plans to increase its eventual enrollment to 10,000 students per year; property values skyrocketed and investors began clamoring to get in on the housing market.[33] In order to finance this building boom, the Goleta Valley Savings & Loan was created in 1962. This highly unusual financial institution lent 85% of its capital to developers (as opposed to the typical 15%), and had a board of directors with a rather auspicious roster: Samuel Mosher, Daniel Frost (Mosher's attorney and Signal Oil director), John Harlen (local developer and Signal Oil's property manager in Isla Vista), Thomas Storke, Bert Lare (Storke's general manager), and Vernon Cheadle, the new Chancellor at UCSB.[34]

One of these men, John Harlan, also served on the county board of supervisors' committee to "investigate" zoning for Isla Vista, along with I.V. realtor Jack Schwartz, and Carl Chandler, an Isla Vista property owner and the assistant to Dan Grant, the County Supervisor for Isla Vista and Goleta. The committee suggested the creation of a unique zoning designation, called "Student-Residential" zoning. This custom-designed plan meant that "Student-Residential" areas did not have to conform to the usual standards regarding distance from the street or the bluffs, number of parking spaces per room, and so forth. It also allowed for the construction of larger apartment buildings than would have been allowed in other parts of the county. Although the plan did meet with some resistance, the committee won out, arguing that UCSB students "arrive here with a sleeping bag and a surfboard," and therefore did not require the same allocation of space and amenities required in residential zones elsewhere in the County.[35]

Despite the already-lax minimum standards of the zoning plan, grants of variances from those standards were continuously given by the Santa Barbara County Board of Supervisors. A disproportionate number of those variances were granted to outside developers who never intended to live in Isla Vista. The result is a half-square mile area with a capacity to house about 13,000 residents (a population density which in those days did not exist anywhere West of the Mississippi) in housing that is largely owned by absentee property owners with little or no vested interest in the community.[36] Despite the fact that the majority of the buildings were constructed by spraying a framework of chicken-wire with plaster, and that many are perpetually plagued with such nuisances as cockroaches, mildew, mold, thin and often crumbling walls, water damage, and general disrepair, [37] rent prices remain relatively high.

According to Jackie Mattice, a UCSB Community Housing Office listing coordinator, the average rent for a studio in Isla Vista (as of January, 2005) is $830 per month, $1012 for a one-bedroom apartment, and so on, ranging up to five-bedroom houses, the rent for which can run as a high as $5077.[38] Due to these high prices, and to a perpetual shortage of housing, students are often forced to share a room with as many as two or three of their peers.

As a Teaching Assistant, I have seen the impact of these living conditions on my students' work firsthand. Student claims that they were unable to finish an assignment due to sleep deprivation, intolerable noise levels, disrespectful roommates, etc., are positively epidemic at UCSB. At first, I dismissed this phenomenon as nothing more than students making excuses for not applying themselves, despite the fact that many of the students making such claims were among the brightest and most engaged in my classes. Now, after having spent a considerable amount of time observing the Isla Vista scene, I must say I find it remarkable that students who reside there manage to accomplish anything at all. Not only are students deprived within their living spaces of that most basic of intellectual necessities, quiet solitude—the "room of one's own" prescribed by Virginia Woolf and so many others—they are unable to find it anyplace else. With the exception of the UCSB library, there is no place within reasonable walking distance of Isla Vista that offers students an appropriate environment for studying. And even the library is not open 24-hours (except during finals week), meaning that there is *no* appropriate study environment available for those students who prefer, or who are forced by circumstances, to study at night.

The living conditions in Isla Vista also affect the ways in which students treat their neighborhood. On a Friday afternoon in the spring of 2003, a visiting friend and I witnessed a group of probient males playing an impromptu soccer game on Sabado Tarde with what appeared to be a shower head. When my companion inquired what they were doing, one of the fellows held up the dented shower head and told us: "This fucker fell off and hit me in the head, so we're teaching it a little lesson."

This scene made a lasting impression on my friend, and on me. As I watched these boys kick the offending faulty shower head at various objects such as a fence, a dumpster, a Stop sign, etc., their laughter poised between vengeful bitterness and liberated glee, it was very clear to me that the disrespect with which students treat Isla Vista is in direct proportion to the disrespect which they are shown by property owners, police, and County and University officials.

According to figures collected by Professor Harry Nelson of the Isla Vista Action Group, per person per year spending within Isla Vista is considerably lower than that of the rest of the county. For every Santa Barbara county dollar spent on those living outside of Isla Vista, only thirty four cents is spent on planning and development, and only six cents on road maintenance, within Isla Vista.[39]

The result is an apparent lack of such public amenities as adequate lighting, traffic signals, and, perhaps most glaringly, sidewalks.[40] Again, Strand's description of Isla Vista in 1984—"A capricious distribution of sidewalks forced pedestrians, stray dogs, and skateboarders out into the streets with cars, buses, bicycles and motorcycles where they encountered a Darwinian struggle for right of way"[41]—remains disconcertingly familiar as I write this in 2006.

WHERE THE SIDEWALKS END

SPATIAL RESISTANCE AS SOCIAL RESISTANCE

"Although they use as their *material* the *vocabularies* of established languages (those of television, newspapers, the supermarket or city planning) […] these 'traverses' remain heterogeneous to the systems they infiltrate and in which they sketch the guileful ruses of *different* interests and desires. They circulate, come and go, overflow and drift over an imposed terrain, like the snowy waves of the sea slipping in among the rocks and defiles of an established order."

- Michel de Certeau[1]

In my quest for spatial awareness, I have realized that my own daily commute across Isla Vista is remarkably consistent.

Generally speaking, I tend to vary my paths, subscribing as I do to the "variety is the spice of life" philosophy of urban existence. Yet this place has become the exception to my rule: having carved a relatively "safe," passably direct route through this labyrinth of apartment complexes and parked cars, I follow it faithfully, day in and day out.

Still, as I criss-cross these misaligned streets in a joyless game of connect-the-sidewalks, I am occasionally struck by the absurdity of my stubborn adherence to rules of circulation that apparently do not apply here. I watch children from the working class families living on the edges of Isla Vista, playing in the cul-de-sacs of dead-end streets. I see groups of students walking arm-in-arm down the center of the street, motorists and bicyclists casually veering around them and continuing on. I feel the scoffing glances of those who brazenly stroll along the other side of this row of parked cars. Yet I cannot bring myself to abandon this illusion of pedestrian safety, these rare and precious slabs of concrete set just slightly above the dark and dangerous street.

That is, until Halloween.

For a confirmed walker such as myself, there is something gloriously liberating in the collective reclaiming of a city street. During Halloween, we bodies drastically outnumber the vehicles in this strange little seaside village, and at last I can unabashedly join the rebellious ranks who have long since claimed this space as their own. By sheer force of our number, we make a sidewalk of the street, and it is difficult not to let that kind of power go to one's head.

As I make my way down Del Playa on Halloween, surrounded by elated pedestrians, I understand why people come from far and wide to take part in this rather uneventful event: because ultimately, spatial resistance *is* social resistance.

1. Isla Vista and social resistance

Social resistance has long been part of the cultural fabric of Isla Vista. The geographical factors described above, combined with the substandard conditions of the housing, roads, and so forth, and the political disempowerment of a transient student population living on unincorporated county land, all contribute to the ongoing unrest among the student population of Isla Vista. This unrest is augmented by the fact that students living in Isla Vista have always been a close-knit group, literally and figuratively. Living in such close proximity, separated only by notoriously thin walls, Isla Vista's student population, a group already very close in terms of age and often background, quickly created a unique cultural space. As Tom Bulgin, then Assistant Editor for the *El Gaucho* wrote in his October 23, 1964 opinion piece "The Isla Vista Problem,"

Isla Vista makes Santa Barbara unique among the campuses of the University of California. No other campus offers students an opportunity to reside in an isolated private housing area. This combination of freedom and isolation, a privilege afforded by the geography and growth pattern of this area, should be jealously preserved.[2]

The uniqueness of their situation was not lost on Isla Vistans, who quickly began to take advantage of the cultural freedom afforded by isolation. Counter-cultural movements flourished in Isla Vista: a lively Beatnik culture was in evidence in the late 1950's through the mid-1960's, at which point those seeking an alternative lifestyle were no longer referred to as "Beatniks" but rather "Hippies." Drug use increased considerably in the mid-to-late 1960's, and along with it came an increase in crime, as well as police presence.

The response of University administration and the campus police to the nascent problems in Isla Vista was a peculiar mixture of *in loco parentis* paternalism and free-market *laissez-faire*.[3] As a result, Isla Vista's student population often criticized the University for being too involved in their day-to-day lives, *and* for not being involved enough. In other words, students wanted the administration to support them in their struggle to receive fair treatment from landlords and lawmakers, but to allow them to make their own choices in terms of lifestyle. Conversely, administrators made it clear that they felt Isla Vista to be beyond their jurisdiction in all senses save student conduct. As a result, students felt simultaneously abandoned and harassed by the University's policies, as enforced by the campus police.

As enrollments increased, however, the role of surrogate-parent proved impossible for the administration to maintain within the crowded, chaotic parameters of what soon came to be known as "I.V.", and *in loco parentis* disappeared, leaving only the *laissez-faire* portion of the equation.

Yet the legacy of *in loco parentis* remained. As students increasingly adopted lifestyles of which the University administration and much of the surrounding community did not approve, a psychological gap began to develop between the student population of Isla Vista and the surrounding institutions. As that gap widened through the mid-1960's, one group struggled to promote unity: the Isla Vista League. In 1967 the league was led by George Keiffer and Paul Sweet, who began to conceptualize Isla Vista as a spiritual and intellectual center for UCSB and the community at large. Aside from being the first association to seek a unified community of students, homeowners, businesspeople, University personnel, and others, the I.V. League pointed out the urgent need to establish a local body of governance for Isla Vista. This warning, however, was to go unheeded for another four years, during which time the residents of Isla Vista would learn a tragic lesson about what can happens in the absence of structured advocacy against established power-structures.

2. The radical student movement

At first, the anti-establishment energy in I.V. was largely aimed at cultural rather than political transformation. The atmosphere was one of experimentation and exploration, rife with possibility and the hope of discovering more appealing options than those offered by mainstream American culture. Artistic expression was an important ingredient in this burgeoning alternative culture, and a local renaissance of sorts was organized by student entrepreneur Robert Borsodi and his wife Lisa. Offering a free stage for plays and poetry, and stalls for artisans, the Borsodi's hoped to transform Isla Vista into a "mecca" for the hip and the talented. Their enterprise, "The Arts in Congress," succeeded in creating a vibrant artistic community, which in turn inspired organizations like the I.V. League to stage cultural events in Isla Vista, such as the 1968 Community Fair.[4]

Eventually, however, political events began to intersect with personal concerns, blurring the line for many Isla Vistans between lifestyle choices and political activism. One such event came in January 1966, when the Selective Service discontinued the automatic student deferment, leaving college students eligible to be drafted into the war in Vietnam. Another was the assassination of beloved nonviolent civil rights leader Dr. Martin Luther King Jr. on 4 April, 1968. The restless political climate of the era, opposition to the war and to the draft in particular, concerns over race relations, and reactions to some of the University's policies on these and other issues all converged to create a volatile atmosphere which, by fall 1968, had already begun to manifest into direct action. Influenced by student resistance movements in UC Berkeley and elsewhere in the United States, UC Santa Barbara students began to make public their concerns and opinions in the form of student organizations such as the Student Non-Violent Coordinating Committee (SNCC), Students for Free Political Action, Students for a Democratic Society (SDS— eventually phased out and replaced by the Radical Organizing Committee or ROC), Young Americans for Freedom (YAF), and the "United Front," a group comprised of the Black Student Union (BSU), United Mexican-American Students (UMAS), and the SDS. At first, the radical tactics employed at places like Berkeley were condemned in the *El Gaucho*, but a series of incidents set UC Santa Barbara toward one of the most extreme radical actions undertaken by American university students in that, and perhaps any era: the burning of the Isla Vista branch of the Bank of America in April of 1970.

The first incident to set students onto this more radical trajectory was the October 14, 1968 occupation of North Hall, which housed the only existing UCSB computer center, by sixteen member of the BSU. These black students were frustrated by the Chancellor's lack of response to their accusation that white Athletic Director Jack Curtice and his assistant Arthur Gallon were mistreating black athletes, and took over North Hall, renaming it Malcolm X Hall. They refused to surrender the building until a list of eight demands had been addressed, most of which focused on increasing minority enrollment, eliminating institutional racism, and expanding the curriculum to include more minority-based studies. Much to the chagrin of Governor Ronald Reagan, Chancellor Cheadle negotiated with the students, and ceded to all but one of their eight demands.[5] This successful take-over was an inspiration to many groups on campus, who were also feeling frustrated by their lack of control over the administrative decisions made on their behalf by University officials.

In January of 1969, the United Front was formed, and frequent rallies were held to promote awareness of the presence of racism at UCSB and in Isla Vista. Oppressive actions and racist statements on the part of police officers and landlords offered plenty of fodder for these rallies: on February 3, six BSU members were arrested during an early-morning raid by Santa Barbara County Sheriffs, who were quoted as using nasty racial epithets such as "damned niggers."[6] Twelve hundred students turned up at the County Courthouse the following day in protest of the arrests. Three days later, a prominent black athlete was evicted from his apartment by notoriously unpopular Isla Vista Realty. Spokeswoman Mabel Schultz poured salt on the wound by publicly announcing that "our major defaulting tenants are E.O.P.'ers."[7] The insinuation that minority students were less responsible than their white counterparts ignited the already-volatile situation, and, as the "Malcolm X Hall" occupiers had done the previous October, United Front leaders decided to take matters into their own hands.

At the head of a parade of 1000 students, the United Front marched into the University Center, declaring it a "liberated zone" and re-naming the building the New Free University. Unlike the brief North Hall takeover, the occupation of the University Center lasted about three months, from mid-February to early May. During that time, the occupying students offered an alternative curriculum, covering such timely topics as women's liberation, violence and social change, Marxism, and American capitalism.[8] Chancellor Cheadle allowed the students to maintain possession of the University Center, and even defended their actions to the UC Board of Regents, saying they must respond to "the needs of the times and the tremendous resentment, particularly of our minority groups," once again garnering the criticism of governor Reagan.[9] In fact, the New Free University ultimately disbanded not due to any outside pressure but to internal conflicts such as the presence of numerous transients who had taken up residence in the occupied building. Although their ideology would not allow participants to refuse entry to anyone, to limit their stay, or to charge any sort of rent, the New Free University was apparently not equipped to function as a homeless shelter, and the United Front was ultimately forced to return the University Center to the UCSB administration in order to free themselves from this unexpected and unsolicited responsibility.[10]

Meanwhile, ecological disaster struck the region when an oil drilling platform in the Santa Barbara Channel experienced what was at the time the worst oil spill in the United States to date. The resulting slick covered over 800 square miles, blackened local beaches, and killed vast amounts of marine wildlife. This horrific dramatization of the dangers wreaked by capitalist greed and industrial "progress" vividly drove the point home for UCSB students, dragging an abstract issue into their own backyards—or rather, their beaches. The radical environmentalist energy stirred up by the oil spill resulted in protests of a proposed extension of Highway 101 to campus via the Goleta slough. These student-led protests, along with some well-timed budget cuts, were ultimately successful in squelching the project.

As activism spread across campus, a more violent branch of radical action was also beginning to surface in Isla Vista. The windows of three Isla Vista real estate offices, including Isla Vista Realty, were shot up by unknown assailants. An unknown person in a moving car shot at, and missed, an SDS member who was walking through Isla Vista.[11] Most tragically, at 6:30 a.m. on 11 April, 1969, live-in custodian Dover Sharp opened a mysterious box inside the UCSB Faculty Club, and was flung violently backward, his body riddled with bits of glass, when a bomb exploded from within the box. Two days later, Sharp was dead.[12] Although the SDS, UMAS, and the *El Gaucho* all issued statements condemning the bombing as a senseless act of random violence, the SDS nonetheless felt the need to clarify their position further by underlining that it had "never… claimed a position of nonviolence."[13] Apparently, there was at that point no consensus within the activist community at that time regarding the use of violence as a means toward social change.

After Sharp's death, county police presence in Isla Vista became more pronounced than ever before. By fall, 1969, the tension between students and officers was palpable, as evidenced in a mid-August melee that began when an unknown man sprayed mace through the window of the Campus Cue, Isla Vista's pool hall. As people poured from the building, more students came to investigate, prompting the two deputies dispatched by the Sheriff's Department to call for reinforcements. Students lobbed bottles at the arriving officers, prompting them to request further backup until fifty-seven law enforcement officers from three policing districts were on the scene in Isla Vista. The crowd of students also grew to about five hundred, mostly due to curiosity about the phenomenal number of police officers pouring into their neighborhood. During the three-hour confrontation, bottles were thrown, trash cans and a wooden cable spool burned, and finally the streets were "swept" clean via the advancement of a line of officers carrying clubs and shields. Ultimately, the officers made three arrests, and left behind them a good deal of resentment and hostility.[14]

However, it was not at county police that students vented their frustrations next, but at the UCSB administration. When a tremendously popular Anthropology professor, William "Bill" Allen, was denied tenure by his department, student activists claimed it was due to his leftist politics rather than academic merit, and demanded an open hearing. They circulated a petition which eventually garnered over 7,000 signatures. Regardless, acting Chancellor Buchanon (and eventually Chancellor Cheadle, who was at the time away on an official visit to Europe and Africa) refused to compromise the integrity of the tenure process by relaxing standards of confidentiality. Students staged several rallies before the administration building, during which campus and county police were called in, prompting further student-officer skirmishes. Allen eventually lost much of the student support he had garnered, as students began to suspect that the Anthropology professor was more interested in provoking the administration than in seeking long-term change. In the end, the university not only denied his tenure but filed disciplinary charges against Allen.

By that time, though, the central issue for students had already shifted from the injustice of their academic institution to the invasive presence of police officers on their campus and in their neighborhood. Some believe this to have been a conscious tactical move on the part of the student organizers; as former activist Robert Langfelder put it:

"The demonstrators in the Allen case wanted the off-campus police called in. It was a concentrated strategy to radicalize the students. If they saw the police busting heads, then they'd get involved."[15]

Meanwhile, nineteen activist students were signaled out for arrest, despite the fact that several of them had been calling for nonviolent protest throughout. They were quickly labeled the "Santa Barbara 19" by sympathizers, and became the subject of many an impassioned speech in the almost-daily rallies that followed the first demonstration staged in support of Allen, on January 30th.

3. The Isla Vista riots

On February 24, 1970, full-scale violence broke out in Isla Vista. This was the date on which the "Santa Barbara 19" were scheduled to appear in court in order to determine the date of their trial. That afternoon, officers arrested Lefty Bryant, a black activist who was arrested during the August melee, outside the Campus Cue. A crowd of sympathizers gathered, throwing rocks at the patrol car and slashing its tires. James Trotter, a known supporter of Bill Allen, was among this crowd and officers singled him out for arrest. Trotter fell to the ground and eye witnesses insist that the officers beat him as he fell. Enraged at what they perceived as police brutality, members of the crowd set fire to the patrol car. As officers arrested four more crowd members, the scene quickly grew into the beginnings of a full-scale riot: patrol cars were pelted with rocks and bottles, windows were smashed in realty offices and the Bank of America, and flaming trashcans and mattresses were in evidence all along the Embarcadero Loop.

The following day, William Kunstler, principle defense attorney for the Chicago Seven, along with defendant Jerry Rubin's wife Nancy, spoke on campus. Infused with the spirit of resistance and unity, students made their way back into Isla Vista, heading toward a planned gathering in Perfect Park. Officers in riot gear lined the streets, preparing for a disturbance, and students became incensed at what they saw as an unnecessary invasion of their space. Ex-student Richard Underwood was seized by officers who believed the wine jug in his hand to be a Molotov cocktail, and when he resisted arrest, officers began to beat him with their clubs, in full view of the crowd. Immediately, students retaliated by pelting officers and patrol cars with rocks. The rock-throwing quickly spread to realty offices and the Bank of America, and dumpster fires broke out soon after. The crowd in Perfect Park grew to about 1500 by 9:30, at which time the students suddenly shifted their tactics: rather than the usual geurilla-style disobedience, the crowd suddenly charged at the 79 officers sent to quell their disquiet, hurling rocks and bottles as they did. Although the officers did attempt to use tear gas to disburse the crowd, a strong ocean breeze thwarted the tactic, and the officers were forced to retreat back onto the bus from which they had come.[16] By 10 p.m., students had effectively driven police from the area.

What happened next remains shrouded in mystery. What is amply clear, however, is the sense of euphoria at having driven the police out of the area, and the roiling animosity toward "the system," coursing through the gathered crowd. Said one anonymous participant:

> "I can't begin to tell you what it was like, that moment when we realized our liberation. It was as if time had ceased, we had spun off from the rest of the world [...]. There was this inexpressible animal feeling."[17]

In that moment of "liberation," when the students recognized that they had successfully rescued the territory of Isla Vista from foreign (read: police) occupation, possibility seemed endless, and experimentation began in earnest.

Soon after the officers' hasty exit, collective attention turned to the Bank of America, "the biggest capitalist thing around."[18] "Of course everybody began looking at the bank, with all its trashed windows," noted the same anonymous participant.[19] Still-unidentified students rolled a dumpster through the front doors of the bank, and someone tossed in a lit match. That fire was eventually extinguished, however, by students who were opposed to violence.

Having effectively opened the bank to the public, the protesters made themselves at home, parading through the bank, some even lounging in the Board of Directors meeting room and the vault antechamber, eating ice cream cones and smoking marijuana. "The scene," wrote John James Whelan in his 1984 dissertation, "was a surreal mélange of revelry and insurrection."[20] The highly symbolic act of penetrating the inner sanctum of what participant Warren Newhouser called "the (corporate) sanctuary of sanctuaries" was clearly an extraordinarily empowering experience for the victorious protestors. "It was a cultural event," said Newhouser, an opportunity for these students who had felt so powerless in the face of the institutions purported to "serve" them, to bring one such institution back down to their level.[21]

Eventually, the novelty wore off, and people began to wander away. It was at this point, sometime between 11:30 and midnight, when most folks had already headed home, that the bank began to burn in earnest. This fire appears to have been started by a small group of die-hard activists (still unidentified) who remained upstairs in the Bank of America board room, piling furniture and papers into gasoline-soaked heaps, and then bringing in burning material from a bonfire that had been set on the sidewalk.

The fire brought the community back out in droves. One observer said of the flaming bank, "it was like this carnival, this blazing carnival [...] an I.V. pagan ritual!"[22] Others described the burning bank as an enormous bonfire around which a circle of euphoric protestors laughed, danced, and sang. Although there were many observers who were shocked and dismayed by such flagrant destruction of private property, and many more who were just plain terrified of the repercussions that would surely come from such a monumental act of defiance, it is that vision of the bank burning as a sort of pagan celebration that has survived as the dominant lore. And it is this alluring image of an impromptu carnival, a crowd of liberated merrymakers reveling in the destruction of the old world and heralding hope for the new, that may well have prompted students to try and recapture some sliver of that bank-burning magic during the wild Halloween celebrations of later years.

The burning of the bank would later come to be known as "Isla Vista I." Isla Vista II occurred on April 17, after a state of emergency had already been declared and lifted, the National Guard long since come and gone. A crowd of students attacked the temporary Bank of America, confronting not only police officers but anti-violence students, who were attempting to defend the bank from damage. One of these bank-defending students, Kevin Moran, was accidentally shot by a police officer while attempting to douse a fire set by his peers.[23]

Isla Vista III began as a peaceful protest of the 7:30 curfew imposed on the community and the unnecessarily brutal methods employed by the Los Angeles Special Enforcement Bureau (SEB) in enforcing it.[24] The violence and destruction of property that had characterized Isla Vista I had estranged many potential supporters, causing them to sympathize with the outnumbered officers and to look upon the students as dangerous radicals, or simply as spoiled little vandals. But the death of Kevin Moran and the subsequent reign of terror at the hand of the L.A. SEB caused the pendulum of public opinion to swing back in the direction of the students, so that by early June the community viewed the police not as protectors but as the enemy. Local business owners, UCSB faculty members, clergy, and other Isla Vistans joined students in a nonviolent sit-in at Perfect Park. For the first two hours after curfew, police made approximately three-hundred peaceful arrests.

However, once the darkness set in, the officers switched tactics, suddenly firing pepper spray directly into the crowd. Officers in gas masks and wielding nightsticks then charged into the disoriented crowd, beating and arresting protesters at random until the park was cleared. It was the *pièce de resistance* for the SEB's spectacle of brutality, after which the UC Board of Supervisors would insist that Governor Reagan call in the National Guard to replace the SEB.[25]

4. The aftermath

The damage done to Isla Vista went much deeper than the expensive and unsightly aftermath resulting from the massive destruction of property. These superficial wounds were merely symbolic manifestations of the internal disintegration that had been brewing in Isla Vista for nearly two decades. The University (and to some extent, the county) appears to have understood this, since University of California president Charles J. Hitch commissioned a group of external researchers to investigate the underlying problems of Isla Vista soon after the riots. The 1970 "Commission on Isla Vista," chaired by Martin Trowe, would later come to be known as the "Trowe Commission." The final report of the Trowe commission is remarkably thorough, examining many of the historical factors I have listed here, its observations are highly astute and its recommendations apparently pragmatic and feasible.

Yet the prescient warning of the Trowe commission, that "the University can no longer ignore, if it ever could, the conditions under which the bulk of its students live and spend the greater part of their time while at the University,"[26] appears to have gone largely unheeded. A February, 2005 report compiled by the Isla Vista Action Group (IVAG), a group of concerned faculty, administrators, students, and community representatives formed in November, 2003, states that it "has found that most of the problems noted in the 1970 Commission Report persist today, and that most of its recommendations, which were specific and practical, were never implemented."[27]

While they recognize that the chronic problems of Isla Vista are as stubborn as they are complex, the authors of the IVAG report (professors Catherine Cole, Harry Nelson, and Walter Yuen) express a good deal of frustration and bewilderment at the lack of University response to the Trowe report, and to later reports such as the 1992 Isla Vista Enhancement Committee report, which reiterated many of the Trowe report's recommendations. It would therefore not be unfair to state, from the vantage point of the present, that the University's interest in creating a commission at that time was not, as many had hoped, to tackle the chronic problems of Isla Vista, but to address the acute symptoms of unrest and to save face within the community.

5. Community (re)development

Unlike the University administration, which was still looking backwards, struggling to understand the factors that had led to the unrest in Isla Vista, Isla Vista residents were already surging ahead, taking specific action toward community (re)development. So dramatic was the rise of Isla Vista's grass-roots community rebuilding effort that more than one commentator has compared it to a phoenix rising from the ashes of the burned Bank of America. Residents were determined not simply to reconstruct Isla Vista as it was, but to create an unprecedented community structure, a self-sustaining student utopia.

In the July 1970 issue of *Ramparts*, Tom Hayden listed Isla Vista among several "liberated zones" where radical culture had begun to blossom in the United States. He listed four characteristics of these cutting-edge communities, all of which had already begun to take root in Isla Vista before the disturbances: First, liberated zones were intended to be "utopian centers of cultural experiment" where traditional social relations could be deconstructed and re-examined; second, they would be internationalist in spirit, celebrating cultural diversity and nurturing industrializing nations in their struggles for liberation; third, they would be battlegrounds where the values of capitalism and mainstream institutions would be endlessly challenged; and fourth, they would offer support to revolutionaries in need.[28] This was precisely the kind of community that many of the students had in mind, and there was a great deal of optimism in the year or so following the bank burning that it was within their grasp. As one young Sociology professor put it, "We have a magnificent opportunity to follow a signal act of destruction with a spectacular act of construction."[29]

That change was not only necessary but long overdue appears to have been beyond question by spring, 1970; discussions revolved around a few stubborn barriers to the creation of the ideal Isla Vista. The most fundamental and urgent issue was the lack of any kind of governing structure that specifically represented Isla Vistans. Thus among the numerous institutions created during this exciting era in Isla Vista's history was the community's first governing body: The Isla Vista Community Council (IVCC). Although the IVCC had no real political power, it did have a certain legitimacy to make recommendations to, and sway the opinion of, the representatives and political structures governing Isla Vista. It remained in operation until 1983, when the county voted to de-fund the program, and UCSB Chancellor Robert Huttenback followed suit, repealing not only its annual grant to the IVCC, but all its funding to Isla Vista service programs, save law enforcement. And even there, Huttenback shifted the University's half of the Isla Vista Foot Patrol's funding from administrative sources to student fees, meaning that UCSB students were, for a time, paying for their own policing!

Next on everyone's agenda was the terrific animosity between police officers and students. Members of the newly-created "Ad Hoc Committee for a New Isla Vista" identified several contributing factors, among these the over-saturation of patrol cars in the area, and the anonymity of officers on patrol. Thus the idea was put forth (not for the first time) to create a fleet of accessible foot-patrolling officers who would get to know the community and whom the community would get to know in return. Thus the birth of the Isla Vista Foot Patrol (IVFP) on December 1, 1970; a unique operation jointly staffed and operated by the University Police department and the County Sheriff's office, the IVFP was specifically designed to meet the needs of the unique Isla Vista community.[30] At first, Isla Vista residents were suspicious of this new branch of law enforcement, even going so far as to fire-bomb the original IVFP office. Likewise, officers were mistrustful of the IVCC, and wary of students, particularly large groups of them. Eventually, the Foot Patrol was accepted into the community, and remains a prominent Isla Vista institution.[31] Tensions have not dissipated entirely, however, and tend to resurface most vehemently in the fall, when the IVFP mounts its annual "fall offensive," and when students stage their annual Halloween carnival (see section two).

Unfortunately, nearly all of the institutions created during this community-oriented chapter in Isla Vista's history were ultimately de-funded by the County and the University. Furthermore, over the course of the 1970's and '80's, a major cultural shift took place among the student population. Alison Zuber, UCSB alumnus and long-time resident of Isla Vista, explained to me in a March, 2005 telephone interview that, after the rioting of 1969-70, the University made a concerted effort to de-politicize its student body. This was not the first time I had come across this particular theory, and so I thought it worth looking into.

Unfortunately, it has proved a rather difficult task to assess whether or not the University consciously set out to recruit less politically-minded students in the wake of the Isla Vista riots. The only "recruitment" activity practiced at UCSB is, and has been for as long as anyone I spoke with can recall (Britt Ortiz, who works at the Early Academic Outreach office, has been at UCSB since the mid-1970's), the sending of representatives to high schools and junior colleges in the surrounding counties. According to Lisa Prezkop, Associate Director of Admissions, School Services, there is no record of who was sent to which schools, or even how many representatives were sent out and to which counties. In fact, Prezkop insists that the School Services office has no records whatsoever reaching back further than the mid-1980's.

I *have*, however, unearthed some intriguing information in the University archives which does seem to suggest, at the very least, that

UCSB took a greater interest in, and allocated a good deal more funding to, undergraduate admissions and recruitment following the events of spring, 1970. In the UCSB budget for the school year 1968-69, and every year before that, admissions is merely a subheading under the Registrar's office, with a total budget allocation of $3,468. But in the 1970-71 budget, "Undergraduate Admissions" is listed separately and features the newly-created positions of "Admissions Officer," five "Admissions Clerk(s)" and seven "Admissions Assistant(s)," with an allocation of $165,402.[32]

Although there is no information in the archives on how this money was spent, such a drastic increase in the resources allocated to admissions (a $161,934 increase to be exact) certainly suggests a sudden preoccupation with recruitment. It could be argued that this is to be expected, given the anticipated drop in enrollment numbers following the riots. However, it certainly leaves room for speculation regarding the role of this new Undergraduate Admissions office in the apparent ideological transformation that took place during the decade that followed on the UCSB campus and in Isla Vista.

By the mid-1980's the campus-by-the-sea had lost its notoriety as a hotbed of political activity, and regained its original reputation as a laid-back party school. This new batch of students was apparently less interested in fostering a spirit of community—let alone experimenting with alternative lifestyles—than in enjoying their probient years and securing themselves a financially stable future. Thus Isla Vista reverted to its previous state: a conveniently located, though over-populated and poorly maintained neighborhood where students could sleep, study, and socialize, not necessarily in that order.

6. The sweetest little slum on the west coast: Millennial Isla Vista

In looking at both the history and the current state of Isla Vista, several things become clear, even to a casual observer.

First, that this place which ought by every right to be a beautiful and invigorating place to live is instead a beachfront slum. The overall crime rate in Isla Vista exceeds that of the surrounding area by five hundred percent, and the rate of reported sexual assault is four hundred percent higher.[33] In 2003 there were forty sexual offenses *reported* in Isla Vista, and Carol Mosely, Director of the UCSB Women's Center's Rape Prevention Education Program estimates that this is not even close to the actual number of assaults occurring. "I think in our community [of Isla Vista], we probably have five hundred [sexual assaults] a year," stated Mosely in a March, 2006 interview.[34]

In addition to sexual assaults, in the year 2003 there were one hundred and twenty seven [non-sexual] assaults reported, three hundred and eighty six recorded property offenses, and three thousand seven hundred and eighty four complaints lodged against loud parties and similar disturbances.

There are twenty-two liquor licenses in a neighborhood where much of the population is not of legal drinking age; two thousand and ninety nine alcohol-related arrests were made in Isla Vista in 2003.[35] The term "ghetto" occurs fairly frequently in studies such as the one put together by professors Potter and Sullivan for the President's Commission on Campus Unrest.[36]

Second, that the blame for Isla Vista's current condition rests somewhere between the private developers who turn a profit on it, the county within whose jurisdiction it lies, the renters that endlessly cycle through it, the attitude of the community surrounding it, and the University that prompted its creation and continues to provide its *raison d'être.*

Third, that the inconsistent architectural, social, and managerial infrastructures of Isla Vista encourage an attitude of lawlessness and disrespect for the neighborhood itself, an attitude that is exacerbated by the self-focused experimentalism that characterizes its largely probient population.

I argue that it is this rebellious, experimental attitude and unusual emphasis on social performance and spectatorship, largely products of the specific cultural-geographical space of Isla Vista, that have created an ideal environment for the Halloween carnival that has in many ways come to define the community.

Although the days of overt political protest in Isla Vista are apparently over, and the content of the Halloween celebration is in no way comparable to that of the late 1960's-early 1970's unrest, I insist that the spirit of resistance is alive and well in Isla Vista. And although the carnivalesque thrives to a certain degree throughout the year in Isla Vista, the revelers' use of masking and parody (which I explore in the next section), plus the sheer magnitude of the crowd, make Halloween the carnivalesque pinnacle of the Isla Vistan social calendar.

7. Re-actualizing public space

Regardless of its content, I believe the *form* of Halloween in Isla Vista constitutes an increasingly rare—and therefore increasingly critical—form of political resistance: the willful reclaiming of public space.

Michael Hardt and Antonio Negri assert in *Empire* that in the post-modern world public space has become privatized to such a degree that, "the place of politics has been de-actualized."[37] Even political activism itself has increasingly retreated into virtual space. Web activism, email petitions, and political listserv groups are quickly becoming the modus operandi for contemporary activists. In other words, we are moving into what Guy Debord termed the "Society of the spectacle."[38] Such a society blurs the distinction between inside and outside, public and private, to such a degree that the liberal notion of the public as an outside space where we act in the presence of others, has lost its meaning. As Hardt and Negri put it: "The end of the outside is the end of liberal politics."[39]

This theory is already being borne out in the public-spaceless city of Los Angeles, where police have adopted a "containment strategy," criminalizing vagrancy in all areas of the city save the confined area of Skid Row, as described by Mike Davis in his fascinating portrait of that sprawling postmodern metropolis, *City of Quartz*.[40]

A similar, though more subtle, containment strategy appears to be at work in regards to Isla Vista: although students are certainly not subjected to the same sorts of harassment and abuse as are the home-less and the destitute in Los Angeles, many of the probients with whom I spoke noted that they are often made to feel unwelcome within the public and private spaces of the surrounding communities. Griped graduating senior Jamie Birkett of downtown merchants:

> "As soon as they're done taking our money, they pretty much toss us back on the trash heap. They're all like, 'oh, yeah, y'all are cool, we looooove UCSB students,' until closing time. Then its, 'get back to I.V. ya lousy bums.' I hate that shit."[41]

In other words, the largely commercialized spaces of Santa Barbara and Goleta are only open to those who have money to spend, and only during business hours. Those who lack the requisite resources, or who keep unusual hours, are expected to remain within the marginalized, "graffiti wall" space of Isla Vista.[42]

Thus corralled and insulated from the world at large, it is little wonder that the student population of Isla Vista would celebrate its internal openness, and welcome with open arms the one moment of the year when the world begs for entry at its guarded gates.

Through the blatant high-jacking of public space that is Halloween, participants reclaim their territory (both literal and figurative), rejuvenate their collective power, and reaffirm their very right to exist, and to take action, within the space of Isla Vista. Put simply: the party isn't just *on* Del Playa, the party *is* Del Playa. Participation in the simple, defiant act of collective loitering is all that is required to be a part of this infamous event.

In conclusion: as a re-actualization of public space, a reaffirmation of the right to free assembly, and a rare example of genuine face-to-face interaction, the massive physical presence of college-aged revelers on Del Playa Drive on Halloween must be taken seriously as a site of cultural resistance, if not political action. In the following section, I zoom in on this sea of student revelry, investigating the myriad miniature performances that combine to make up this extraordinary example of recurrent-yet-spontaneous street theatre.

PART V
SLEAZY BEAUTY AND PIMP CHARMING

PARODY AT PLAY

"Just keep swimming! Just keep swimming!"

- "Dory," *Finding Nemo*

"Just keep drinking! Just keep drinking!"

- "Nemo," Halloween in Isla Vista

1. Refin(d)ing Nemo

The impromptu reunion scene described in section one offers a good deal of insight into the nature and purpose of the improvised enactments performed among Isla Vistan revelers at Halloween time. Like the Disney / Pixar computer animated film to which it referred, the short scene, played out between the young man dressed as Nemo and his self-declared surrogate father (a video camera-toting sailor), was simultaneously humorous and heartfelt, sardonic and sincere.

While apparently intended to lampoon the simplified sentimentality peddled in this and so many other Disney features, the perfor-

187

mance nonetheless betrayed an underlying emotional honesty on the part of the actors. The palpable excitement in the voice of the sailor when he first spotted and called out to Nemo, the look of delighted surprise on Nemo's face when he recognized that he was being sought after by name, and the unfettered warmth of their brief embrace all colluded to reveal a genuine connection to the material.

In investigating the nature of that connection, it will be necessary to take a closer look at the film itself.

Finding Nemo (2003) recounts two simultaneous tales: that of a neurotic, overprotective father (Marlin) who loses, and seeks out, his only son (Nemo); and that of a young boy (Nemo) who must endure exile in order to find his strength and to mature into adulthood.

In a sense, it is a double coming-of-age tale, since both Nemo and Marlin must confront their greatest fears in order to be reunited, and in doing so, both discover an inner strength that neither previously knew/believed himself to possess.

Although this parable is set in the underwater realm of fish and other sea creatures, its creators have gone to great pains to assure that we will recognize the story as a middle-class domestic drama. The opening scene between Marlin and his wife (Nemo's mother), clearly establishes theirs as a nice, normal, suburban family: the dialogue revolves around home ownership, child rearing, and the couple's rather standard-sounding heterosexual courtship. Their domestic bliss is cut short, however, by the appearance of a rather nasty-looking barracuda, who knocks Marlin out and, we assume, proceeds to devour his wife and all but one of her incubating eggs. Upon waking, Marlin promises to protect the surviving progeny, whom he dubs "Nemo" in honor of his late wife's wishes.

This tragic opening serves several purposes. First, it assures that the audience will sympathize with Marlin's quest to protect the only surviving member of his once-happy family, forgiving him his excesses and his often misguided methods. Second, it offers an explanation for Nemo's damaged fin, the locus of Marlin's anxiety over his son's ability to function independently. Third, it provides a pretext for yet another motherless family, the Disney domestic structure *par excellence.*

A number of critics, such as Janet Wasko, Lynda Haas, and Mark Axelrod, have pointed out this remarkably consistent feature of Disney's animated films: that nearly every hero(ine) is motherless. Though there is occasionally a step-mother (invariably evil), or some kind of surrogate mother-figure (usually non-human), the mother is rarely given even the cursory appearance which she is granted in *Finding Nemo.* The nurturing function of the mother having been neatly excised from the equation, what we are left with is unmitigated patriarchy. In this case (as in *The Little Mermaid*) this translates to the controlling, disciplinarian approach of the well-meaning but over-bearing father. Consequently, the audience understands that Nemo has little choice but to forcibly separate himself from the incapacitating protection of his father, if he ever hopes to properly come of age.

Nemo's behavior signals to the audience that he does desire to attain maturity, almost desperately. Although his exile is not intentional (having disobeyed his father's orders to stay away from an anchored boat, Nemo is captured by a scuba diver and imprisoned in an aquarium in Sydney), it soon becomes apparent that a separation from the Oedipal father is precisely what is needed in order for Nemo to reach his goal of adulthood.

His desire for competence and autonomy is recognized and nurtured by the surrogate father-figure he discovers in his new environment: Gill, a surly, sea-caught fish who is bound and determined to escape and return to his ocean home. Having gotten himself caught in the aquarium's filter-tube, Nemo calls out for help.

Unlike Marlin, who, in a similar situation earlier in the film, told Nemo not to move and promptly pulled him out, Gill instead instructs Nemo to swim out by himself, telling him "you got yourself into this, you can get yourself out of it." Thus invested with the requisite confidence, Nemo does indeed manage to escape from the tube.

Having passed this initial test of strength and courage, Nemo, the archetypal neophyte, is then put through an initiation ordeal in order to be fully accepted into his new "family." His reward for completing the requisite task is to be given a tough-sounding nickname ("Shark-bait") and offered a pivotal, highly dangerous role in Gill's latest escape plan.

As I hope I have made clear by this point, the parallels to the (middle-class) college experience—a desire for autonomy, separation from family, nostalgia for nurturing, adjustment to an unfamiliar environment, seeking to prove oneself before one's peers, undergoing (official or unofficial) ordeals and initiation rituals, homesickness, acquiring new skills, forming new relationships, etc.—are numerous and apparent.

Furthermore, the domestic backdrop of this classical prodigal son plot encourages audience members to relate their own experiences to those of the protagonists. It seems clear that this strategy was successful in the case of the reveler who dressed as Nemo and the sailor who made such a show of "finding" him. What is even more notable is that both of these ad-lib actors recognized Halloween as an appropriate moment to express their emotional connection to *Finding Nemo*'s classical coming-of-age narrative, re-enacting for their peers that archetypical sequence of events: recognition of a separation/loss, the quest for reconnection (complicated by the literal obstacles of the other revelers' bodies), and finally, reunion.

Yet the scene is not, *must* not be played "straight." Rather, it is exaggerated and mocked by the actors, who recognize that they, too, are taking part in an initiation rite of sorts. By deriding this childish tale, as well as their own boyish delight in consuming and re-creating it, they are demonstrating for the crowd their willingness to symbolically annihilate their child-selves to make way for the adults that will take their places.

The performance is thus revealed as part of the larger rite of passage that is Halloween in Isla Vista; in order to gain acceptance into the post-adolescent world of college probience, revelers must parody these once-worshipped icons of childhood before a highly-critical audience of peers.

· · ·

2. The Process of Parody

I have chosen the term "parody" carefully, since it implies a contingent, ambivalent relationship to the target text. Whereas other forms, such as satire or burlesque, may be understood without prior knowledge of the object of criticism, parody's reception is dependent upon some degree of familiarity with the text being parodied.

The humor displayed at Halloween in Isla Vista is frequently dependent upon a certain pop-cultural vocabulary: the more one knows about the figure(s) being imitated, the greater one's amusement.

For example, a fellow graduate student named Hank Willenbrink was very excited to see a young man dressed as the title character in a recent film, *Napoleon Dynamite*, and called out, "Hey Napoleon! What's your favorite animal?" Without missing a beat, the young man picked up his cue, answering "It's a liger!" He continued to speak to us in character for several minutes, performing some of Napoleon's trademark speech patterns and mannerisms, much to the hysterical enjoyment of Hank and a handful of others who stopped to listen. Some of my other cohorts and I, on the other hand, had not seen the movie, and while we did find the fellow's antics amusing, we commiserated on the side that we were clearly not quite getting the intended joke.

As in the case of "Napoleon," the imitations at Halloween in Isla Vista are at times more celebratory than critical of the original text. Whereas satire and burlesque are necessarily derisive forms, parody often implies a kind of admiration for, and desire to dialogue with and build upon, its target text. Even the most derogatory performances witnessed at Halloween display some degree of ambivalence: the performers often betray a simultaneous affection for, and disillusionment with, their chosen character-object.

This conflicted quality of parody allows the performer to work *with* the target text, rather than solely against it. As Margaret A. Rose writes: "This ambivalence may entail not only a mixture of criticism and sympathy for the parodied text, but also the creative expansion of it into something new."[1]

In the case of Halloween in Isla Vista, I believe this "something new" will offer valuable insight into the culture of these probient performers. By examining the unique texts that are created through the parodic imitation of existing childhood lore, I intend to provide a clearer understanding of how, and more importantly, *why* revelers make use of parody in their Halloween performances.

I argue that the revelers' use of parody functions as a kind of "lower-frequency" politics, as described by Gerard Aching in regards to Caribbean carnival (see section two). Rather than seeking any sort of recognizable revolution, I believe the revelers are using the act of masquerade as a means of circulating, questioning, resisting, espousing, and generally playing with various socio-political ideas, values, and representations. They are performing for each other, and anyone else who is willing to watch, what (they think) they are, what they are told to be, what they are told not to be, what they would like to be, what they once thought they wanted to be, and so on.

My strategy is as follows:

First, I will examine the texts that have been selected as parodic objects, theorizing the possible reasons why these texts might have been chosen over other, equally available objects. In other words, I will endeavor to explain why revelers might feel a particular connection or attraction to the selected texts. In the case of *Finding Nemo*, for example, I have argued that the archetypal "hero's journey" undertaken by the protagonist shares many common elements with the (middle-class) collegiate experience.

Second, I will interrogate the specific changes wrought upon these once-beloved texts, noting the elements that have been exaggerated, highlighted, excised, inverted, invented, or otherwise altered. Although they are often subtle and may at first appear insignificant, I believe it is these alterations that hold the key to understanding *why* the revelers have chosen parody as their expressive mode of choice.

> Rose names two major effects of parody upon its readers: 1. "Shock or surprise, and humour, from conflict with expectations about the text parodied," and 2. "Change in the views of the reader of the parodied text."[2]

I understand this to mean that revelers use parody not only to create humorous and/or shocking incongruity, but to make their audience take a second look at the object of their parody. Their intent in doing so may be, but is not necessarily, critical. A performer may simply wish to bring to his or her audience's attention something they might have missed on a first reading—particularly if they were very young at the time. The best way to ascertain whether a parodic performer is offering a criticism of the original text or simply shedding new (and quite possibly positive) light on it, is to examine which aspects of the text have been altered, and in what way. As Bakhtin writes:

> "It is the nature of every parody to transpose the values of the parodied style, to highlight certain elements while leaving others in the shade: parody is always biased in some direction, and this bias is dictated by the distinctive features of the parodying language, its accentual system, its structure."[3]

Though their specific methods vary, Isla Vistan revelers do display fairly coherent trends regarding what is highlighted and what is hidden at Halloween, betraying measurable cultural biases. By describing in detail the "parodying language" through which the revelers communicate, I will show how the revelers make use of parody as a means of inducing recognition, and introducing ambiguity into accepted visual texts and narrative tropes.

As I argue in the final chapter of this section, "Defining We; Defining Me," the sign systems adopted in these performances are intended as insider communication codes, a means of circulating multilayered social and sexual messages among the initiated.

Halloween in Isla Vista thus proves to be a cultural performance *par excellence*: "a story [the revelers] tell themselves about themselves," in the much-quoted words of anthropologist Clifford Geertz.[4] In offering this reading of the story being told by, to, and about this remarkably homogenous sampling of (largely white, middle class) probients living in the United States, I hope to illuminate the culture of a group that has come to represent the most important market in the global economy, the protagonists of so many foundational myths of capitalism.

In asking readers to take a second (and perhaps a third or fourth) look at this much-misunderstood and -misrepresented group, I am admittedly hoping to trigger the "demasking" effect described by Aching—that is, "an unexpected and undesirable self-recognition [...] that is brought on by contact with a masked subject."[5] It is my hope that readers will come away not only with a better understanding of this much-misunderstood and –misrepresented group, but perhaps even with a better grasp on their own cultural norms and the ways in which they are complicit with, resistant to, and ambiguous about those norms.

THE GROTESQUE REALISM
(RE)GENERATION

1. 'Toon Town

Nemo is in good company on Del Playa drive; the past three years' celebrations have been awash in cartoon characters, fictional heroes and heroines from television and movies for children, and more general incarnations of childhood games and fantasies.

Standing at the corner of Del Playa and Camino Pescadero at around 10 p.m. on Sunday, October 31, 2004, my cohorts and I [1] take a moment to marvel at the number of animated characters populating the streets of Isla Vista. We call out the names of cartoon icons as they go by, a list which I will dutifully transcribe from my hand-held tape recording the following morning:

> "Little Red Riding Hood!" "Tigger." "Is that–? Hey, Ernie from Sesame Street!" "Another Snow White." "Tigger again." "Homer Simpson." "More Ninja Turtles – girls this time." "Gumby?" "Yup. And Spongebob." "An Asian Pocahontas." "Fred Flintstone – a whole pack of Fred Flinstones!" "I think that guy is supposed to be Smurfette." "Pooh. I mean, *Winny* the Pooh." "Cinderella in a very short skirt." "The Cat in the Hat. Oh, and there's Thing One and Thing Two! Awesome!"

"A guy in a Tinkerbell costume." "Robin (of Batman and Robin)."
"Superman." "Pillsbury Dough Boy." "That's all I can see for now."[2]

In fact, the roll call in Isla Vista differs very little from the cast of
characters one might find at a grade-school Halloween party or trick-
or-treating in an average, middle-class residential neighborhood: girls
are mainly dressed as angels, fairies, cheerleaders, cats, bunnies,
princesses, dancers, movie stars, and cartoon heroines, while the most
popular costumes for boys are cowboys, firemen, athletes or sport
heroes, Vikings, gangsters, rock stars, movie stars, cartoon characters,
and sailors or pirates.

Yet these costumes, which appear at first glance to be nostalgic
throw-backs to days gone by, are no longer direct replications of these
childhood icons. Rather, they are painstakingly vulgarized versions of
once-beloved figures: exaggerated and degraded *parodies* that fore-
ground the hidden subversive transcript of this kind of childhood
lore.

The Halloween revelers' manipulation of the idyllic images offered
them in childhood—their blatant foregrounding of the bodily, sexual,
and scatological aspects which are underplayed, disguised, or erased
outright by the mainstream media—serves as an outstanding example
of what Bakhtin referred to as "grotesque realism." He defines this
important element of cyclical regeneration as:

> "...the essential principle of grotesque degradation, that is, the
> lowering of all that is high, spiritual, ideal, abstract; it is a transfer to
> the material level, to the sphere of earth and body in their dissoluble
> unity."[3]

Grotesque realism, in other words, refers to the foregrounding of
the material body and its myriad functions that is a common element
of all carnivalesque celebrations. Via this carnivalesque aesthetic, the
unspoken is not only made manifest, it is magnified to a grotesque
extreme. Bakhtin goes on to explain the function of grotesque realism

as being one of necessary destruction that makes way for new growth. He writes:

> "Degradation digs a bodily grave for a new birth; it has not only a destructive, negative aspect, but also a regenerating one. To degrade an object does not imply merely hurling it into the void of nonexistence, into absolute destruction, but to hurl it down to the reproductive lower stratum, the zone in which conception and a new birth take place."[4]

Thus the revelers' willful destruction of childhood fantasies through the device of degradation is equally an act of regeneration. As these old fantasies are being laid to rest, new fantasies are being created and enacted via the tactics of parody and bricolage.

2. Scavenging sacrilege

No doubt there are those who will argue that these students are simply wearing what is most readily available to them. There is certainly evidence that a significant number of them buy their Halloween costumes from the same downtown retailer—"Scavenge"— and that the majority of the ready-to-wear costumes sold there (year-round) are sexy, cute, or kinky / fetishistic outfits for women, and goofy / funny, macho, or scary outfits for men. I personally witnessed the overwhelming popularity of this costume/clothing shop when I attempted to make a last-minute wig purchase on October 28, 2004. The line just to get in the door stretched to the end of the block, and the wait at the counter was over an hour.

Yet the mere fact of the store's popularity (there are, after all, other costume shops in town, with quite different selections available) is an indication that these are the kinds of costumes students *seek* to wear, and not simply what they end up with by default.

Furthermore, having perused the available selection at Scavenge, and having attended several Halloweens, I can safely say that certain costumes are considerably more popular than others. This would imply that students are not merely taking the first available option, but carefully selecting from what is offered. UCSB student Ethan Roberts, who coordinated with friends to dress up, and perform as, Mexican wrestlers, explained that they had ordered the masks for their costumes on e-bay two months in advance. When asked if he thought most students were already thinking about their costumes when they arrived at UCSB in the fall, Ethan offered the following reply:

> "Oh absolutely. You have to have an idea beforehand. 'Cause like come Halloween there's no costumes left. And you know the thrift stores are out of everything, like, even the ugly shit at the thrift stores is gone. So you kinda have to have a plan and know what you want to do. And people spend *money* on Halloween, like, girls'll spend upwards of a hundred dollars just for a costume, and they'll wear it one time. It's pretty insane."[5]

This assessment was consistent with other student interviews: clearly, many of them invested a good deal of time, money, and thought into their costume, and would not take kindly to the suggestion that they simply put on whatever they could find.

The very act of "scavenging," of picking through and choosing from the offered selection, is one that requires volition, critical thought, and creativity. In other words, while students are inevitably choosing from what is available, they are nonetheless *choosing*, and I believe those choices are worth studying. In addition, many of the costumes purchased at Scavenge and elsewhere had apparently been altered by the purchasers. Thus even those costumes that appear to be "ready-mades" may in fact be Isla Vista originals.

Furthermore, in addition to the act of putting together a costume, the revelers then layer on a physical embodiment of the given character: voice, gestures, dialogue, etc. Through the combined creative efforts of choosing (and perhaps altering) costume elements, placing them on the body, and giving them a physical life via embodiment, a parodic *performance* is composed. Although this performance may have its basis in a pre-packaged outfit purchased at Scavenge or some other retail shop, the end result is inevitably unique and worthy of closer examination.

3. That old Disney magic

Given its continued stranglehold on the children's media market, not to mention an increasingly global popular imagination, it is little wonder that Disney in particular is so well-represented at Halloween in Isla Vista. As Elizabeth Bell, Lynda Haas, and Laura Sells argue in their introduction to *From Mouse to Mermaid: The Politics of Film, Gender and Culture*, we as audience members have all, to some degree, internalized the "Disney magic." Indeed, watching Disney movies has become a pseudo-sacred activity for American families, the secular equivalent of going to church. As Mark I. Pinsky notes in *The Gospel According to Disney:*

> "In the Western world in particular, the number of hours children spend receiving moral instruction in houses of worship is dwarfed by the amount of time spent sitting in front of screens large and small, learning values from Disney movies and other programming."[6]

Thus "criticizing Disney" has become "a kind of secular sacrilege."[7]

That is not to say that cultural critics are afraid to speak badly of the Disney empire—on the contrary: Disney-bashing has become something of a favorite pastime in intellectual circles. In fact, the pendulum seems to have shifted to the opposite end of the spectrum for the moment: I must agree with Douglas Brode that the whole of Disney's repertoire has too frequently been unfairly dismissed as excessively conservative, conventional, and saccharinely sentimental.

Disney's earliest films, his silent shorts, were quite the opposite. As Sean Griffin points out in *Tinker Belles and Evil Queens: The Walt Disney Company from the Inside Out*, "Disney's early work celebrates the spirit of the carnivalesque, including the constant reveling in the function of physical assault of the body."[8] In the silent era, Disney cartoons were dominated by the decidedly "lowbrow" aesthetics of vaudeville, farce, and burlesque. Popular gags included losing one's drawers, getting stripped to nothing more than a bra and panties, losing body parts, and getting squirted in the face by a cartoon cow's enormous udders. In addition, many early Disney figures displayed strongly libidinal characteristics: Oswald, a popular early Disney hero, was an incorrigible skirt-chasing rabbit, often compared to another notoriously licentious cartoon figure of the era, Felix the Cat. Of course, none of this was deemed particularly scandalous at the time: rather, it was quite in line with the norm of silent-era animation. What is noteworthy is not how bawdy Disney cartoons once were, but how and why they were sanitized, and the early animation all but erased from public memory.

Around 1930, Disney came under attack in the press when mothers started a campaign of complaint to censors, claiming that their children, among whom the cartoons were unquestionably gaining popularity, were being harmed by the licentious content and immoral messages in the Disney shorts. Foundering financially and desperate for good publicity, the Disney studio consequently underwent a major overhaul in regards to its "attitudes toward sexuality and the representations of the body in Disney's product" between 1931 and 1933.[9] The character of Mickey Mouse, originally selfish and sadistic, was thus transformed into a clever but guileless Midwestern boy-next-door—innocent, romantic, and moral—much to the delight of mothers across the country.

In accordance with public demand, Disney cartoons in the latter 1930's began to revolve exclusively around male-female courtship, naturalizing the American middle-class ideal of romance as innocent, chaste, heterosexual interaction. The quintessential example of this kind of essentially asexual courtship is the ubiquitous image of Mickey and Minnie Mouse singing at the piano in the evenings, sustaining absolutely no physical contact. Meanwhile, as Griffin explains,

"At the same time as Disney's animation was being laundered of its more burlesque elements, Disney's public relations went into high gear, to make sure that everyone knew how wholesome Disney's films were."[10]

Within the cutthroat market of the post-silent era, this new wholesome Disney was warmly welcomed both by the press, and by consumers. The earlier Mickey was soon forgiven, and subsequently forgotten, his childlike replacement embraced with open arms—and wallets. In direct consequence of this drastic shift in image, the Disney studio soon came to be known among its staff as "Mickey's Monastery" due to its strict dress and behavioral codes. Women working in the Ink and Paint department were segregated from, and given a different lunch hour than, the male workers, prompting them to re-dub their sequestered workspace "The Nunnery."[11]

There was, however, opposition to this enforced "family" atmosphere, often expressed in the form of bawdy, anatomically correct Mickey Mouse cartoons posted anonymously on the studio bulletin boards. Also, a studio-wide "weekend getaway" in 1937, celebrating the phenomenal success of *Snow White and the Seven Dwarfs*, quickly turned into an orgiastic scene of carnivalesque excess, a direct reversal of the restricted atmosphere of the Disney studios. Walt and his wife reportedly fled the scene early the following morning, and the incident was not spoken of at the studio for many years afterward.[12]

In the Eisner era, Disney films have perhaps become bolder in terms of direct depictions of (hetero)sexual desire, and more willing to cater to a growing homosexual market. Yet they remain eerily evacuated of direct references to sexual activity of any kind.[13] Although, as Griffin argues, audiences are more than willing to interpret, and elaborate on, the subtle sexual hints and double entendres proffered in Disney cartoons for themselves, cultural critics have been quick to point out that Disney—as a major purveyor of American culture to the global market—must nonetheless be held accountable for its consistent denaturalization of human sexuality.

And this failure to deal directly with the question of desire is only one of the myriad complaints lodged against the Disney corporation by its critics, among the ranks of which can be counted Henry Giroux, Jack Zipes, Susan Hines, Brenda Ayres, and a growing roster of others. I would argue that Disney films do indeed construct communities that are disturbingly divided and unequal in terms of class, race, and gender, and frighteningly homogenized in terms of sexuality (or lack thereof) and naturalized capitalism and patriarchy.

At the same time, I would argue that they simultaneously encourage a certain degree of independent thinking and rebellion against the status quo through the relentless individualism of the hero or heroine.

As Brode argues, Disney films comprise a children's literature that "champions one's growth as an individual entity over conformity to the crowd and its current code," and that "offered us alternative possibilities *not* in the end rejected by the hero."[14]

However, this celebration of the individual is not without its suspect political underpinnings; that the divine right of the individual to seek out his or her own version of happiness is held up as natural, universal, and wholly sacred within the Wonderful World of Disney is testament to Disney's strong ideological ties to capitalism and the "American Dream." As Pinsky and others have argued, Disney's "magic" provides a peculiarly American vision of morality: personal wish fulfillment as the highest possible good.[15]

It should come as little surprise, then, that these films remain close to the hearts of college students in hot pursuit of their "American Dream" of permanent acceptance into the middle class. Having worked hard to secure the necessary grade point average—and perhaps the necessary capital—to attend college, these students are doing precisely what Disney told them to do: wish upon a star, whistle while you work, have faith in your dreams, and be grateful for the bare necessities.

At the same time, however, they are in a prime position to critique the values of the society for which they are being groomed. From their liminal vantage-point, probients are able to take stock of the messages they were given as children, and to measure them against the life-lessons they are currently receiving (both in and out of the classroom). The discrepancies that are inevitably uncovered are then highlighted via specific patterns of alteration in the appearance and behavior of the childhood icons revelers choose to inhabit at Halloween.

By manipulating key aspects of the characters' costumes and self-presentation, the revelers at Halloween in Isla Vista seem to have found a means of simultaneously honoring and mocking, worshipping and critiquing, the pseudo-sacred animated icons on which they were raised. These patterns are relatively consistent, focusing squarely, and unsurprisingly, on issues of gender and sexuality.

The most popular type of alteration made to Halloween costumes in Isla Vista is the massive reduction/removal of fabric; weather not withstanding, copious amounts of bare flesh are inevitably displayed on Del Playa. After a stroll across Isla Vista on October 31, 2003, professor Harry Nelson said he was "struck by just how pervasive skimpy costumes were for women," estimating that eighty or ninety percent of the women present were wearing "outfits [that] were revealing to an embarrassing degree."[16]

Even participants themselves are quick to note the pervasive tendency to sexualize costume choices. One woman in attendance at the 1999 celebration calling herself a "Charlie's Angel" aimed her plastic revolver at passing women, and proclaimed that she was "slut hunting." "But I'll never be able to shoot them all," she lamented, "there's just too damn many of them."[17] Jenn Lotz also shared with me a running joke between herself and a friend about this phenomenon:

> "We'd be like, oh, what are you dressing up as tonight? And some girl would be like, 'I'm gonna be a pirate,' and then me and my friend would go, 'a *slutty* pirate.' And then someone would be like, 'I'm gonna be a bumble bee,' 'a *slutty* bumblebee.' [...] Because, it was true, every single girl [...] skankified their little outfit."[18]

The convention of "skankification" to which Lotz refers is so widely understood that the modifiers "slutty" or "sexy" are often looked upon as redundant, even when there is no suggestion of sexiness in the costume's basic theme. In fact, the women at Halloween in I.V. are not, by and large, simply masquerading as something or someone innately sexy. Instead, the overwhelming trend is to take an icon of innocence or modesty, and to sexualize it; the Britney Spears look-alikes, and even the showgirls and belly dancers, [19] are now vastly outnumbered by the hordes of once-beloved characters in outrageously inappropriate attire.

4. Skankerella and the Seven Whores

Let us explore one very popular choice for Halloween "skankification": Disney's Cinderella. This icon of femininity is associated with a host of popular myths and fantasies about what women want, or are supposed to want, and how they ought to go about attaining it. The romantic-rescue fantasy represented by Cinderella and her fellow distressed princesses, Snow White and Aurora, has become so thoroughly imbricated onto our social fabric that many women must consciously work *against* its seductive sway, attending workshops and reading books on the so-called "Cinderella syndrome"—pop psychology shorthand for the pervasive tendency for otherwise independent and capable women to expect a charming prince (or at least a romantic man) to come along and sweep her off her feet. And yet, ironically enough, this popular poster-girl for romantic rescue was originally intended as an antidote to Snow White's excessive passivity.

Walt Disney described Cinderella as more assertive and "practical" than her pale predecessor. "She believed in dreams all right, but she believed in doing something about them. When Prince Charming didn't come along she went right over to the palace and got him."

In a similar vein, screenwriter Maurice Rapf described the Cinderella he helped to create as "a rebel who fights for what she wants," and who, as a result "is locked up in the tower and is never going to be able to try on the glass slipper when the guy comes around."[20]

Indeed, a close reading of *Cinderella* reveals this plucky heroine to be a hard-working pursuer of upward mobility, rather than the passive recipient of a grand stroke of romantic luck. She does everything within her control to secure the right to attend the ball and meet the prince, and we are made to understand that the appearance of her fairy godmother is the direct result of Cinderella's good behavior. Furthermore, Cinderella goes to the ball with the full intention of winning the heart of Prince Charming: her ball gown and glass slippers are, for all intents and purposes, the trappings of seduction. Her coquettish dropping of the slipper may not have been a calculated move, but it was apparently successful in securing her the man, and the social standing, of her dreams. In this sense, Cinderella is less a prototype of passivity than a shining example of the power of feminine seduction.

Probient women attending college have good reason to admire Cinderella: she stands as a sort of secular patron-saint of upward mobility. Whether a coed hopes to improve her class standing, to escape the drudgery of traditional "woman's work" (like the endless stream of household chores Cinderella was forced to perform for her stepmother), to expand her (social and intellectual) horizons, or simply to attract a future life-partner, Cinderella's is the archetypal success story for each. Yet Cinderella, as a character, as a film, and as a fairy tale, is dated; the norms and expectations of femininity, and of gender roles and relations more generally, which were taken for granted in the '50's are no longer viable.

The probient women who choose Cinderella as their Halloween avatar are apparently aware of this discrepancy. They recognize that to publicly admit to seeking what is no longer deemed desirable, or even possible—that is, the romantic rescue fantasy exploited by those three Disney "classics": *Cinderella, Snow White and the Seven Dwarfs*, and *Sleeping Beauty*—would be considered "childish," and therefore inappropriate within the strongly anti-childhood social space of Isla Vista. Instead, one must *play at* playing Cinderella, hacking off her ball-gown to miniskirt length and plunging her neckline to blush-worthy depths, so as to invoke Cinderella's symbolic and fetish value without actually inhabiting her (now outmoded) persona.

Of course, the shortening and tightening of Cinderella's gown could simply be viewed as an updated version of the classic tale, since it is apparently worn with the same intent as the original: to seduce a suitor of the wearer's choice. Yet the decidedly un-feminine, non-seductive behavior of many Halloween Cinderellas suggests more than a mere transposition across time and through fashion trends. There is something of the burlesque in the raunchy comments and lewd gestures offered by the Disney princesses parading down Del Playa. This calls to mind Elizabeth Bell's assertion that the latter-day counterparts to these classical princesses, the Eisner-era Disney heroines such as Ariel, Belle, and Jasmine, share the common aesthetic of the striptease.

While the earliest (Disney) folk heroines move in the stilted lines of classical dance, the latest folk heroines tease with the conventions of burlesque. While the first approach distances the audience in the guise of artificiality and elitism, the second approach entices with the implicit warning, "look, but don't touch."[21]

In "Stripping Beauty," Kellie Bean explains this striptease aesthetic as a means for the assumed masculine audience member to view these heroines both as sexual objects and as innocent, "good," marriageable women.

Narratives of sleeping beauties argue that remaining unattainable (either through direct refusal or deep sleep) functions as a kind of modesty, and insist on this modesty as a term of appropriate female behavior. Remaining unattainable is, therefore, the equivalent of being chaste.[22]

The "look-but-don't-touch" attitude is palpable at Halloween in Isla Vista: although the scantily clad coeds striding down Del Playa are certainly inviting onlookers to see, and to admire, their physiques, anyone who attempts to cross the unspoken but understood line of propriety will receive a strongly negative reaction. This is, in fact, the source of much of the un-princess-like behavior emanating from these partially-stripped Cinderellas, Snow Whites, and Sleeping Beauties.

For example, on Friday evening, October 29, 2004, one such scantily-clad Cinderella was spotted at the corner of Camino Pescadero and Del Playa making obscene gestures and repeatedly yelling "you wish!" to a group of males gathered on a balcony, in response to their shouts of "Flash!" and "Show us your tits!" Her repeated taunt directly inverted Cinderella's trademark song, "A Dream is a Wish Your Heart Makes," implying that her would-be audience should not "keep on believing" but should rather abandon all hope that their inappropriate wish would be fulfilled. The accompanying gestures, which included turning around and pointing to her derriere with both middle fingers, were clearly intended as a physical retort to an audience that had attempted to force the terms of her exhibitionism. Although this Cinderella may have voluntarily transformed herself into a "Skankerella" for the evening, she did so on her own terms, and her hostile response to the desiring balcony voyeurs made it amply clear that those terms were non-negotiable.

This sort of immodest inversion of the classical Disney princesses' coveted naïveté can also serve as a social commentary on the unrealistic norms/expectations of beauty and behavior for women. As an example, let us examine more closely the Snow White described in my introduction. Though her costume was recognizably that of Disney's Snow White, the "skirt" was in point of fact little more than a large ruffle: the entire length of this Mexican-American coed's burnished-copper legs stood in defiant contrast to the covertly racist appellation of Disney's original milky-white heroine.

Furthering the parody were the sexually charged lyrics she sang to her audience of cartoon combatants: "My milkshake brings all the boys to the yard / and their like / is better than yours / [...] / I could teach you / but I have to charge..."[23] Again, the "milkshake" image provides an ironic reference to Snow White's glorified pallor, once again inverted by the defiant confidence of the dark-skinned singer.

Meanwhile, the lyrical narrative suggests three things to this Snow White's audience of "boys" (dressed, not insignificantly, as the *Teenage*

Mutant Ninja Turtles). First, it is not her physical appearance, but her "milkshake"—i.e. her sexual potency and skill—that "brings all the boys to the yard." Second, it is the "like" (i.e. presentation or appearance) of her male listeners, rather than her own, that leaves something to be desired: "their like / is better than yours." Third, although she *could* pass on her (sexual) skills to these boys, her knowledge is simply too valuable for her to go passing it out for free. This confident claim to sexual prowess subverts the Disney character's trademark modesty and passivity. Thus the impromptu performer is able to pervert this symbol of racial and sexual "purity" into an emblem of subversive power and social/sexual liberation.

We have seen how female revelers at Halloween in Isla Vista have re-fashioned the iconic figures of Cinderella and Snow White, cashing in on their cultural value as classically desirable women, while making ironic comment on their outmoded codes of beauty and femininity. But what of their more recent counterparts, the Ariels and Jasmines, the Belles and Esmereldas?[24] Surely these newer, "feminist" models of young womanhood can be adopted wholesale, rather than being inverted and (subtly or pointedly) commented upon?

Unfortunately, to believe that these latter-day Disney heroines are somehow immune from the Disney meta-narrative of (heterosexual) domesticity and deference to patriarchy is to have fallen too deeply under the Disney spell. As Janet Wasko notes in *Understanding Disney*, very little has changed in terms of the portrayal of women from *Snow White* to *The Lion King*: they are consistently "portrayed as weak, pristine, and incapable of independent action." She answers analysts who claim that these newer heroines have been "updated and modernized," by pointing out that:

Ariel [of *The Little Mermaid*] is a sensual, aggressive, mischievous, adventurous, savvy, independent teenager, in contrast to Snow White, who is shy, obedient, hesitant, naïve, innocent, and motherly. However, both are surrounded by male characters, are dissatisfied with their current lives, and wish to marry a prince. Some things obviously have not changed.[25]

It seems to me that what has not changed, above all, is the number of options made available to—and, more importantly, deemed acceptable for—these young women in a patriarchal social system. Although these newer heroines frequently dream aloud of achieving something beyond domestic tranquility ("There must be more than this provincial life!" laments Belle in *Beauty and the Beast*), after the lightening-strike of love-at-first-sight, nearly every one of them eventually succumbs to a sudden, overwhelming desire to marry a man and start a family.

Kellie Bean similarly warns against falling for the "feminist" veneer of these newer Disney heroines. Although many of them do appear to characterize themselves as "independent, unconventional, even feminist," Bean counters that

> "In the Disney world, independence functions not as an indication of female power or self-determination, but rather as a strategy for seduction: Reluctance functions in a Disneyfied courtship as the lure with which the chosen woman finally attracts a husband."[26]

Furthermore, despite Disney's purportedly anti-erotic ethos, the latter-day Disney heroines are clearly intended to satisfy the masculinized public's libidinal preoccupation with the eroticized female form. Calling them seemingly "deliberate illustrations" of Laura Mulvey's now-classic theory of "woman as image, man as bearer of the look" in mainstream cinema,[27] Bean denounces these new Disney heroines as little more than sanctioned, soft-core fodder for heterosexual male fantasy.

> "[*The Hunchback of Notre Dame's*] Esmerelda and her Disney sisters [...] are male-defined fantasies of female biological perfection. Drawn according to the same impossible dimensions of the Barbie doll—or any number of surgically altered Hollywood actresses—Disney's heroines all feature tiny waists, large breasts, curvy hips, and sensuous hair."[28]

Despite their purportedly progressive personas, the shell-clad

Ariel, short-skirted Pocahontas, and bare-midriffed Jasmine and Esmerelda are better remembered for their fantastic physiques than their assertive behavior, which is in any case undercut by their eventual wholesale adoption of a traditional domestic role of wife-and-mother.

Nonetheless, their apparent aesthetic appeal and sassy, "girl-power" attitudes would seem to make these newer heroines, at least comparatively speaking, ready-made models for Halloween masquerading, no reassembly required. It may then be surprising to learn that only two of these latter-day Disney characters were witnessed with any frequency in the years 2003 to 2005: Ariel and Pocahontas. It is my belief that these two characters carry meanings for these probient women that go beyond the eye-candy possibilities of their skimpy costumes.

First, let us examine Ariel, the redheaded title character of *The Little Mermaid*. Ariel, like Cinderella before her, dreams of access to a world that is off-limits to her because of her station in life. Pining for entry into the human world above her from her undersea home, she is, as Laura Sells puts it, an "upwardly mobile mermaid," both literally and figuratively.[29]

As I have already argued in the case of Cinderella, this makes Ariel an understandably popular icon among the upwardly mobile college crowd. In both cases, however, the patriarchal universe of Disney must subsume these young women's desires for social advancement under the auspices of their "natural" longing to be wives and mothers.

The recurring, unstated theme of Disney movies from *Snow White* onward is the grooming of ("naturally" beautiful) adolescent females into acceptable marriage partners for men. In order to be properly domesticated, both Cinderella and Ariel must be costumed and directed by an older female figure (*not* a mother) in the theatrical art of womanhood (Cinderella by her Fairy Godmother, Ariel by Ursula the Sea Witch). Furthermore, Ariel, like Cinderella before her, is instructed that she must silently seduce her prince within a given time period in order to permanently escape her present circumstances.

Although Cinderella is not specifically instructed to remain silent, she knows that she cannot reveal her true identity and therefore relies on non-verbal cues. Ariel is literally silenced, her voice traded for human legs—though, as Ursula tells her adolescent pupil, men are much more interested in a woman's "body language" than in anything she might have to say.

In fact, as Laura Sells points out, Ursula's exaggerated (and at least partly ironic) demonstration of how to look and act like a woman comes across as a drag show, teaching Ariel that "gender is a performance" in which she will have to become proficient if she wishes to be accepted into the human world.[30] Thus, despite the overarching phallocentric narrative of *The Little Mermaid*, Ursula's campy portrayal of human womanhood does manage to destabilize Disney's painstakingly naturalized vision of the gender binary.

Ursula's sardonic instructions call to mind Luce Irigaray's assertion that "One must assume the role of the feminine deliberately. Which means already to convert a form of subordination into an affirmation, and thus begin to thwart it."[31] Ursula, whose ultimate goal is quite literally to undermine patriarchal rule by taking King Triton's powerful scepter-phallus, encourages Ariel to mistrust her father and the system for which he stands by drawing a direct connection to the Little Mermaid's current dilemma. Only by consciously playing her part as a "woman," Ariel is instructed, will she succeed in subverting the patriarchal system that has kept her from fulfilling her (again, perfectly "natural") heart's desire.

It is important to note that all of the Ariels witnessed over the course of these two Halloween weekends were mermaids rather than women. Admittedly, this is Ariel's iconic state, and any legged versions might have been mistaken for some other attractive young redheaded character. Nonetheless, the presence of so many pre-transformation Ariels, despite the apparent inconvenience of having to take much smaller steps than usual in the restrictive mermaid costume, suggests that it is this early Ariel which holds the most attraction and appeal for contemporary probient women.

I propose that these barely post-adolescent, upwardly mobile coeds relate to Ariel's desire for transformation, her passionate longing for access into the "real/human" world. Their transition, like Ariel's, is not painless, and often involves sacrificing, or at least masking, portions of their previous identity.

Like Ariel, these young women surely tire of the unrealistic expectations and unreasonable restrictions that are placed upon them, and long to break free of the ties (or rather, the fins) that bind them. At Halloween, one can watch this metamorphosis taking place quite literally over the course of each evening, as the "mermaids" begin to tire of their restrictive costumes and start to tear, hike up, modify, or remove altogether the narrow "fin" below their seashell bras.

One such Ariel even went so far as to frame this activity as a burlesque performance, having recognized that her frustrated fin-ripping had attracted an eager audience on a balcony above. What appeared to have begun as an annoyed reaction to having tripped, yet again, over the "fin" protruding from the bottom of her dress, was subsequently transformed into a deliberate striptease. To delighted shouts of "take it all off!" and "show us what you got under there!" from above, and cheers and applause from her companions below, the red-wigged mermaid ripped upward along the side-seam of her dress in small, calculated spurts, twice stopping altogether and pretending to walk away (under much protest), only to return (accompanied by much cheering) and continue the tauntingly slow revelation of one leg, followed by another. As we have seen, seductive striptease is hardly a perversion of the new Disney aesthetic.

Yet this Little Mermaid was able to write an alternate ending to her transformative tale/tail: rather than succumbing to the persistent request from her (mostly male) audience to come up to the balcony and join their party, our protagonist instead flung her freshly-freed legs around the waist of one of her female companions, who was dressed as a "Gangsta Grrrl." She then threw back her head in defiant, jouissant laughter and, with a final wave to her disappointed fans, dove back into the sea of costumed probients beyond, quickly disappearing from view.

Pocahontas (1995), like *The Little Mermaid*, tells the story of a young woman caught between two worlds. Unlike Ariel, however, Pocahontas has no prior interest in, or even knowledge of, the world from which her love interest has come. Although she is painted as a "free spirit," going "wherever the wind takes her," she displays an apparent love for her home, and shows no desire, let alone intention, to leave it. Thus it is only her romantic interest in Captain John Smith that places her in the precarious position of bridging the cultural gap between her people (the Algonquian) and his (British settlers). Her love for the handsome young Captain, portrayed as the usual Disney instantaneous variety, carries with it a kind of magic, indicated by a sudden gust of wind that blows around their clasped hands. This love-magic carries both a gift and a curse. The gift is that of instant understanding between the young lovers: Pocahontas is granted the sudden ability to understand and speak fluent English, and John Smith's ingrained racism quickly evaporates thanks to Pocahontas's words of wisdom. The accompanying curse is that of all star-crossed lovers: their people are at war, and their love for each other puts both—and all who care for them—in grave danger.

This "colonial adventure tale" is, as Pushpa Naidu Parekh and others have argued,[32] extremely problematic in terms of its reliance on stereotypes and historical inaccuracies. Even more troubling is its wholehearted embracing of the romantic myth of the "noble savage" whose sole purpose in life appears to be to aid in the enlightenment of the kind-hearted, though misguided European.

The "politically correct," "multicultural-ist" message of the film, that everyone is the same underneath the surface and that we must therefore learn to tolerate each others' differences, is perfectly captured in a single image from the film's bittersweet conclusion. Standing side-by side, we see Meeko the raccoon, Pocahontas's long-time companion, and Percy the pug, prized pet of the gold-grubbing British governor Ratcliffe. Meeko and Percy are cross-costumed in the stereotypical trappings of the other's culture, conveying an end (or at least a momentary truce) to what has been an ongoing war between the two throughout the film. Stretched between them is the previously-destroyed necklace that once belonged to Pocahnotas's mother, offered up to Pocahontas as a tribute to the peace she has ostensibly inspired by saving John Smith's life. Their joint reparation and presentation of the necklace, broken during a skirmish that resulted in the death of the handsome warrior Kocuom, is apparently intended to serve as a symbol of inter-cultural cooperation, evidence that it is indeed possible for "the Native Americans and English settlers [to] learn to live side by side," as claimed by the film's back-of-the-box blurb.

This simplistic retelling of the legend of Pocahontas is a clear example of what has come to be known as "Disneyfication": the process by which cultural products are simplified, cheapened, sentimentalized (etc.) for mass consumption.[33] The film suggests that simply by following "her heart," which, "naturally," led her to fall in love with the Fabio-esque captain John Smith, Pocahontas was able to establish peace between two peoples who are still to this day embroiled in conflict. This is, at best, an oversimplification of historical events, and would more accurately be deemed an outright misrepresentation.

Nonetheless, the protagonist that Disney has created, one-dimensional poster child for sentimentalized multiculturalism though she may be, does appear to hold a strong fascination and appeal for probient viewers. Aside from the obvious aesthetic appeal—Pocahontas is drawn with perhaps the most impossible dimensions of any of the latter-day Disney heroines, her waist barely larger than her neck, and her remarkable mass of jet-black hair following no natural laws that I can recognize—she is imbued with a good deal more wisdom and self-possession than most of her Disney sisters.

Despite her incriminating resemblance to the colonialist fantasy of the savagely beautiful wild-woman longing to be tamed by a brave European explorer, Pocahontas did what no other Disney heroine before her dared to do: she chose *not* to marry her handsome prince. At the end of the film, rather than follow her white knight back to England, as he invites her to do, Pocahontas chooses to remain with the people, the animals, and the land that she loves.

Unfortunately, what might otherwise be viewed as a victory for single women everywhere is marred by the fact that the lovers' separation undermines what first appeared to be an endorsement of inter-cultural marriage. Given the racially-charged dialogue of the film, the audience is unable to view Pocahontas's choice to remain among her people as an empowered decision to cling to her beloved independence. Rather, they are left with the feeling that Disney is endorsing the passively racist doctrine that "birds of a feather [should] flock together." Pocahontas, however, does not seem to view her decision in those terms, and so the integrity of her character is preserved from the contaminative racism of the metanarrative.

The frequency with which Pocahontas appeared at the last three Halloween celebrations alone would seem to confirm her popularity in the young feminine imagination: on Halloween 2004, for example, over fifty coeds were spotted on Del Playa dressed as the scantily-clad Algonquin maiden.[34]

Moreover, I hardly believe it accidental that the overwhelming majority of revelers seen dressed as Pocahontas were non-white. Rather, it seems apparent that Pocahontas holds an important place in the imaginary-symbolic of probient young women of color. Yet Pocahontas, like the rest of her Halloweenized Disney sisters, has not been spared a few requisite alterations. Although her outfit in the Disney film is already scarce, revelers tend to downsize her costume even further, so that those masquerading as "Pocahontas" are in fact clad in little more than a beige, tight-fitting, fringed tube top and matching loin cloth. This emphasis on the character's sexy-savage appeal suggests that one main reason she is such a popular choice for young women of color is that she is one of a very few non-white sex symbols that will be widely recognizable to their peers. Interestingly, though, Princess Jasmine and Esmerelda, who would also seem to fall into this category, were considerably less popular, suggesting that there are other considerations involved.

Another common alteration suggests a rather different appeal: although Disney's Pocahontas never appears with a weapon in her hand, and in fact spends the entire film working toward the goals of peace and nonviolence, multiple Halloween revelers in Pocahontas garb chose to add a bow and/or quiver to their costume. I do not know how many of them would also have carried arrows or daggers, as these items are banned and would have been confiscated by the police had the revelers walked out into the street with such weapons on display. Still, the significant number of makeshift bows and/or felt sacks slung over the shoulders of Halloween Pocahontases certainly suggests that her image conjures "warrior princess" associations for many of these (largely non-white) young women.

Like all Halloween alterations, the addition of a weapon, or at least the suggestion of one, serves to correct an error or oversight on the part of the Disney company, and by extension the American culture it so faithfully reproduces. Pocahontas, so these young women seem to be implying, *should* be a warrior: she should have the ability, and the resources, to fight for what she wants, what she believes in. Perhaps many of these coeds of color view themselves not only as diplomats—human bridges, precariously stretched between two or more cultures—but as warriors, forced to fight for the right to subjecthood in white society, and at the same time to defend their ties to the culture(s) they have left back home. Said Ana Vasquez, who dressed as Pocahontas during the 2004 celebration:

> "I dressed as Pocahontas because she totally kicks ass. She doesn't apologize for being who she is, she totally calls [John Smith] on his racist shit and stays true to her people but also to herself and what she wants. I think that's awesome and that's what I try to do, too."[35]

Rather than choosing between the equally repugnant roles of the self-sacrificing martyr or the self-centered traitor, these young women insist upon carving out a new space: that of the confident, cosmopolitan warrior-princess. Furthermore, by inhabiting the role of Pocahontas, popular symbol of love, peace, and desirability, and arming her with the ability (and, by implication, the right) to defend herself, her beliefs, and her loved ones, these revelers are able to re-establish a sliver of the original heroine's complexity, and to create a new icon all their own.

· · ·

5. Mucho macho men

For male revelers, machismo is simultaneously emphasized and mocked. I argue that, through humorous exaggeration, the male reveler is able to come to terms with the impossibility of ever achieving his childhood fantasy of manliness. Faced with a social climate that is increasingly hostile toward unbridled masculinity, the male probient must content himself to play at being a cowboy, a pirate, or a superhero, while at the same time openly mocking such a fantasy as unrealistic or even inappropriate. In "The Curse of Masculinity," Susan Jeffords describes how Disney's *Beauty and the Beast* serves as a modern morality play on the subject of masculine reformation.

> "It is as if, the Beast's story might suggest, masculinity has been betrayed by its own cultural imagery: what men thought they were supposed to be—strong, protective, powerful, commanding—has somehow backfired and become their own evil curse."[36]

In order to liberate themselves from this "evil curse," contemporary males must resort to the tactics of humor and parody, choosing costumes that allow them to inhabit, while still deriding, the beastly persona of the macho man.

One of the most popular costumes at the 2004 celebration, for example, was Fred Flintstone, that comical icon of American masculinity. I asked one reveler dressed as Mr. Flintstone why he had chosen this stone-aged Everyman as his character of choice. He replied that "Fred is THE MAN," and beat his chest a couple of times in appropriately mock-Neanderthalic fashion.[37]

This response suggests a kind of nostalgia for the days "when men were men," as well as a vague sort of guilt—masked by self-reflexive humor—about such nostalgia. Also well-represented were "The Village People," a 1970's musical group who masqueraded in exaggeratedly manly attire to sing "Macho, Macho Man." During the course of the Halloween weekend, I heard no less than three spontaneous renditions of "Macho, Macho Man," only one of those from a group actually dressed like The Village People.

Mingling among the comical icons of American masculinity is a noteworthy addition to the childhood repertoire: the pimp. A significant perversion of the classical male role-model, the pimp figure foregrounds the hidden heteronormative transcript of so many socializing narratives: that a successful man is one who is able to have unlimited sexual access to, and to maintain control over the sexual activities of, multiple women.

One 2001 reveler, calling himself "Pimp Charming," illustrated this process by combining elements of the classical Disney prince—the white suit, complete with gold buttons and a plastic sword (eventually confiscated by an attendant police officer), with the Hollywood conception of a 1970s pimp—fuzzy, wide-brimmed hat and long, frilly coat, copious gold jewelry and platform shoes. "Has anybody seen Sleazy – I mean, Sleeping Beauty?" he asked passersby, and added – accompanied by a none-too-subtle grinding of the pelvis, "I've got something here that'll wake her right up!"

Although in one sense this is a parodic perversion of Disney's Prince Charming, in another sense it is simply an exaggerated exposition of the heteronormative, patriarchal subtext already present in Disney's feminine rescue trilogy: *Sleeping Beauty*, *Cinderella*, and *Snow White and the Seven Dwarfs*.

In all three films, happiness is directly equated with heterosexual marriage (to someone of equal or greater class standing). Despite the heroines' declared desire to meet and marry a handsome prince, all three are prevented from making that dream a reality via the evil deeds of jealous older women. As a result, the prince-hero must carry the burden of securing happiness not only for himself, but for the princess-heroine as well.

The films therefore naturalize the right—nay, the *duty*—of a man to chase, woo, win, and take as his prize whatever woman he desires. The pimp figure simply updates this logic: women (now read as prostitutes rather than princesses) need protection and desire happiness (still equated with a heterosexual alliance); therefore, it is not only the pimp's right, but his *duty* to please and protect as many women as he can manage, in exchange for their indentured labor (now in the form of sex with strangers rather than housework and child rearing).

Furthermore, the pimp, like his princely predecessors, is exceptionally allowed to primp, preen, and decorate himself with ostentatious evidence of his wealth and power, without being accused of effeminacy. Whether or not "Pimp Charming" consciously made this connection when he decided to interbreed these two purportedly contrasting icons of masculinity, he certainly incited onlookers to do so.

6. Sex in the spotlight

The activity of exposing hidden heteronormative transcripts is hardly limited to Disney-based parodies. One remarkably popular costume at the 1999 and 2000 celebrations was that of a doctor in scrubs, sporting an exaggerated, and apparently prosthetic, erection. Equally popular was the female counterpart to this type of "dirty doctor," the busty, short-skirted "naughty nurse."[38] Thus the childhood game of "playing doctor" returns to the young adult repertoire at Halloween time, its covert transcript of sexual exploration exposed and amplified. Again, these performances betray an ambivalent attitude toward the target text: by "playing doctor" with such explicitly sexual intent, revelers expose simultaneously their nostalgia for a lost age of innocence, and their jaded awareness that such games were never entirely innocent.

The foregrounding of sexuality, particularly deviant or "inappropriate" sexual behaviors or images, has remained a common thread throughout the history of costumes at Halloween in Isla Vista. Judging from the photo-spreads and descriptions provided in the *Daily Nexus*, it appears that religion was the parodic object of choice in the early days of Halloween in Isla Vista. Popular costume choices from these early days include (male) nuns reading copies of Penthouse magazine, partly-undressed monks, and religious zealots proclaiming, "the end is near – party while you can!"[39]

Political parodies have come to the fore on a cyclical basis, during presidential election years, or during other politically-charged moments, such as the outbreak of a war, but do not appear to have increased or decreased significantly over the years.[40] Thus the most recognizable transformation in parody object is a steady shift from pregnant nuns and perverse prophets to figures such as a marijuana-smoking Cat in The Hat and a licentious Oscar the Grouch, which began to appear in the early 1990's.[41] This trend has steadily continued throughout the last decade: the 2003 and 2004 celebrations yielded few religious send-ups, the vast majority of costumes instead parodying childhood texts.[42] The objects have changed, yet the revelers' parodic technique—that is, the sexualizing of sacred iconography—has remained remarkably consistent throughout the event's history.

Much of the costuming at Halloween is not based on any specific character, but rather is constructed on the basis of a *type*: an archetype of attraction that can be simultaneously exploited and exploded by the wearer. And as many observers have pointed out, much of the costumes and behavior at Halloween in Isla Vista evoke a "soft-core" pornographic sensibility of the *Animal House, Porky's, American Pie* variety.[43]

And in keeping with the "boys-chase-girls" genre, much of the intended humor is pointedly androcentric, and markedly homophobic, in nature. Of course, this is true of many carnivalesque festivals, particularly Caribbean Carnival. As Richard Burton points out, in the Caribbean, women who dare to carry themselves with "'manlike' autonomy and assertiveness," also known as "higglers," are mercilessly derided at carnival time. Also, before the 1884 clampdown by British colonial authorities, many a Trinidadian male was known to don a flimsy woman's nightdress and/or "a menstrual cloth liberally daubed with 'blood'," and to engage in "a variety of sexual antics" which particularly lampooned sexually aggressive females.[44] Equally ridiculed is the figure of the "batty man" (homosexual), or "auntie man" who simply fails to act with requisite manliness. These figures, as Burton puts it, have "no place in the West Indian social world." He writes:

"The 'auntie-man' is by definition the 'anti-man,' the negation of everything it is to be a man, just as the higgler is the negation of everything it is to be a "'lady.'"[45]

Because the system of the strong, (hetero-)sexually aggressive man, and the demure, submissive female primarily benefits straight men, it stands to reason that heterosexual male revelers would be invested in mocking those who fail to conform to those norms. Furthermore, due to the inherent instability of such a system, the authority to lampoon behaviors and identities must be closely guarded. Thus any attempt on the part of female or gay male revelers to mock straight male sexuality is taken as an attack and publicly shamed.

Judging by the sense of humor witnessed during Halloween time, it seems that straight male revelers in Isla Vista are equally invested in protecting their privileged sexual status. The following examples, witnessed at various Halloween celebrations from 1990 to 2004, amply illustrate this androcentric slant:

- A man dressed as a vagina who told passersby, "I'm a big pussy"
- A man in female drag who hung a stuffed beaver between his legs so that it was clearly visible beneath his miniskirt, and asked passersby, "You wanna see my beaver?"
- A host of six-foot phalli
- A compulsive masturbator with an enormous fake phallus in his faux fur-lined palm, pretending to have gone blind
- "Trojan Man," a giant condom
- The "fallopian tube swimming team," a group of men dressed as sperm squiggling their way through the crowd.[46]

To my knowledge, no female revelers have chosen to dress as a vagina, a giant breast, or a pair of ovaries.

Furthermore, the ubiquitous male genitalia is rarely victim to the same kind of malicious visual punning to which the female sex organs are so frequently subjected. Women at Halloween don't tend to walk around with roosters in their pants, or to put on one of the many giant penis costumes floating around in order to proclaim to passersby, "I'm a big dick!" The overarching rule seems to be that it is funny to reproduce aspects of male sexuality, or to mock aspects of female sexuality, but not vice-versa.

As Carol Mosely of the UCSB Women's Center put it in a March, 2006 interview, "Isla Vista is very much a boy's town."[47]

However, let me be clear that I do not take this as evidence that the media has somehow perverted these probients, inducing them to reproduce the frequently androcentric, almost inevitably homophobic, tropes of this kind of mainstream, soft-core porn. Such an assumption recalls Catherine MacKinnon's inflammatory claim that, "sooner or later, in one way or another, the consumer wants to live out the pornography further in three dimensions. [...] It makes them want to; when they believe they can [...], they do."[48] This kind of simplistic monkey-see, monkey-do equation not only denies agency to consumers of pornography, it makes a vast and unfounded generalization about human behavior. Furthermore, it blatantly ignores the polysemicity of pornographic images, offering only one possible interpretation of the pornographic image, one possible set of behaviors that will "sooner or later" result from exposure to it.

What the presence of a soft-core pornographic aesthetic at Halloween in Isla Vista *does* evidence in my mind is the fact that the material apparently resonates with this particular audience. Something about the characters and situations reproduced by the revelers —the naughty secretary, the horny plumber, the stylized, almost scripted encounters between toga-sporting frat boys and kitten-eared coeds—speaks to them; they find in these iconic images of eroticism something they recognize as being true, or amusing, or desirable, or perhaps all of the above.

This stands to reason, since there is much to be said about Halloween in Isla Vista as a specifically *sexual* event. The Del Playa scene is often compared to an enormous, outdoor singles' bar, and I don't think it would be overstating the case to claim that most, if not all, of the revelers, consider the Halloween ritual an elaborate form of foreplay, or at least flirtation. "College is [...] your prime," Jenn Lotz, a UCSB sophomore from New Orleans, noted in our March, 2004 interview, "most of [the revelers] are out to get ass [Halloween] night."[49] Anyone who has had even minimal exposure to the Halloween event would have a very hard time refuting Lotz's claim.

Indeed, a successful Halloween is frequently measured in terms of sexual interaction. When responding to the question, "What is your fondest memory of Halloween in I.V.," the majority of revelers surveyed recalled a memory directly related to sexual activity.[50] Male respondents tended to focus on sexual encounters with strangers, or virtual strangers; Tyler Whalen, for example, stated that his favorite Halloween happening was "bringing like 10 girls from the street up to my buddies' balcony, having all my BEST friends cheering me on as I did so, then making out with the hottest one of the group!" Sophomore Bruce Gordon relayed a similarly anonymous encounter as his all-time favorite Halloween memory:

A woman in a gothic-looking costume walked up to me and said, "come." "Where?" I asked her, so she told me, "In your pants." I told her I was going to need some help on that one, and she started unbuttoning my pants, when suddenly someone called to her and she took off running. I was like, "no, dream woman, come back!" But alas, she was gone.

Some women also described anonymous encounters; Carrie Awalt, for example, said the best thing about Halloween 2003 was "Making out with Satan. Too bad he doesn't go here," and Colleen Bingham fondly recalled getting a lap dance from an unknown Chippendale dancer. Most of the female respondents, however, relayed intimate encounters with known partners; Christina Ossa and "Briana," for example, both wrote about having kissed their current boyfriends for the first time on Halloween. Nearly all respondents, however, mentioned some sort of sex-related memory or activity (be it positive or negative, desired or undesired), ranging from mild flirtation and incidental voyeurism to actual sexual contact with fellow revelers.

Furthermore, sexual propositioning is one of the few activities which one could refer to as being "traditional" at Halloween in Isla Vista. Carried out both verbally and visually, propositioning at the event has become an art-form that provides much of the entertainment value for participants. Among the cleverest come-on schemes witnessed (either by myself or my informants) over the past five years are:

- The ever-popular kissing booth costume
- A superhero who went around "saving" female revelers
  from certain danger
- A group of topless firemen who doused attractive women
  with water, saying, "You are just too hot!" and the like
- A group of female fire-fighters wearing tiny white T-shirts
  reading "We find them hot and leave them wet"
- A man dressed as Inspector Gadget who announced "to all
  the ladies in the crowd," that they were welcome to "inspect
  [his] gadget"
- A young woman in pigtails whose baby T-shirt read "I been
  bad," and who invited passersby to "punish" her (usually in
  the form of a spanking)
- A man dressed as a baby who attempted to get passing
  coeds to breast feed him
- A fellow dressed as TV's "Crocodile Hunter" whose (live)
  pet snake provided endless fodder for licentious humor;
  and a man wearing a shower curtain who encouraged every
  woman he met to "save water" by showering with "a friend"
  (preferably himself, we assume).

ONE INTERACTION I witnessed on Halloween night, 2004 was particularly apropos to the college setting: A man dressed as a "Scantron" (an electronically graded answer sheet) tapped on the shoulder of a woman dressed as a naughty schoolteacher, saying, "Excuse me, can you help me out? I don't know the answer to number four!"

The Schoolteacher slowly pulled out the two pencils that had been keeping her hair in a bun, allowing a mass of brown, wavy hair to tumble around her shoulders, punctuated by a campy shake of the head. She then leaned forward, giving the crowd an excellent view down the front of her white, button-up blouse, as well as up her short black skirt, as she carefully filled in the letter "A" on the Scantron's cardboard costume. Meanwhile, the Scantron reacted as if she were rubbing his skin rather than his cardboard coating, making exaggerated facial expressions that mimicked sexual ecstasy. Once the circle was filled, the crowd gave an appreciative cheer, and both actors raised their arms in triumphant acknowledgement of their impromptu performances.

This foregrounding of sexuality makes a good deal of sense within the university setting; college is traditionally understood as an excellent place to find one's eventual mate, or at least to accrue a good deal of sexual experience in the attempt. Since, as Marcel Danesi has pointed out, adolescents are discouraged from acting on their sexual urges, the exploration and experimentation which might have occurred at puberty is instead pushed into probience. It is therefore unsurprising that Halloween in Isla Vista has, for many participants, come to represent communal sexual liberation and experimentation, albeit within certain culturally-defined limits.

7. An aggressively heterosexual scene

Those limits, at this point at least, are largely defined and enforced by straight males. Any behavior that is taken as a threat to heterosexual male sexual privilege receives an immediate, strongly negative reaction, and often threats of violence. For example, sexual battery (i.e. "ass grabbing" and "boob grabbing") is so ubiquitously practiced by men at Halloween that, in response to a survey in which women and men were asked if they had ever been touched in a way that made them feel uncomfortable, 40% of women's responses were directly related to Halloween. One woman simply wrote: "Halloween… I think that's pretty self-explanatory."[51] Women are also frequently spotted grabbing the asses of men at Halloween. However, the results of a Sexual Battery Survey conducted by the UCSB women's center revealed that "women [are] more often victims of uninvited grabbing (38% of women vs. 21% of men surveyed)." Furthermore:

> Female victims are much more likely than male victims to say that they always feel uncomfortable when they experience uninvited grabbing—41% vs. 4%. Moreover, 18% of males say they never feel uncomfortable.[52]

What does appear to make (straight) men uncomfortable is being ass-grabbed by a man when that man is believed to be a homosexual. On Halloween, 2001, I witnessed a scuffle between a man in fairly subtle female drag and another man dressed as a construction worker. Apparently, the man in drag grabbed the other man's ass and made a sexual comment, in a clear reversal of the cliché scene of the horny construction worker sexually harassing female pedestrians. The construction worker got very angry, repeatedly calling the man a "fag," and warning, "I'll kick your cock-loving ass if you ever touch me again." I later spoke to the man in drag, who identified himself as "Kevin." Kevin agreed that his major offense was to have been so convincing in his portrayal of a woman.

> "A boy can walk around with his dick hanging out of a mini skirt, no problem. But if you actually have the balls to shave your legs and really […] look the part, you're asking to have your ass handed to you, apparently."[53]

Had Kevin's costume been less convincing, had he left off the wig or kept the five-o'clock shadow, had his makeup been less masterfully applied, or had he refused to wear the high heel shoes, the construction worker may have read his performance as humorous and perhaps even played along. As it was, he had clearly overstepped the line of propriety by daring to publicly erase his masculinity. Worse still, he went so far as to mock male sexuality by performing a parody of sexual harassment in reverse. These were the crimes for which he was instantaneous judged and punished by his (straight male) peers.

In an informal discussion about Halloween in Isla Vista, Dr. Catherine Cole made a statement that gave me considerable pause to think. The Halloween scene, insisted Cole, "isn't just predominantly heterosexual; it's *aggressively* heterosexual."[54]

The distinction here is an important one: it isn't simply that there is a pervasive assumption of heterosexuality at the event (which there is); any kind of homosexual behavior that cannot be re-absorbed into the heterosexual economy (and here I am thinking specifically of the spectacle of two women kissing for the benefit of a male audience) will receive an immediate, and strongly negative reaction.

Unfortunately, this kind of strictly-enforced heterosexuality is not reserved for Halloween. "I.V. is so homophobic," noted UCSB graduate Angie Eng back in 1991, "It doesn't get worse on Halloween, there's just a lot more people."[55] I can corroborate Eng's assessment: walking down Del Playa on a Saturday afternoon in May, I witnessed the following, rather disturbing interaction. Two women were walking a ways ahead of me, and at one point they linked their pinkies together. A man riding by on a bicycle called to them, "Hey *fellas!*" and made a lewd gesture involving his tongue and two fingers. The women said nothing but promptly unlinked their pinkies and stepped slightly away from one another.

Openly gay friends and acquaintances of mine have reported similar occurrences, including the following tale, recounted by a UCSB student whom I will call "Joe." On a warm evening in September, 2003, Joe and his boyfriend were standing together on the balcony of Joe's apartment on Trigo Road. Although they were not kissing, they were being openly affectionate with one another, standing very close with their arms around each others' waists and speaking in intimate tones. Suddenly, Joe heard a male voice yell, "This Bud's for you, Faggot!" and felt his boyfriend lurch forward, knocking Joe to his feet and landing on top of him. Joe heard a good deal of laughter and cheering from below, and looked up to see a mixed group of probients congregating in the street. It was at that point that Joe noticed the (full) can of Budweiser that had apparently hit his boyfriend full in the back, hard enough to knock them both to the ground. The gathered crowd refused to identify the assailant, except to claim that he had been riding by on a bicycle and was now long gone.[56]

Just as Eng suggested, the larger crowds on Halloween make for an unfortunate mob mentality that seems to encourage conformity and to exacerbate mockery of the marginal. As with men in relatively convincing female drag, the few women who choose to dress in male drag are often the target of marked hostility and heckling, particularly from male revelers. At the 2000 gathering, a bold young woman strutted around decked out in "homeboy" garb, her T-Shirt reading "Whatz up, bitch?" and a realistic-looking latex penis hanging out from her open fly, cat calling coeds and mock-fraternizing with nearby men. Although the women she approached generally took her come-ons with good humor, and often reciprocated the attention, men appeared much less willing to play along.

One young man, whom she had approached because he was dressed in a similar outfit to her own, told her to "get the fuck outta here," and added, pointing to her faux phallus, "Jesus, keep that shit away from me!" Another man called her a "crazy-ass dyke" and instructed his girlfriend not to touch "that crazy bitch."

In 2003, a woman in fairly convincing male drag was singled out by a group of males dressed as firefighters. "Hey guy," they called to her, "what's a bull-dyke like you doing in a place like this?" The woman did not respond but was visibly shaken by the antagonism.

I received a similar reaction when, on the final night of Halloween, 2004, I decided to dress as a storybook prince. My costume consisted of a home-made paper crown, a velvet tunic (over a sports bra), white tights, knee-high boots, and a cod-piece. Because I left my hair down and rouged my cheeks in imitation of a fairy tale illustration, the character did not always immediately read as male. Thus I had a number of male revelers approach me, asking whether I was supposed to be a princess or a queen. When I told them that I was in fact a prince, and parted my tunic to show off the cod piece, I got a range of reactions, none of which were particularly favorable. Some simply laughed and said, "Oops, never mind," while others made a major production of stumbling backward, yelling out expletives and generally treating me like a side-show freak.

The most strongly negative reaction I received came near the end of the night, from one of the stragglers at Alice's party. The young man, who was dressed as a "redneck" in roughed-up overalls and boots, approached me with a couple of friends, asking, "Hey Princess, what Kingdom do you come from?" "Prince," I corrected, and showed them my royal "package" to illustrate. The three men began hemming and hawing loudly, one side-kick repeating over and over, "that is fucked up," the other lamenting, "what a waste." Most alarming, however, was the reaction of the "redneck" ringleader. With what appeared to be genuine hurt and anger, he shook his head for a moment before asking me point-blank, "Why'd you have to go and ruin the mood like that, huh?" The three then turned their backs to me and proceeded to commiserate with the other men at the party about my offensive costume choice.

The redneck's statement, along with his and his friends' behavior in general, told me a number of things about the expectations placed upon female revelers at Halloween in Isla Vista. As a woman, I was expected to create and maintain a romantic/sexual mood for the benefit of this male audience. My failure to do so was viewed as a direct and deliberate attack on the ego, and the libido, of the men present. The fact that I was wearing a cod piece made me, in the minds of these young men, an inappropriate object for their sexual attention, and my failure to make my unsuitability immediately apparent was deemed a kind of entrapment. In other words, they seemed to feel that I had tricked them into believing that I was sexually available, and they felt quite betrayed by the discovery that, by their definition, I was not.

Furthermore, as the evening wore on, it became apparent that they were quite unprepared to relate to me, or any of the women present, on any other level than that of flirtation. I and another woman who had turned down a sexual proposition earlier in the evening were pointedly ignored; the clear message was that the young men present felt sexually unavailable women to be *de trop*, that is, useless: simply unavailable bodies taking up space and unfairly wasting their time and attention.

8. The female grotesque

In addition to dressing in male drag, there is another way in which women may arouse the disapproval of male revelers, and that is to deny them the pleasure of objectifying them by pushing their own sexuality to a grotesque extreme. Like performance artist Karen Finley, who presented her body to audiences as degraded and deviant, an object already consumed and excreted, some female revelers have chosen to emphasize the messy, unpleasant, undesirable side of womanhood. For example, a woman at the 2001 celebration covered her body in "bloody" tampons and sanitary napkins. Another dressed as a rather menacing-looking package of yeast: a "yeast infection." Women have also chosen to dress as victims of domestic violence, mistreated sex workers, or as grotesquely fat, frighteningly skeletal, or otherwise unappealing female forms. While it is fairly standard for men who are cross-dressed as women to push femininity to a grotesque extreme (perhaps by over-doing the make-up, over-stuffing the chest and derriere, or performing a parody of pregnancy, and even the act of giving birth), such an unappealing caricature of womanhood is considered offensive, even "disgusting," when enacted by an actual female. The implication is that women are not allowed to participate in the performance of grotesque realism as *subjects*, only as its primary *objects*.

That is not to say that female revelers are not commenting upon mainstream representations of girlhood, womanhood, and female sexuality. On the contrary, as I have shown in regards to women's portrayals of Disney characters, such commentary is fairly ubiquitous, albeit often deeply ambiguous, and always transmitted on Aching's "lower frequency."

Another common site of ambivalent commentary is the mainstream media's tendency to juxtapose girlhood innocence and sexual desirability: sexualized versions of the catholic school girl, the Girl-scout or Brownie, and the pig-tailed toddler in leg-revealing baby-doll dress are all common sights on Del Playa.[57] Equally common are non-human symbols of sexualized innocence: angels become Victoria's Secret angels, bunnies become Playboy Bunnies, and cartoon heroines are unveiled as surreptitious sex symbols. On one level, these young women are indeed playing into the paradoxical, media-endorsed fantasy of the forever-young virgin-whore. On another level, however, by exaggerating and often mocking the paradox, they are also challenging the image and emphasizing their new-found sexual agency. The revealing costumes and raunchy behavior of the revelers constantly undercut the coveted virginal innocence of their personae, and this provocative incongruity serves to isolate and to comment upon the media's fetishization of girlhood.

Although it is not always apparent that this incongruity is consciously undertaken, there are incidences in which the commentary on contemporary girlhood seems more intentional. For example, one "troupe" of women at the 2004 celebration wearing Girl-scout uniforms called themselves the "Sexy Scouts" and showed off the merit badges they had earned in such areas as "blow jobs," "bong packing," and "'69." On one level this could be seen as simply a titillating and humorous parody of a trope that is familiar to many young people (i.e. the Girl-scout merit badge). However, it can also be read as a sardonic commentary on the skills girls are now expected to garner in order to become successful women. This latter interpretation is supported by a brief exchange I shared with one of these "Sexy Scouts:"

Adrienne: Did you earn all these yourself?

Scout: Hells yeah! This is pretty much everything I learned in college right here.

> **Adrienne**: Really?
>
> **Scout**: Well, this is what I remember, anyway. [laughter]
>
> **Adrienne**: And what else does a girl need to know, really?
>
> **Scout**: [more laughter] Exactly! These are important skills, yo. Life skills.
>
> **Adrienne**: (*Reading off one of the badges*) Wilderness survival skills?
>
> **Scout**: Yeah, that's for surviving four years in this fucking jungle.
>
> **Adrienne**: I.V., you mean?
>
> **Scout**: Isla Fucking Vista. Four fuckin' years out here. 'S rough, you know? No place for little fuckin' […] Campfire girls. […] But the real world is worse. So I hear.[58]

Despite her ironic tone, the Scout's comments suggest an awareness that the skills she has learned in the "jungle" of Isla Vista are the only skills she will actually need to survive in "the real world." This certainly implies intent on the part of at least one "Sexy Scout" to humorously comment on contemporary womanhood and perhaps even higher education.

Another popular target for irony among female revelers is iconic femininity, such as the perfect wife-and-mother, the ballerina, and the beauty queen. A few examples: one Donna Reed-style 1950's housewife was spotted popping pills from an enormous bottle marked "Mother's Little Helper (a.k.a. Valium); a young woman dressed as a ballerina had painted ribs onto her leotard to emphasize the anorexic, even skeletal silhouette so revered in the world of classical dance; and several bloodied beauty pageant contestants were seen haunting the streets of Isla Vista, their (powdered) white faces, (greasepaint) bruises and trails of dried (fake) blood all standing in stark contrast to the iconic elegance of their gowned, bannered, high-heeled bodies. These readings emphasize the dark underside of these icons of female beauty and goodness, bringing to light the steep price that is often paid in exchange for recognition as an ideal woman.

The place of the feminine in the theory of grotesque realism has, until recently, gone largely unexplored by scholars of the carnivalesque. Mary Russo writes in "Female Grotesques: Carnival and Theory," that

> "Bakhtin, like many other social theorists of the nineteenth and twentieth centuries, fails to acknowledge or incorporate the social relations of gender in his semiotic model of the body politic, and thus his notion of the Female Grotesque remains, in all directions, repressed and undeveloped."[59]

Though I agree with Russo that carnival scholars have historically underplayed the place of female sexuality in the aesthetic of grotesque realism, this may be due to the enforced subtlety of performances of the female grotesque by women. Clearly, there is much progress still to be made in terms of experimentation with alternative representations of gender and sexuality within the United States carnivalesque. And just as clearly, the androcentric, heterosexist culture of Isla Vista (and, sadly, the United States more generally) currently limits the potential for free exploration in these areas at Halloween. However, thanks to these and other lower-frequency masquerading tactics, female revelers are able to suggest some rather subversive ideas without subjecting themselves to the social sanctions levied against those who take a more brazen approach.

Furthermore, ironic commentary on idealized, heterosexist images of gender relations and sexuality is not limited to female revelers. Certain male revelers' exaggerated performances of a media-defined ideal of manliness serve to comment both on the absurdity of that ideal, and on the unfair, and often contradictory expectation that they should conform to it. At a party at which a number of Dramatic Arts majors had gathered, I witnessed an exemplary performance of satirized machismo.

First, a reveler dressed as "He-Man," a popular cartoon/action figure for boys in the 1980's with an exaggeratedly masculine physique, decided to put on a show of his manliness. He invited everyone to watch as he alternated between swigging large gulps of Vodka from a 40 oz. bottle and crushing empty beer cans against his forehead. This started off well enough, eliciting much laughter and cheering from the crowd. Predictably, however, he eventually became dizzy and disoriented, causing him to drop the bottle. When the bottle hit the floor, shattering loudly, he first looked embarrassed, covering his mouth with one hand. After a moment, however, he put his hands on his hips, stuck out his chin and declared, "I am He-Man, smasher of cans and breaker of bottles!" This, too, garnered laughter and cheers from the crowd. At that point, a reveler dressed as "Mr. Clean," the bald-headed, broad shouldered, excessively macho mascot of a line of commercial cleaning products, materialized from the crowd.

Taking charge, he asked the gathered audience to step away from the crash site, ceremoniously sweeping up the shattered glass. "Hey," He-Man called to Mr. Clean as he dumped the broken glass into a recycling bin, "what are you doing, man? That's woman's work!" As if this contradiction had never before occurred to him, Mr. Clean suddenly jumped away from the broom and dustbin, sending them clattering to the floor. "Woah," he answered, "I don't know. Habit, I guess." At this point, Mr. Clean's date, who was dressed as a Gypsy, interjected, insisting that she found sweeping to be a rather sexy pastime for a man. This prompted a number of nearby males to grab for the broom simultaneously, accompanied by much grunting and growling, and overlaid by another explosion of laughter among the gathered crowd.

What I would like to emphasize in particular about this scene is the male revelers' willingness to poke fun at ideals of masculinity, and even to emphasize the confusing contradictions underlying them. He-Man recognizes that his comical display of machismo has led him to look the fool, yet he feigns pride in his ludicrous accomplishment, emphasizing the inability of the "ideal man" to own up to his mistakes. Meanwhile, Mr. Clean, that macho superhero of domesticity, swoops in to save the day, only to be forced to come to terms with the contradiction upon which his masculine identity is based. The question lingers for a moment: can sweeping be considered a masculine activity? Finally, the riddle is solved when Mr. Clean's Gypsy-girlfriend demonstrates this simple principle of heteronormative manhood: if it attracts the feminine, then it is masculine.

By foregrounding and mocking the absurd contradictions underlying traditional conceptions of masculine and feminine, revelers of both genders do appear to be challenging the narrowly-defined options for adult (sexual) behavior presented by the media. In this sense at least, it does seem that some revelers are defining—or attempting to define—the terms of their own sexual maturity, rather than simply following the templates provided via the androcentric, heteronormative media, Disney most certainly included. Although the revelers' ability to do so openly is currently limited by the social sanctioning intended to safeguard straight male sexual privilege, these ideas *are* being transmitted to those who can to tune into their frequency.

9. Blackfaced brothas, transparent Caucasians

In addition to sexual privilege, many of the revelers also appear to be invested in defending racial and/or class privilege. This is made apparent through the practice of ethnic stereotyping and mimicry.

A remarkable (read: disturbing) number of the costumes witnessed on Del Playa are essentially walking ethnic jokes: Caucasian men seem particularly predisposed to don, for example, an exaggerated sombrero and poncho, Japanese "Ninja" gear, a Hawaiian shirt with fake grass skirt and plastic lei, a Hollywood-style "Indian" loincloth and headdress or, perhaps most disturbingly within the context of the current political climate, a Middle Eastern tunic and turban with faux, Osama Bin-Laden style beard.

Even more prevalent are ethnic stereotypes of non-white cultures from within the United States. In 2004, the streets of Isla Vista were awash with Caucasian boys dressed as jive-talking "Homeys," Chicano gangsters, and blaxploitation-style, Afro-sporting pimps. Another fairly ubiquitous costume piece, for both men and women, was a Bob Marley style hat, complete with attached dreadlocks.[60] Some simply wore the hat, while others actually went so far as to walk the length of Del Playa in blackface.

Shockingly, this was not the only instance in which white students painted themselves "black": in 2001, for example, a Caucasian man used charcoal to blacken his face, arms, legs, and midriff and, sporting a white skirt and stuffed tank top, and jovially bandying a racket, declared himself African-American professional tennis star Venus Williams. Another young man, witnessed that same evening, had painted his entire body dark brown before donning war paint, a loin cloth, and tying a bone into his hair.

As a number of authors have pointed out, among them Catherine Cole, Ralph Ellison, Eric Lott, Marlon T. Riggs, David Roediger, and Robert Toll, the practice of performing in blackface began as a means of marking African Americans and other non-Caucasian peoples as inferior Others, and continues to signify racial / ethnic difference and discord within the United States.[61]

Blackening one's face and parading around in public would be an extremely dangerous proposition in nearby Los Angeles, yet these white students enjoy a comfortable majority in Isla Vista which cushions them from the consequences of such inflammatory acts. The presence of blackface (both literal and figurative) on Del Playa, therefore throws up a red flag regarding race and class relations within Isla Vista.

However, as Homi Bhabha argues, "the discourse of mimicry is constructed around an *ambivalence*."[62] The act of masquerading as the Other contains simultaneously a fear of, and a desire for, that Other. The stereotype, Bhabha argues, is not inherently negative, rather, it encompasses the full range of colonial ambivalence, "from the loyal servant to Satan, from the loved to the hated."[63]

Like the fetish, the "good object" that "makes the whole object desirable and lovable, facilitates sexual relations, and can even promote a form of happiness," the stereotype acts as a metonym, a point of fixation that facilitates colonial relations by rendering the whole object exploitable. The mimicry witnessed at Halloween in Isla Vista betrays precisely this ambivalence: the stereotypes adopted by the revelers simultaneously reveal both their fears and their desires.

One apparent point of fixation is potency: many of the ethnic stereotypes presented by the Halloween revelers hinge upon sexual, physical, or financial prowess. The Latin lover, the Indian warrior, the black athlete or rap star, the Saudi oil millionaire: all of these express what is most attractive, and most threatening, about the imagined Other.

Another common theme is serenity: the peace-loving, ganja smoking Rasta, the laid-back tropical beach dweller, the wise Yogi, and so forth. These identities have come to represent those things that Euro-Americans view as lacking in their lives: balance, harmony, and calm. The portrait of the Other painted by these revelers is an ambivalent one: representations of strength are often accompanied by the insinuation of unscrupulous or sinister behavior, and peaceful portrayals tend to include an implied laziness and/or lack of intelligence. In this way, stereotype allows maskers to simultaneously transcend, and implicitly reaffirm the superiority of, their racial subject-position.

Although my colleagues and I did not see any Euro-American women in blackface, we did note prolific examples of exoticized portrayals of non-white sexual stereotypes: Middle-Eastern Belly dancers, Japanese Geishas, Indian Princesses, Chinese Concubines, etc. We also noted a pervasive tendency for non-white women to masquerade as white icons of femininity, including Madonna, Marilyn Monroe, Britney Spears, and of course, the ubiquitous (classical) Disney Princesses. We also witnessed such inter-cultural creations as a Japanese Pocahontas, a South American Alice in Wonderland, and an African-American Carmen Miranda.

It seems that, for female revelers, **sex appeal trumps all**: race is only important insofar as it is able to increase one's sexual desirability.

Embodied racial stereotypes are hardly new within the University setting. The Native American mascot controversy has brought critical attention to the ways in which intersections of race, power, and performance play out both on the field (or the court) and in the class-room. C. Richard King and Charles Fruehling Springwood write in *Team Spirits*,

"Native American mascots are masks, which when worn enable Euro-Americans to say and do things they cannot in everyday life, *as though by playing Indian they enter a transformative space of inversion wherein new possibilities of experience reside.*"[64]

Playing Indian, in other words, is viewed by Euro-Americans as a liberating act of carnivalesque masquerade. For the Isla Vistan revelers, the same appears to be true of playing Mexican, or Middle Eastern, or African-American, (etc.): these ethnic "types" are seen as vehicles for Euro-Americans both to transcend and to reaffirm the boundaries of racial/ethnic identity.

Even more revealing were those non-white students who chose to masquerade under some other racial signifier. Although a number of non-white males were seen dressed as various ethnic stereotypes—for example, an Asian-Pacific Islander in an Afro wig as a "Harlem Globe-trotter," and a Mexican-American masquerading as a Middle Eastern "terrorist," non-white men seem to avoid specifically Euro-American types.

Whereas I noted a number of Caucasian men dressed as "white trash"—mullet-and-overalls-sporting stereotypes of the Southern bumpkin—or in the khaki pants-and-Alligator-shirt uniform of the New England prepster, I saw almost no non-white revelers in compa-rable outfits. The only recognizable "white" trope any significant number of non-Caucasian men appeared to be willing to take on was that of the white woman: an Indian man, for example, paraded up and down Del Playa dressed as Dorothy from The Wizard of Oz in 2004, and in 2003, a black man donned a blond wig, low-cut dress, and matching feather boa.

These observations suggest that while non-white ethnic stereo-types and icons of white womanhood are fair game for mimicry and mockery, the Euro-American male remains more or less untouchable territory. The handful of brave souls who ventured into this arena were chastised for their lack of creativity, or simply harassed on principle.

For example, one black reveler who was dressed in a suit and tie was repeatedly asked by a group of white males "Are you supposed to be a Mormon or something?" When he declined to reply, the group taunted him loudly, and made rude gestures behind his back.[65] Yet the same group greeted a white man in fake dreadlocks with an enthusiastic high-five, saying, "What up, my brotha?"

From all this I conclude that the white male is still considered the invisible, unspoken "norm" in Isla Vista. Therefore, to dress as a "white guy" is not to be dressed up at all.[66] This process of "whiting out" Caucasian male identity is intricately linked to the calculated Othering of non-white, non-male identities via caricature.

The notion of Othering comes from Edward Said's foundational Post-colonial text, *Orientalism*. "Only an Occidental could speak of Orientals, for example," writes Said, "just as it was the White Man who could designate and name the coloreds, or non-whites."[67] Possessing the power to "designate and name"—in other words, to *objectify*—the Other, the White Man is able to cast himself as the invisible, unspoken *subject*.

10. De-Disneyfication?

Halloween in I.V. does display certain characteristics of Disneyfication—among these nostalgia, heteronormativity, racial Othering, and commercialism. For all its taboo-twisting pretensions, in practice Halloween in I.V. is much more closely linked with consumer culture than many UCSB students would care to acknowledge.

Take for example the pervasive presence of product-related costumes, such as the women dressed as "Budweiser Girls," "Playboy Bunnies," or "Victoria's Secret Angels" and the men dressed as beer cans of various marks, or in fast-food related costumes such as "Ronald McDonald," "Jack-In-The-Box," and even a box of Wendy's French Fries.[68] The presence of these brand-name endorsements seems particularly out of place given the remarkable fact that Halloween in Isla Vista remains in essence a non-commercial event, lacking in any kind of sponsoring body or organizational structure. The fact that students will voluntarily provide free advertisement for their favorite products provides compelling evidence of the profound psychological effects of advertising on children, and serves as a powerful reminder of the vulnerability of probients to commercial exploitation.

Nevertheless, I propose that the unsentimental, "edgy" re-appropriation of characters at Halloween is in fact an example of *De-Disneyfication*. By re-inserting complexity, using childhood icons to project images and tell stories of their own making, revelers are reversing the process of Disneyfication that was practiced upon them as children. Having deconstructed the intended messages encrypted within the entertainment on which they were raised, the revelers then create bricolage "remixes" that convey meanings more to their liking, and more suited to their purposes.

Here I use "bricolage,"—a term first coined by anthropologist Claude Levi-Strauss, but now widely employed by philosophers, sociologists, cultural theorists, and others—to refer to the process by which consumers collect cultural artifacts, partially or wholly strip them of their original meanings, and reassemble them in order to express alternate meanings.

What I would like to emphasize above all is probients' central role in creating, and re-creating, culture. Like Dick Hebdige, author of *Subculture: The Meaning of Style*, I aim

> "...to acknowledge the right of the subordinate class (the young, the black, the working class) to "make something of what is made of (them)" – to embellish, decorate, parody, and wherever possible to recognize and rise above a subordinate position which was never of their choosing."[69]

The revelers' adoption and manipulation of the signs and symbols of the childhood lore on which they were raised illustrates the subcultural process to which Hebdige repeatedly refers: refashioning the very symbols which mark the group members as "other," those indicators of difference imposed through the institutions of family, school, media, the law, etc., into useful tools of insider communication.

Slicing up Cinderella's ball gown and splicing elements of "pimp" into Prince Charming's suit are indeed provocative acts within the larger social space of Southern California (home, let us not forget, to both Disneyland and Hollywood). More to the point, though, they are creative and self-affirming acts, enabling the slicers and splicers to deconstruct the identities imposed upon them and, from the resulting fragments, construct meaningful alternatives.

DEFINING WE; DEFINING ME

1. **What's the password?**

As we have seen, semiotic and linguistic codes are effective means of marking territory. In terms of the parodic performances staged by the revelers, decoding their multilayered meanings relies heavily on a common pop-cultural and experiential vocabulary, as well as a willingness to look beyond the sexy spectacle of the courtship ritual. The semiotic codes adopted by revelers thus serve not only to communicate ideas, but to solidify group identity and insulate insiders from exploitation by external people and power structures. These codes, in other words, protect the much-contested boundaries of probient territory from encroachment by outsiders. As Jagodzinski argues:

"'Youth' in postmodernity has become a conflicted fantasy-object, a source of hope as well as anxiety by adults who wish to stay young, yet find themselves competing with young people, as the very Thing that they deny about themselves."[1]

Thanks to the media's commercialization, and accompanying

glamorization, of post-adolescent youth, membership must be carefully monitored. Since, as Sarlo puts it, "we all want to dwell indefinitely the territory constituted by youth," that fantasized space of (albeit largely illusory) unbridled sexuality and infinite freedom, those who "rightfully" belong there must find ways of defending its borders. "The 'young' expel all phonies from this territory," writes Sarlo, "casting out those who do not fulfill the conditions of age."[2]

I would argue, however, that the requisite condition is not that of *age* per se, but of *culture*: more specifically, the collective unconscious formed upon common ideas and images circulated in the mainstream media. Although the formation of such a bank of common imagery and ideology is in some senses generational, it cannot be so neatly tied to numeric age. I must agree with Jagodzinski's assertion that

> "Youth is a fetishistic object that has an immaterial existence. It can only exist in the unconscious [...] where, being endowed with magical qualities, it remains indestructible and immutable, a transcendental signifier that is beyond both language and the imagination."[3]

Youth being immaterial, its boundaries existing only in the social imaginary, and carrying as it does so many social benefits (both material and ethereal), it is no wonder that its membership is so hotly contested.

It further stands to reason that the creation and circulation of these signs and symbols is not necessarily a *conscious* process: rather, revelers are collectively drawn to images and ideas that will mark them as insiders. When asked why they have chosen a given costume, revelers tend to respond not in terms of what the costumes *mean*, but of what they *do*.

Halloween revelers are extremely focused on the question of *reception*: what effect a given costume will have on its intended audience of fellow revelers. Popular criteria for costume choice (aside from the ubiquitous consideration of availability and ease) included: what would attract the most (positive) attention; what would attract the highest number of potential sexual partners; and what would get the most laughs. In other words: whatever social commentary might be embedded within their costumes and accompanying performances, the bottom line for revelers is to achieve social affirmation from their peers. To be recognized, in short, as *insiders*.

The power of such recognition should not be underestimated. Unlike on campus, within the carnivalesque space of the Halloween street-stage, social hierarchy is suspended and attention is fair game for all.

Constanza Berardi, who dressed as Harry Potter on Friday, October 28, 2005, was amazed by the amount of attention she was getting from people who would not normally associate with her. At one point, a group of women she assumed to be sorority sisters stopped to fawn over Berardi for a couple of minutes, and took several pictures with "Hah-rry Pottah!" Pleased, if somewhat mysti-fied, the openly lesbian Computer Science major said later of the experience, "Those sorority girls who practically tackled me? On a daily basis, if they saw me in normal clothes, they wouldn't give me the time of day."[4] It seems that, at Halloween time, the quotidian criteria for insider status are collectively suspended and rewritten.

This re-writing of the rules of acceptance relies on a kind of collective critical engagement: if Halloween is to be successful as a means of defining and defending the boundaries of probience, there must be some common criteria upon which judgments of "in" or "out" can be made. In the following section, I describe one way in which I believe the revelers to be setting, communicating, and contesting those criteria, as well as providing useful insight on the purpose of masquerade within the United States Carnivalesque.

2. The judgers and the judged

In spite of the "festival ordinance" banning any kind of organized entertainment, revelers in Isla Vista have invented a number of permissible ways to amuse themselves, and each other, at Halloween.

One of the most widespread activities is the rating of, and/or providing a running commentary on, costumes and their wearers. Some of these self-appointed judges—whom I will call "judgers," so as to emphasize their unofficial status—hold up home-made cards bearing either numbers (usually one through ten), or pithy adjectives ("Hot!" "Lame," "Cute," etc.). During Halloween weekend, 2004, I spent a good deal of time observing groups and individuals involved in this activity, in an attempt to better understand the criteria upon which their judgments were made, and what this might signify about the larger purpose of the event.

My first encounter with a group of costume judgers came fairly early on Friday night, October 29. A group comprising both male and female revelers, all of them in costume, had stationed themselves on the back of a parked flatbed pick-up in a Del Playa driveway to rate the costumes of those passing in front of them.

Nearly all judgers in Isla Vista station themselves up above street level, either on balconies, fence-height platforms, raised couches, parked vehicles, or standing upright on chairs or benches. This lends both visibility and perspective; like de Certeau's exalted pedestrian who escapes the labyrinth of the city by looking down on it from a skyscraper's summit, a judger's "elevation transfigures him into a voyeur [...] looking down like a god."[5]

I watched these particular judgers, who made their opinions known via numbered cards, for about twenty minutes, and returned several times that evening to observe a few minutes more. I noted a marked difference in the methods of male and female judgers. Eventually, I concluded that any decently attractive female would receive a ten from the (apparently intoxicated) male judgers, while those deemed unattractive were given a number ranging from zero to three. This suggests that, in the case of males evaluating females, physical attractiveness is the most important criterion for acceptance into the privileged space of probience.

Men, on the other hand, were generally ignored by the male judgers, unless they spotted a costume they found particularly funny, at which point they would hold up the "10" and comment grudgingly that they wish they had thought of that. This suggests a competitive element among male revelers, who seem loathe to admit when they have been outdone.

The female judgers were also concerned with the matter of attraction, though not so exclusively, and not in such black-and-white extremes. The female judgers reserved the ten for costumes they found especially clever, labor-intensive, flattering to the wearer, or which conjured a particularly strong emotional or intellectual connection for the judger. Women were also less inclined to use the lower numbers than their male counterparts, usually staying within the range of seven to ten. These observations proved to remain consistent throughout the weekend: while men were more likely to judge the wearer than the costume, often judging in extremes of "hot" or "not," women seemed more concerned with the costumes themselves, particularly with their personal connection to the chosen material.

Not insignificantly, similar dynamics appear to be at play when it comes to determining who is eligible for entry into private parties. During Halloween weekend, 2005, I stood at the entrance to three separate parties for approximately one-half hour each, taking note of who was allowed entry, who was turned away, and for what [stated] reason. The designated "bouncers" at all three parties were male (probably due to their more intimidating physical presence), but in one case, one of the female hostesses stood nearby and was given the final word on who gained entry to her abode.

At the two parties where the doors were guarded solely by men, any decently attractive female was allowed in, whereas men were routinely turned away. In fact, unless a man was accompanied by a large group of women, he had little chance of gaining entry. By contrast, at the party where one of the hostesses was present, all potential guests were submitted to the same scrutiny, regardless of gender. Unless he or she could identify which resident had invited him or her, a reveler seeking entry had better have a phenomenally interesting costume, an intriguing accent, or an acceptable addition to the wet bar. Otherwise, hot or not, the hostess would have no compunction about telling the bouncers to remove the uninvited guest from the premises.

These observations suggest that the criteria for judging insider status are not wholly consistent among male and female revelers. Men are as stingy about accepting other males into the fold as they are lenient about allowing entry to women. So long as a woman is considered—to use the judgers' term—"fuckable," then she is a welcome addition. Women, on the other hand, appear to have consistent criteria for both males and females: to be an insider, they must speak the correct symbolic language, conveying messages that the judgers can decode and appreciate.

3. The Ref

Even more revealing than the rule, in this case, were the exceptions: those who dared to step outside these remarkably consistent gender norms in judging costumes.

One such deviation came in the form of a female "referee" who was stationed on a platform that had been built above the fence-line of a Del Playa residence. This dark-skinned, sharp-tongued judger used her referee's whistle to draw mocking attention to those outfits she saw as "foul," inevitably following the shrill whistle with a stream of humorous insults directed at the offending party.

"The Ref," as I will call her, soon drew a crowd of amused revelers, who joined in her game of pointing out "bad" costumes, either to hear her deride them, or to offer their own commentary. After observing The Ref's activities for nearly an hour on two consecutive nights, I came to the following conclusions regarding her standards, which differed quite drastically both from the benign encouragement of most female judgers, and from the "hot" or "not" rule of many of her male counterparts.

Firstly, her greatest pet peeve appeared to be "cop-outs"— costumes that were not really costumes at all, but merely apparent excuses to wear next-to-nothing, to look glamorous/sexy (women), or to look macho/tough (men). On Friday night, I heard her berate several young women, asking them, "Are you supposed to be hookers, or did you just forget to put on the rest of your costume?" The bra-and-panty clad ladies responded by flipping off The Ref, who yelled after them, "Oops, sorry, didn't realize those were your work clothes!"

She threw a similar taunt out to a group of young men in "Gangsta" gear, asking them, "You thugs forget to buy costumes, or what?" The young men did not respond, prompting The Ref to twist her long, black ponytail around one finger in little-girl fashion, and to squeal in falsetto, "Please don't let the bad men hurt me!"

By contrast, The Ref's favorite outfits were those that demanded a certain amount of courage and bravado on the part of the wearer. Those who had taken a social risk, such as women dressed in un-feminine attire (i.e. [non-sexy] Ninjas, construction workers, etc.) and men in convincing female drag, or proffering political humor (such as the young man dressed as the recently-recalled California Governor Gray Davis, bearing a sign reading "will govern for food"), were greeted with cheers and thumbs-up signs from The Ref. Her most frequently bandied compliment was "That's bad-ass!" which provides a much different brand of affirmation than does the ubiquitous (largely male) shouts of "That's hot!"

So, thus far, it appears that according to The Ref, it is more important to be brave than attractive.

However, The Ref was also quite concerned with whether or not a given costume suited its wearer. For this sharp-looking, mini-dressed, soccer-socked judger, the key to a successful outfit was clearly a matter of compatibility: what looked fantastic on one reveler might look abominable on another, and no amount of creativity or hard work could make up for simple suitability. In this sense, she served as a kind of on-duty fashion-police officer, attempting to maintain some basic standard of fashion-sense among the Halloween crowd.

She was especially quick to jump on overweight revelers who had chosen to display what she considered to be an excessive amount of flesh. "Oh my god, put that thing away!" she was heard to call out to a "boxer" with a severely protruding beer belly, "Nobody wants to see that—all hanging over your belt and shit. That is nasty." Similar comments were tossed to young women whose bellies or buttocks were seen to be hanging over the edge of their costume-bottoms, or whose thighs she deemed too large for public display.

Also ridiculed were those whose costumes, however well put-together, were deemed poorly matched to the wearer in terms of style or genre. For example, The Ref blew her whistle on a young woman in rather elaborate Little Red Riding Hood gear, calling out, "Red is NOT your color, Babe." This attitude stands in stark contrast to the general principal of "carnivalesque disguise," as described by Beatriz Sarlo in reference to costumed youth lined up outside a Buenos Aires nightclub:

"There is a counterpoint between the body and its costume. *The clothes are not chosen to flatter the body* [...]. On the contrary, the girl first chooses her costume and only then layers, swathes, and drapes it on a body that has to adapt to the costume because *the costume is deemed more important than the body*, even though the body is freely on display. The girl's choice is not based on what suits her best. Instead, she has put on the costume that she likes best or, simply, the one she ought to wear. The idea of carnival takes precedence over other ideas, and *in the carnival what flatters bodily beauty has to give way to the imperative that bodies should come out transfigured by costume.*"[6]

Has The Ref simply misunderstood the purpose of costume at carnival? Or do the costumes at Halloween in Isla Vista serve some slightly different purpose than those at other carnivalesque celebrations? Also, is not this enforced adherence to Hollywood-style beauty codes inconsistent with The Ref's affirmation of socially deviant costume choices? I believe my third and final observation regarding The Ref and her standards will offer further insight on these questions.

The Ref was apparently of the opinion that, if a reveler was willing to wear a given costume, he or she should be ready to play the corresponding part on demand. At one point, she called down to a male reveler dressed as a Chippendale dancer: "Show us some moves!" The young man, apparently not much of a dancer, gave a half-hearted pelvic thrust and then shrugged his shoulders, as if unsure how to continue. The Ref blew her whistle loudly and shouted "FOUL!" to much laughter in the crowd. "You got no business wearing that costume til you learn some *moves,*" she lectured to the embarrassed reveler's receding bare back.

A similar rebuke was given to a Santa Claus who failed to produce a convincing "Ho ho ho!" and to a Cowgirl who was too intoxicated to come up with any kind of Cowgirlish behavior, even when prompted by her friends ("just yell out 'yee-ha' or something!" suggested a 1950's housewife on whom she was leaning for support). This emphasis on a willingness to fully inhabit or correctly perform one's adopted role suggests that the question of compatibility goes beyond the aesthetic realm. The Ref seemed to feel—and, judging by her crowd of enthusiastic followers, many others appear to agree—that Halloween is not merely an excuse to put on an unusual outfit and parade around in it, but an opportunity to publicly display some heretofore hidden portion of one's personality in the form of an alter-ego/avatar.

This notion of Halloween embodiments as alter-egos is supported by the way that revelers speak about their performances. Ethan Roberts, for example, described a kind of double-awareness, of being a character, and of being oneself:

"It's just like being on stage, like being an actor; you're aware that you're an actor, *and* you're aware that you're playing this role... Like [if you're dressed as a jogger] you have to play up the jogger part, like, "hey I'm a jogger I'm gonna go running, I'm not paying attention to you, but I'm totally paying attention to you while I'm running." And not only that, but you have to interact with people in a way that a jogger would interact with people. But of course you're also interacting with them in a way that you want to interact with them, because you're really still yourself."[7]

The jogger in Ethan's example performs the necessary task that will mark him as a jogger, while at the same time performing his role as a Halloween reveler by paying attention to, and interacting with, other revelers. This marks the type of performance involved as what Richard Schechner terms "simple acting." This Schechner describes as, "when a performer simulates the speech and behavior of a character," as opposed to "complex acting," in which, "the performer's entire physical, mental, and emotional capability is involved in the portrayal of a character."[8]

The Halloween performer in Ethan's example is not wholly focused on creating and portraying the character of the jogger, rather his attention is divided between simulating joggerly behavior and interacting with fellow revelers in a way that is appropriate to the Isla Vista social scene.

This double-awareness could also be described as "Brechtian," in that it serves as an example of Bertold Brecht's *verfremdungseffekt* or "Alienation Effect."[9] By distancing himself somewhat from his character, purposefully emphasizing that he is not really a jogger but is merely playing at being a jogger, the actor in Roberts' example reminds his audience that they are witnessing a performance.

In addition, as Ethan notes, the jogger is not only interacting with other *revelers*, but with the *characters* they portray. In other words, the Halloween actor must not only perform two simultaneous roles (himself and the jogger), he must also be prepared to interact with anyone he encounters on two different levels: as a fellow reveler, and as a character. In this sense, Ethan saw Halloween as being comparable to the Comedy Central cartoon "Drawn Together,"

> "...where they put eight cartoon characters into a house and it's sort of like a fake reality show? That's sort of how Halloween is, it's just these really out-of-place characters, all thrown together. You know like, you see a Playboy bunny, and you go up to talk to her like she's just like some normal person on the sidewalk, but she's a *Play*boy bunny, she's got on ears and like, almost nothing else. You're both playing these roles, but at the same time you're conscious that you're playing them,

that you're still who you are and you're still interacting as people underneath it all."

Although Schechner deems this kind of acting "simple," the double-awareness Ethan describes here is more complex than simply recognizing that there are people interacting beneath the character-masks of the jogger and the Playboy bunny. It is the simultaneous awareness that the jogger *is* a jogger, and is also himself; that the woman he is speaking to *is* a Playboy bunny, and is also herself. In other words, Halloween characters are not masks that disguise or obscure the "real" identity of the wearer. Rather, they are embodied representations of some aspect of the wearer that he or she has chosen to project before the public.

In short, these masks are no more masks than those which their probient wearers don in the course of their everyday lives. They are avatars, identity fragments that have been carefully selected and projected via embodied performance.

Ethan and other revelers' ability to articulate this phenomenon suggests that Halloween participants are aware, at least to some degree, that the "roles" they adopt for the occasion are not so much disguises as advertisements announcing some aspect of the wearer's personality to the crowd at large.

Take for example the following opener to a *Daily Nexus* story by students Christine Bai and Matt Cohen, about alternative Halloween entertainment: "There are alternatives to the often seen ritual of dressing in next to nothing and trying to score as your *self-perceived alter-ego* parades down Del Playa Drive."[10] That Bai and Cohen felt the need to state that there are alternatives to this ritual suggests that projecting an alter-ego in hopes of "scoring" with peers is the Halloween norm.

Another *Daily Nexus* article that describes Halloween costumes as alter-egos is an opinion piece by Kevin McFadden entitled, "No More Treats, Just More Tricks." "Halloween isn't just an excuse [...] to change into a costume for a night – or weekend," writes McFadden, "It's an excuse [...] to magically change" into one's Id, an unbridled collection of "carnal instincts." He even goes so far as to suggest that Halloween masks are perhaps even more "real" than those worn in everyday life:

"Perhaps it is the other 364 days out of the year that you are pretending to be someone that you're not, and only on Halloween do you get to be who you are."[11]

This recalls Oscar Wilde's famous quip: "Give a man a mask, and he'll tell you the truth."

Although I feel this dichotomy of "real" versus "false" to be an oversimplification, I do feel that Halloween costumes function more as revealing than obscuring agents in terms of the wearer's self-identification.

Jagodzinski describes the tactic of adopting alter-egos among "youth" (probients) as one of the "ways in which territorialized capitalist space has been invaded and evaded by youth."[12] He describes the practice of masking (even when the mask is not "worn" but rather "dealt with" on what he calls the "imaginary mirror") as "a form of self-protection" for young people. Through the creation of an alter-ego, argues Jagodzinski,

"They are able to directly address the struggles within their psyches [...] so as to be able to deal with authority figures in their own terms, especially the institutional authorities like school, family, and the state."[13]

College students, such as those attending Halloween in Isla Vista, surely rank among the most directly affected by institutional authority figures: their daily lives are defined by continual interactions with, and enforced submission to, these power structures, in addition to continued (if transformed) relations to family and other social structures. It therefore stands to reason that they would make use of the time-tested tactic of masking/disguise as a means of temporarily escaping/manipulating the system within which they find themselves more or less trapped for most of the year.

This is a *tactic* in Michel de Certeau's use of the term: a means of "making do" within the "technocratic *strategies* that seek to create places in conformity with abstract models." Strategies, de Certeau explains, "are able to produce, tabulate, and impose these spaces [...] whereas tactics can only use, manipulate, and divert these spaces."[14] In this case, the masking tactics used at Halloween do not produce, tabulate, or impose a social system within the space of Isla Vista. Rather, they serve as a means of navigating the system, or *strategy*, within which students must operate and from which there ultimately appears to be no escape.

I believe The Ref understood this aspect of Halloween masking better than most of her fellow judgers, which explains the seeming contradiction in her critical standards for costume choices. If Halloween costumes are intended to be avatars/alter-egos, then they must serve a dual purpose. In addition to providing proof of insider status and enhancing their desirability factor among their peers, Halloween costumes should also stretch the bounds of revelers' accepted notions of the self—freeing them, in a sense, to be someone they wish to be, or believe they could be, if given the chance.

This dual purpose mirrors Jagodzinski's explanation of the projected "Ego Ideal" and its double-function within the realm of Cyberspace. The first half of the double-function is the narcissistic projection of an imagined "complete" self, rather than the motley collection of selves that it actually represents. In this sense, Halloween acts, just as Cyberspace does, as "a space where we can try out other points of view, explore other parts of ourselves." The second half is to exhibit "the imaginary perception that we think the (...) community has of us."[15] As the judgers amply illustrate, "not all such exploration is freely permitted, as if our every demand is met." The social space of Del Playa, like the Cyberspace of the world wide web, "acts as an agency of prohibition that prevents access to our full gratification."[16]

The Halloween avatar, like its online counterpart, is a projected persona which the reveler believes to represent not only who he or she is (or ought to be, or may yet become), but also who he or she is expected or desired to be by his or her fellow revelers. Thus the Isla Vista Halloween carnival is a place where revelers are encouraged to embrace their contradictions, to be everything they are, everything they think they are expected to be, and even everything they might be, all at once.

PART VI
CONCLUSION

ENDURANCE, IDENTITY, EXPERIMENT

"THAT is the real test for any burner: can you build a life and community off-playa that is based on the same principles? Can you make a difference in the world? That's the difference between a Tourist and a Participant… a tourist leaves it all in the desert. It's a vacation for them. For a Participant, it's a milestone for change in their life."

- Longtime Burner Christian Jacobsen

"This is Mardi Gras, this is New Orleans, it's what we live for. This is our life."

- "Mardi Gras Bob"[1]

"People just don't get it. If you go to UCSB, if you live in Isla Vista, *especially* if you live on DP—this is, like, *the* most important time of the year for us. […] this is where we *live*, this is what we *do*, this is who we *are. Get used to it!*"

- Kelly Barber, temporary Del Playa resident[2]

BURNING MAN RE-EMBERED

THE LIMITS OF RADICAL INCLUSION

1. **Good Morning, Black Rock City!**
It's morning in Black Rock City, Nevada. You were up so late last night you've lost track of time, but the sun is up, and the techno music has died down, so morning is a solid bet. Your camp-mates are still sleeping, so you ruffle the powdery beige dust out of your hair, grab your playa bike, and go out exploring.

Black Rock is a city like no other. Each year, it is constructed from scratch in the Nevada desert, and each year, it must be just as meticulously broken down and packed back out again by its citizen-participants. At the end of the week-long event, hordes of volunteers comb the "playa" (so called because in the winter months the entire area transforms into a lake), looking for matter out of place, a.k.a. "MOOP." This makes Burning Man the world's largest leave-no-trace event: an ever-evolving experiment in conscious ephemerality.

Black Rock City From Above

As you head for center camp, a voice calls out, "You look positively radiant today!" You wave and smile. Riding by compliment camp is always a delight.

You ride for a bit, then look around. This doesn't seem familiar. You must have taken a wrong turn somewhere. "Welcome to the Inconvenience Store," chirps a woman in a purple tunic and cat ears, emerging from a canvas tent, "How can I inconvenience you?"

"Well… I'm trying to find center camp," you tell her, dismounting.

"Ah. In that case, I definitely won't tell you where it is. Yet. Would you like something to drink?"

You're starting to catch on to the purpose of this camp, but you're up for the game, and quite thirsty. "Absolutely!" you reply.

"Okay cool. Do ten jumping jacks while I go find something for you."

Ten jumping-jacks later, she returns with a can of warm Tab that looks like it expired about a decade ago. You drink it between belly laughs, and she gives you directions to center camp.

Once there, you stop to admire some of this year's artwork. It, too, will only survive the week, and that temporality enhances its poignancy. Even the pieces that are humorous, absurdist, obscene, or downright silly feel meaningful in this context.

You stop to take a selfie by a mural depicting a sunburnt shirtless tourist with the caption: "I'm just here to see boobs." The irony speaks to you.

A fellow dressed in a Speedo, coattails, a bow-tie, and a dust-encrusted bowler hat walks up to you with a tray of chipped mugs and offers you hot coffee from a thermos. You accept, and though reciprocation is neither needed nor expected on the playa, you offer him a tube of your homemade lip balm for his cracked lips. He applies it, and gives you a balmy kiss on the hand before moving along.

You ride out into the deep playa, heading toward The Man.

Who's The Man?

The Man is not burning just yet. He will burn on Saturday night, the Saturday before Labor Day. But he is already constructed (always of wood) and looms large, the focal point of the semi-circular city.

The Man is the throughline that has remained constant since the very first burn, back in 1986. On the summer solstice of that year, Larry Harvey, Jerry James, and a few friends met up on Baker Beach in San Francisco. As an act of "radical self expression," Harvey set fire to an eight foot tall wooden man, as well as a small wooden dog.

Much has changed since that first burn. As illustrated in the interactive timeline on the Burning Man website, the event has grown steadily from less than one thousand to the **2019 population of seventy-five thousand**. In 1990, the event grew too large and unruly for its original location on Baker Beach, and so the burners joined forces with dadaist performance art group The Cacophony Society who were already planning an "autonomous zone" event in the Nevada desert over Labor Day weekend. Thus Black Rock City was born.

The Playa

That first year, the only admission price was survival. If you could get yourself out to the desert and manage to stay alive for a week, you could participate. Starting in 1991, though, a ticket price of $15 was charged to help cover the costs of providing basic safety and sanitation. Ticket prices have risen steadily since.

Tickets for the 2019 event cost $425, but they sell out so quickly (this year all 23,000 main sale tickets sold out in half an hour), purchase is limited to two per person. They've also added a second sale the week prior to the event, appropriately titled the "OMG Sale," for $550 apiece, as well as a pre-sale "FOMO" price for those who want to be *absolutely sure* they'll get in. That price? $1,400 apiece.

But that's just the price of admission. Burners also need to provide for all their own basic necessities: shelter, water, food, and so on (and yes, they WILL turn you away at the gate if you appear unprepared).

If you want to drive your car to Burning Man, you'll need to pay another $100 for a vehicle permit, but you'll have to park it at the gate. The only motorized vehicles allowed in Black Rock City are mobile art installations known as "mutant vehicles" (formerly called "art cars"). So you'll also need to bring a bicycle--the ubiquitous "playa bikes"--in order to get around. And of course you'll want to decorate it. And yourself. And your camp...

All told, the actual cost to attend Burning Man is upwards of two thousand dollars.

2. Burning Man Version 32.0?

Inevitably, the increases in population and price have induced significant cultural shifts over the years. The organizers, however, work hard each year to ensure that the ten principles which form the core philosophy of the event--are at the heart of every iteration.

As long-time burner James G. puts it, the ten principles are like the operating system of Burning Man, and each year's event is a new version. Like the Google Doodle, which is always evolving and adapting to fit its cultural context, the basic functionality of Burning Man remains the same, but the user experience is constantly changing. Some consider those changes to be upgrades. Others not so much.

His first burn was in 1997, when you could still drive up to the gate and buy a ticket, and there was very little in the way of infrastructure. His most recent burn was last year, 2018, and he'll attend this year as well.

"Every year, people complain that it's not as good as it used to be," says James. "But they were saying the same thing even back in '97! 'Oh it's terrible this year, it was so much better ten years ago.' I think there's always that sense of nostalgia, that it was better in the old days. But the reality is that it's alive and well. And that's what's fascinating about it. It's a completely self-perpetuating event, and yet, even at this scale, it still works."

Karen Stewart, who wrote her award-winning dissertation as a non-fiction graphic novel about her experience at Burning Man, says she definitely noticed a shift in 2007.

"That year," says Stewart, "it was obvious BM was going through changes. Awareness of the event was clearly mainstream. Still experienced amazing art, and loved the people we camped with. But the place felt like it was losing its edge. For example, people were dressing 'as burners' (buying prepackaged costumes online vs. creating looks themselves) and the BM Org was implementing more rules and regulations about what art could be created, where it could be shown, and how people could interact with it in the name of public safety.

"2007 was also the year Paul Addis snuck onto the man and set it on fire the opening Monday of the event, as a protest against the commodification of the BM experience. It was fascinating watching how that action rippled through the community as he was both loathed by people who felt he 'ruined things' and loved by those who thought he embraced the 'true spirit' of BM."

One of the most controversial shifts has been the introduction of so-called "plug and play" camps. These all-inclusive luxury camps are created by and for the Silicon Valley tech elite, allowing busy jet-setters who wouldn't otherwise be able to attend to experience the burn in relative comfort. Though they are not technically in violation of the Burning Man code of conduct, the air-conditioned trailers, catered meals, and exclusive, invite-only parties of the billionaire camps have become the target of much scorn; many burners feel that such camps betray two of the Ten Principles: radical inclusion, and radical self-reliance.

Ryan Welliver had been burning for six years when, in 2013, his interest was "starting to flag," largely due to the rise of plug-and-play culture. But the next year, Arctica, the camp that maintains the all-important ice stations at the event, tagged him to come on for production, and he's been with them ever since. "They're an amazing crew," he says of Arctica. "We put a lot of hours in during the day managing the logistics of getting three ice houses stocked and staffed."

"The P&P camps," says Welliver, "tend to present as a group interested in consuming the event rather than contributing to it. These people are paying thousands of dollars for a curated experience. But I'd be thrilled if those same people realized 'Hey, I have ample resources, and this is a cool thing I want to do. Next year I'll strike out and make my own camp'."

Welliver admits, though, that Burning Man isn't exactly "accessible" for the general public, either. Though every year a set number of low-income tickets are made available (this year it's 4,500), they still cost $210, and you still have to get yourself there, and survive.

"Radical inclusion is a tricky thing," explains Welliver. "In the same way that the P&P camps represent a sort of 1% at the burn, the general population has a lot of privilege to be able to attend. Getting time off from work, kids, travel costs… especially for anyone coming from another country. That's where I'm seeing regional burns as a good example of what I think the spirit of the event should be. Recreating the thing in your home, and making a way for more people to experience it. I think we want to bring people to the event to experience this thing we do, take a measure of that home, and reseed the principals."

This attitude was echoed by burner vet Christian Jacobsen. "For me, today, I don't go to the burn anymore," says Jacobsen. "It's EASY to be a burner and live the Ten Principles when you are AT BURNINGMAN. But that's not the point of the event… the point is the bring your expanded mind and learning out into the world and change the world."

Today, Jacobsen is a community Burner. "Building engagement in my local community. Creating community and events. Bringing the Burningman culture to my neighborhood, town, city, county, state, and country.

"THAT," says Jacobsen, "is the real test for any burner: can you build a life and community off-playa that is based on the same principles? Can you make a difference in the world? That's the difference between a Tourist and a Participant... a tourist leaves it all in the desert. It's a vacation for them. For a Participant, it's a milestone for change in their life."

3. Is the future of Burning Man local?

There are now regional Burning Man events all over the world. Will these community gatherings eventually eclipse the main event? After all, the diasporic versions of the pre-Lenten feast of Carnival have certainly given the original Venetian Carnival a run for its money. And if Burning Man continues to grow at this rate, eventually it will outgrow even the playa...

There is certainly evidence that Burning Man is becoming increasingly divided into sub-groups. Which stands to reason, since in any enterprise involving large numbers of humans, the natural tendency is for tribes to develop.

At this scale, every camp at Burning Man becomes its own neighborhood within Black Rock City, and each neighborhood has its own character, its own values, and its own aesthetic. Some are very welcoming and civic-minded, pooling resources into public amenities for all to enjoy. Some are gated communities that focus on maintaining the safety, security, and comfort of their residents. Some are busy, some are sleepy, and some are downright funky. Together, they make a vibrant, living city.

As in any city--actually, any *community*--the trick is to find those pockets where we feel most at home, and offer our unique contribution. Because the bottom line is that **Burning Man is only exactly what participants make of it.** No more, no less.

That's part of what makes the burn so fascinating, and frustrating. It is a blank slate on which a messy masterpiece is created and consumed each year by far too many cooks. Those who choose to collaborate can accomplish incredible feats. Those who prefer to focus on radical self-expression remind us of our innate freedom, and that we all have a unique and precious gift to offer the world. Even those who are just there for the feast offer an important element to this performative ecosystem: an audience.

The result is a kind of funhouse mirror reflection of society in the moment, a concentrated echo chamber for the perpetual struggle between autonomy and cooperation, creation and consumption, the self and the other.

I'll end with an anecdote James shared that perfectly sums up Burning Man's embodiment of this human paradox. One night, when he was out walking on the playa, he realized he was quite far from camp and it was getting uncomfortably cold. A mutant vehicle came by, a fabulous, Victorian-style carriage.

"There were all these people inside [the carriage], wearing steampunk outfits with top hats... very fancy. I remember hailing it down and saying, 'Hey, can you give me a ride?' But they said, 'Sorry. Private party.' And I remember feeling pissed off and rejected and grumbling to myself that that's not what Burning Man is supposed to be as I'm walking home in the cold. But then about ten minutes later, just as I'm feeling the most sorry for myself, this massive, Hong-Kong style junk shows up with a bar, and all these stools on poles all the way around it, and a giant hammock strung up on the front. And the driver says, 'hop on!' So I slide onto one of the stools and proceed to get driven around in this giant boat, chatting with the guy behind the bar with this great Brooklyn accent while he made me a killer drink. And then I get to talking to the guy next to me, who says he's been shirt-cockin' it all day, and his girlfriend chimes in that she's 'free-vaging' too, and in the midst of this delightfully crazy conversation I realize, yeah, some people are going to be pricks. But there are still good people here."

That's the beauty of radical inclusion: the darkness helps us recognize the light.

WE'RE NOT GOING ANYWHERE

MARDI GRAS 2006

1. **Nothing Cancels Mardi Gras**

*"nothing cancels mardi gras. **NOTHING.**"*

So claims a billboard, adorned with a gargantuan bottle of Southern Comfort and strategically located adjacent to the French Quarter of the still-shell-shocked city of New Orleans.

The billboard's claim is, strictly speaking, not true: Mardi Gras has been cancelled thirteen times since 1857, mostly due to wars (including the Civil War, WWI, WWII, and the Korean War).[1] But there is clearly a more symbolic statement being made on this billboard, an advertisement not just for a popular alcoholic beverage, but for New Orleans itself.

The billboard, like the performance of Mardi Gras 2006 as a whole, is intended to remind the people of New Orleans and all the assorted tourists that have converged here to participate in this historical event, that "Nawlins" is not going to let the devastation caused by hurricanes Katrina and Rita, and the flooding and chaos that followed, destroy it. To say, "nothing cancels Mardi Gras," is to say: "Nothing can stop the city of New Orleans from making a comeback. Nothing."

Mardi Gras is not just a holiday, after all. As Robert Tallant wrote in 1947, defending the need for the event in the wake of WWII, "Mardi Gras is a spirit. I believe it is an immortal one." He goes on to describe the irrepressible spirit he labels "Mardi Gras," a term that could easily be substituted in the following citation with "Carnival" or "the carnivalesque."

> "I think if there is any world left in which human beings still laugh and still, even on rare occasions, have fun, there will be a Mardi Gras, and that it will live through whatever catastrophes occur [...]. That is why Mardi Gras is not a trivial matter but a very important one. In a way it is a symbol of the art of being human, and wherever people are still human, wherever they enjoy living, Mardi Gras will exist in some form."[2]

Tallant's defense of Mardi Gras as an embodiment of the immortal spirit of *joie de vivre* is certainly not the first, nor the last of its kind. But his assertion that Mardi Gras will survive "whatever catastrophes occur" is particularly poignant in light of the catastrophic events of 2005, and the widespread skepticism about whether New Orleans could—and more to the point, whether it *should*—recover from such a blow.

Take for example Jeff Jarvis' online poll asking "Should New Orleans be rebuilt? Or how much of it should be?" Although Jarvis recognized the question to be "an indelicate" one, he nonetheless insisted that it is "one that needs to be asked," given the city's widespread poverty, not to mention its vulnerability to flooding, positioned as it is below sea level.[3]

The Mardi Gras krewes of 2006 thus carried the burden not only of defending their own continued existence, but of redeeming the existence of New Orleans itself in the eyes of the rest of the nation. Two parades in particular, Iris and Okeanos, seemed as though they could have been sponsored by the New Orleans Board of Tourism itself. Specifically aimed at vaunting New Orleans, these two krewes's floats represented all the wonderful things the city has to offer, including the cuisine, the jazz scene, and of course, Mardi Gras itself.

Another parade, Thoth, mounted a retrospective of some of the most important Mardi Gras krewes and their date of inception, evoking the one-hundred-and-fifty-year history of parading in the city. This evocation of Mardi Gras as a symbol of all that is good, worthwhile, and historically significant in New Orleans inverts the oft-heard argument, "we need to have Mardi Gras so that New Orleans can survive," reminding the audience that New Orleans must survive so that they can continue to have Mardi Gras.

This is because the survival of Mardi Gras and the survival of New Orleans are inextricably linked within the popular imagination. Most outsiders know only a few things about New Orleans: the food is spicy, the music is spicier, you can drink on the street, and they have Mardi Gras there. For tourists the world over, New Orleans without Mardi Gras would be like Los Angeles without Hollywood, or Pamplona without the running of the bulls.

And for the people of New Orleans, Mardi Gras is much more than merely a symbol of the human capacity for enjoying life: it is a symbol of the city itself. Writes Arthur Hardy, publisher and chief editor of a popular annual Mardi Gras publication,

"On the 150th anniversary of parades in New Orleans, krewe members, despite their own personal and financial losses, continue to feel a civic responsibility to present Mardi Gras to the world as *a symbol of the city's existence*—and, this time, *its refusal to quit existing.*"[4] [Emphases mine]

Mardi Gras has indeed become "a symbol of [New Orleans'] existence"—a metonymic cultural performance that is understood to embody the heart and soul of the place and its people. The performance of Mardi Gras is, in the well-worn words of Anthropologist Clifford Geertz, "a story [the people of New Orleans] tell themselves about themselves."[5] And in 2006 that performance was indeed charged with the task of attesting to the survival of the city it has come to represent, much like a symbolic appearance made by an important public figure in the wake of some threat or disruption (i.e. illness, scandal, political coup, assassination attempt, etc.). The parading of the krewes, the tossing of the beads, and even the influx of tourists during the final week of February, 2006, assured locals and onlookers alike that New Orleans is still alive and kicking.

The importance of Mardi Gras is, of course, not merely symbolic: the annual event is not only a symbol of New Orleans' survival, but an important component thereof, bringing in about $300 million in tourist dollars annually, according to Stephen Perry, president of the New Orleans Metropolitan Convention and Visitors Bureau.[6] To cancel Mardi Gras and forego such a major source of civic revenue would be tantamount to a public declaration of defeat. And every one of the locals with whom I spoke during my five-day stay in New Orleans assured me that their city is far from defeated.

One particularly colorful character, who called himself "Mardi Gras Bob," or simply, "The Bob," made the following emphatic statement about the city's survival:

"This time, right now, everybody that loves New Orleans [is] coming together to make a stand and say 'we are here and we're here to stay.' We're not going anywhere; New Orleans has been here for over two hundred years. We're not going anywhere. So to hell with everybody else who says, 'Hey, you're below sea level, you're gonna...' Well so what! We've been doing it for two hundred years, we've been below sea level for two hundred years, and we're still here."[7]

The Bob's repetition of, and insistence on, the phrases "we're [still] here," "we're not going anywhere," and "[we've been here for] two hundred years" functions in two distinct ways, for two distinct audiences. First, it is a rallying cry to his fellow New Oreleanians, encouraging them to be proud of their city's legacy of endurance and to resist the temptation to capitulate to the doomsayers' implied suggestion that they simply give up and move elsewhere.

This attitude was equally apparent in an overheard conversation at the Endymion Parade, when a woman was heard loudly berating a companion of hers who had apparently announced plans to sell her house and relocate. "Don't you sell your house!" the woman cried out, in apparent distress, "Don't you sell your damn house! We need everybody exactly where they supposed to be." The clear implication was that, if New Orleans is to survive, its remaining residents must band together and insist on staying put. To do so, they must call on their collective quality of endurance, among the most commonly—if not *the* most commonly evoked identifier at Mardi Gras 2006.

Second, The Bob's message was a public refutation to the insinuation that New Orleans is done for, an emphatic answer to Jeff Jarvis' "indelicate question" in the positive: *Of course* New Orleans should be rebuilt, and will be, with a little help from friends like those lining the streets at the Mardi Gras 2006 parades. In fact, The Bob's message— which he believes to be a common sentiment among all those in attendance at Mardi Gras 2006—is that not only will New Orleans be back, she is "still here," and never left. In other words, not only is Mardi Gras "an immortal [spirit]," New Orleans is an immortal city, one whose spirit, whose *identity* cannot be ravaged by storms, destruction, economic disaster, or even death. So long as there are survivors, there will be a New Orleans, and so long as there is a New Orleans, there will be Mardi Gras.

To this I add a further argument: that where there is Mardi Gras, there is the opportunity to re-construct and re-affirm the collective identity of New Orleanians—both among themselves, and for the outside world. As The Bob's speech amply illustrates, Mardi Gras 2006 served a dual purpose. First, as a cultural performance, allowing the people of New Orleans the opportunity to tell themselves who they are, what their city (still) is, and what it might now become; second, as political propaganda, allowing those same New Orleanians to project a consciously constructed image of themselves and their city out into the world. I argue that Mardi Gras is not only a potent symbol for the city of New Orleans, it is an active agent in the creation, re-creation, perpetuation, and projection of the collective identity of the people of New Orleans. And the identity constructed and disseminated at the 2006 event was one of dauntless, even cheerful, endurance in the face of opposition.

Nearly every parade at Mardi Gras 2006 included some kind of tongue-in-cheek reference to the hurricanes and their aftermath. Babylon, for example, presented an underwater theme, including effigies of the sea god Neptune and a multitude of mermaids. The Chaos parade included such floats as the "Homeland Insecurity Office," and the "Pigs of Patronage," which outlined all the various financial scams to which many New Orleanians have lately been subjected.

The Muses (an all-female krewe, at least in theory) presented a satire-heavy parade, themed "Muses Got Game" and aptly subtitled, "if we don't laugh, we'll cry." Floats included a game of "Babble" with the words "flood," "Katrina," and "Rita," spelled out on a giant Scrabble board, and "The Game of Life," on which was painted in bold letters: "To be or not to be? Let's ask the Supreme Court."

Morpheus was riddled with political commentary, such as the "Chocolate City" float, an apparent jab at Mayor Ray Nagin,[8] the "Looter Shooter" float, which highlighted the media's racially divisive coverage of rampant looting in the chaotic aftermath of the flooding, as well as the self-explanatory "Katrina, You Bitch."

Tucks presented such tart offerings as "1001 Nights Without Electricity," "FEMA Fairy Tales," and "Ye Olde Outhouse," a giant toilet above which was written, "The joke is on us: N.O. Takes a Bath."

But the most commentary by far came from Mid-City, whose

parade "Rode Hard and Put up Wet" was literally littered with "signs of the times" sporting sardonic one-liners.

Some quips were apparently political, i.e.

- "What War?"
- "Cheney Rifle Range"
- "Throw me some money, Jon Stewart"
- "Not in my Swimming Pool"
- "New Orleans for sale: Your ad here"
- "Tanks America!"

Others were more locally-aimed attempts to make light of the hurricanes:

- "Don't make me go Katrina on you"
- "Hurricanes happen"
- "This could only happen on South Park"
- "No place like DOME"[9]
- "How blue is your roof?"[10]
- "Raiders in the Lost Trailer Park"
- "Beachfront Property: Dirt Cheap"
- "My toilet was on T.V."
- "My gumbo was insured"
- A giant, frowning refrigerator marked "Free 7 month old gumbo inside"
- "Send Mo' Beans"
- And, perhaps my personal favorite: "Drove my Chevy to the levee, but the levee was gone."

The ironic humor evidenced in these krewes' floats serves a triple-function.

First, it allows a traumatized community to benefit from the healing powers of laughter—as the Muses put it: "if we don't laugh, we'll cry."

Second, it allows for the venting of a good deal of frustration and bitterness, particularly in regards to the official handling and media coverage of the crises.

Third, it sends an emphatic message to and about the people of New Orleans: "not only will we survive, we will survive with a smile."

In other words, the performance of Mardi Gras 2006 willed into existence a people whose most defining qualities are endurance, awareness, and good humor.

Yet despite the overwhelming presence of humor, neither the brutality of the past year, nor the reality of the hard road ahead were absent from the 2006 festivities. Mixed in with the satire was a moving sincerity, evidenced in the following Mid-City placards:

- "Live mindfully"
- "Please come home"
- "Is this enough to save New Orleans?"
- "How do you ever stop dreaming?"
- "There is a great message here for all of Mankind: Love one another!"
- And perhaps most straight-forward of all: "No more tears."

These emotionally-charged messages not only served to evoke pathos and encourage healing among participants,[11] they exemplified another quality intended to define this new People of New Orleans: caring. Thus the New Orleanians conjured by Mardi Gras 2006 are not only a people who laugh in the face of opposition, they are a caring people who feel this loss deeply and who will need the help, and the love, of other caring people, in order to get back on their feet.

This brings me to another frequently-evoked concept at the celebration of Mardi Gras, 2006: that of *family* and togetherness. When asked what Mardi Gras means to him, The Bob answered:

"Mardi Gras means *family coming together*. [...] It's almost like a giant family reunion, like Christmas is in some places, and this year, what with everything that's happened, coming together is even more important than ever." [Emphasis mine]

It seems to me that coming together for Mardi Gras, particularly after "everything that's happened" is important on multiple levels.

First, it offers an opportunity for those who have become separated to reconnect.

Second, it offers a chance for those who are reconnecting to mourn their losses, to celebrate their survival, and to share inside jokes and common experiences.

Third, as The Bob states so explicitly, it provides an opportunity for strangers or near-strangers to experience a sense of commonality, the giddy feeling of togetherness that Victor Turner has named "Communitas."[12]

Fourth, it represents a communal reclaiming of public space, a chance for "everybody who loves (New Orleans)" to "make a stand and say 'we are here and we're here to stay'."

Finally, it offers an opportunity for the people of New Orleans to remind themselves of who they are, and to collectively will themselves into becoming what they would like to be.

2. Bourbon Street West?

Halloween in Isla Vista is frequently compared to New Orleans' Mardi Gras, and for good reason. On a surface level, the Del Playa scene strongly resembles that of Bourbon Street in New Orleans' French Quarter, where costumed revelers drink, interact, expose themselves to one another (sometimes in exchange for some material reward, sometimes just for the attention), and engage in the same kinds of stylized courtship rituals I described in section five. On a deeper level, though, I believe Halloween in Isla Vista provides the same opportunities to participants as those I have outlined above in regards to Mardi Gras.

Halloween, like Mardi Gras, offers an opportunity for those who have been separated—in this case, because they are attending different colleges, or simply because their class schedules do not allow them to see much of one another—to reconnect. It also, as I argued in section five, provides an opportunity for those who are connected through the common experience of college (whether or not they have been previously acquainted) to commiserate, to celebrate, and to comment upon their communal condition.

Furthermore, as I argued in section four, Halloween in Isla Vista is a re-actualization of public space, providing an opportunity for participants to send a collective message to those who oppose the festivities that, in the words of reveler Kelly Barber, "this is where we *live*, this is what we *do*, this is who we *are. Get used to it!*"

Finally, the performance of Halloween in Isla Vista, like the performance of Mardi Gras, offers participants an opportunity not only to show each other, and the world, who they are, but to collectively redefine themselves, as individuals and as a group.

This suggests that, in addition to the negative function of tearing off protective guises and destroying comfortable illusions—the "demasking" effect—carnivalesque events may also provide a positive potential for communities to collectively brainstorm alternative options to the undesirable realities that have been demasked. Within the sanctioned space-time of carnival, participants are exceptionally granted the opportunity to try out modes of behavior and interaction that fall outside the social norms of the community in question.

The degree to which this potential is fulfilled, of course, varies widely, and I have pointed out the factors that currently limit this potential in the case of Halloween in Isla Vista – namely the tacit, though powerful, heteronormative and masculinist biases displayed by many of the revelers, along with alcohol abuse, violence, exploitation, and the (legal and spatial) restrictions placed on the festivities by local law enforcement and University policy.

The bottom line, though, is that the U.S. carnivalesque is here to stay. Though the forms and locations shift and adapt to suit the needs of the masqueraders, the masquerade remains. In the words of Kelly Barber:

Get used to it!

THE U.S. CARNIVALESQUE

ENDANGERED SPACES

The dearth of public space that is impoverishing communities nationwide, what Hardt and Negri describe as the "end of the outside," has consequences that reach far beyond the realm of politics.[1]

Social interaction, from the personal and intimate to the superficial and anonymous, is increasingly technologically mediated, and therefore increasingly regulated. Even socially deviant behavior is frequently re-channeled into the safer, more cushioned atmosphere of the world wide web, where its potential for social disruption is diffused and reabsorbed into the realm of commodification. Although there are certainly virtues to these insulated online communities, they fail to provide the sense of consequence and mutual responsibility that is a necessary prerequisite for meaningful human interaction.

Thus, for a generation bred on inconsequential, indirect exchanges, what is needed perhaps most urgently is an open-air laboratory in which to conduct experiments in direct, unmediated social interaction. I argue that Halloween, and Isla Vista more generally, has the potential to act as one such laboratory environment.

As Isla Vista activist Carmen Lodise wrote of Isla Vista in the 1970's: "The vision was one of a community as *a laboratory of social change*."[2] I believe this vision is still alive today in Isla Vista. And although it can be discerned throughout the year, its most radical expression and blatant manifestation is the annual Del Playa street party.

I further believe that this experimental aspect of carnival can serve an *intellectual* function within the host community by interrupting common sense, de-naturalizing the "natural," and encouraging the communal testing of alternative possibilities.

As Heidegger argued in *Being and Time*, genuine thought requires that the thinker reject the false consciousness of the "they" in order to come into a true, individual consciousness. He writes that "the Self of everydayness is the 'they'. The 'they' is constituted by the way things have been publicly interpreted, which expresses itself in idle talk."[3] This public interpretation, disseminated through "idle talk," I have named *common sense*. Heidegger warns that the Self, in "losing itself in the publicness and the idle talk of the 'they,' [...] fails to hear its own Self in listening to the they-self."[4]

In other words, by listening to the voice of the majority, to the common sense acquired through social contact (and, increasingly, via the media), an individual will lose the ability to think for him- or herself.

This "they" consciousness, the inability of the Self to hear itself over the idle talk of others, has been conceptualized in various ways by different schools of thought: the Marxists called it "ideology"; Semioticians such as Barthes referred to it as cultural "mythology"; Postmodernism has dubbed it "the center"; Feminism has called it "Patriarchy"; Foucault named it "discipline"; and so on.

The unifying theme among all of these concepts is the need to interrupt this pervasive, insidious, invisible force, though the preferred method of interruption varies considerably among and even within these schools of thought.

This need is no less urgent now than it was in the nineteenth century – indeed, it may be more so.

As we become increasingly reliant on technologically controlled and disseminated media as our primary source of information, we become correspondingly vulnerable to manipulation, propaganda, and intellectual mechanization.

Even more concerning, as trust in our media and government erodes, more and more Americans are relying on social media as their primary source of information, a landscape notoriously rife with spurious simulacra of legitimate news articles. Meanwhile video technology is quickly progressing toward the era of "deep fakes" — when it will become all but impossible to distinguish between actual video footage and manipulated imagery.

All of this has been compounded due to the 2020 global COVID-19 pandemic, which has pulled children out of school, adults out of workplaces, and everyone out of public spaces, for an unknown length of time.

If Jon McKenzie is correct that "performance will be to the twentieth and twenty-first centuries what discipline was to the eighteenth and nineteenth, that is, an onto-historical formation of power and knowledge,"[5] as indeed appears to be the case, then the role of performance in the intellectual and social lives of human beings deserves a no less thorough investigation than discipline, ideology, and so forth, have undergone.

There is inevitably some degree of improvisation within the performance of any living ritual, no matter how apparently repetitive, as Margaret Thompson Drewal has effectively argued.[6] Thus the normalizing function of live performance, which I define as a self-conscious display of repetitive/ritualized (or, to use the Schechnerian term, "restored") behavior, is continually undercut by the agency of the performers.

This maxim, as we have seen, also works in reverse: however apparently "liberated" and "liberating" a performance appears to be, it inevitably reifies certain concepts and conditions within the target community. But whereas at other cultural performances, relatively scripted and structured performances are subtly flavored by the interpretations of the individual performers, the street parties that accompany carnivals the world over are *defined* by disruptive, improvised, experimental play.

Much of the appeal and social effectiveness of carnival performance can be attributed to its emphasis on playfulness and imagination, elements that are usually relegated to the realm of "childhood" and considered unnecessary and even dangerous within the adult world. McKenzie dubs this non-serious, non-productive side of performance "perfumance," and argues that it has important intellectual implications which have been effectively described by Nietzche in *The Gay Science*. I believe that this is the element most endangered within contemporary United States culture, with its technologically overdetermined emphasis on speed, efficiency, and product or result. As the writings of G.W.F. Hegel[7] (and many of his fellow philosophers) painstakingly illustrate, intellectual process requires ample time for experimentation, and ample room for repeated failure and catastrophe, neither of which are available within the confines of contemporary (read: corporate) culture. Therefore it is increasingly imperative for intellectuals to investigate those events which value process over product, and which still recognize open-ended trial-and-error as a legitimate investigative methodology.

I argue that carnivalesque street parties are excellent examples of these increasingly rare events, the aim of which is not to produce, decide, or determine anything, but rather to disrupt dominant patterns of thought and behavior and toy with possible alternatives. I further argue that this form of street theatre, when staged by and for students of higher learning facilities, should not be so easily dismissed as wholly anti-intellectual. On the contrary, I believe it may provide a crucial opportunity for innovative thinking and fertile disruption within an increasingly mechanical academic environment.

Even pre-COVID, U.S. universities were in the throes of a massive identity crisis: no longer assured about the primary value, nor even the particular function of higher education, administrators and professors alike are being forced to re-examine what it is, exactly, that they are supposed to be doing here. Roger I. Simon writes in "The University: A place to Think?":

"In neither Canada nor the United States has the university ever been solely a site for the free pursuit of ideas without expectations of utilitarian benefits accruing in exchange for one's time and money. But what is shifting is the degree to which governments are willing to intervene in the articulation of university programs of training and research in regard to specific economic interests in support of particular agendas for "growth" as defined by a specific set of social elites."[8]

These "particular agendas" are rarely in favor of the arts and humanities, or indeed of any part of the curriculum that cannot promise significant economic return. Thus contemporary universities are moving farther and farther from the long-standing notion of the college campus as primarily a place of intellectual inquiry, innovation, and exploration.

If U.S. universities are to avoid falling prey to the market-driven pressure to produce efficient workers rather than innovative thinkers, then the function, the structure, and the value of secondary education must be put back up for debate. Fundamental questions such as what college is, why college is, what it is that students are doing, learning, and experiencing during their college years, and how those experiences are impacting them as individuals and as citizens, must be continually posed and reposed, and creative methods of investigating them must be explored. This project is one such exploration.

I don't delude myself that I have answered all of these questions, nor do I particularly believe there is any one correct answer to be uncovered. Rather, I have pointed to an important resource for exploring the function and meaning of higher education in contemporary society, one that has been thus far overlooked by the academy: student-driven carnivals staged on or near college campuses. I have presented a case-study of one such college carnival, and I hypothesize that other large-scale college parties fulfill similar needs for participants, stir up similar fears and demasking reactions in authorities and administrators, and offer similar opportunities for social experimentation.

I hope this study will inspire similar investigations of carnivalesque events on other college campuses, so that a convincing parallel might be drawn, which could in turn yield important insights about the role of the carnivalesque in higher education, and about the role of higher education within contemporary society.

For now, I can only make speculatory generalizations based on the findings from this singular, highly specified study. One such speculation is that, during college, the majority of students live together in a unique community which offers the development of essential life-skills such as the ability to deal with contradiction, and to embrace complexity. This is particularly important given the complex and contradictory expectations placed upon college students by parents and professors. Caught in the crossfire of adult fears and desires, students are objects of both envy and pity, made to bear the hope and the despair of the generations preceding them. Writes Henry Giroux:

> "Lauded as a symbol of hope for the future while scorned as a threat to the existing social order, youth have become objects of ambivalence caught between contradictory discourses and spaces of transition. While pushed to the margins of political power within society, youth nonetheless becomes a central focus of adult fascination, desire, and authority."[9]

These contradictions become intensified within the privileged space of the university campus: college students are held up as symbols of the best and the brightest, and yet are simultaneously demonized in the press as dangerous, discontented rebels without a cause.

Carnival – unlike most university programs as they are currently structured – is able to encompass these tensions and contradictions. The act of impersonation, as Richard Schechner has pointed out, allows the actor exist in a double negative: although the reveler is not Nemo, he is also not *not* Nemo.[10] Masqueraders are thus able to accept, and to express, mutually exclusive ideas and possibilities as co-existing, and to de-naturalize categories of identity and existence. On

Halloween, the "Girl-scout" is both a child and an adult, the "Teenage Mutant Ninja Turtle" is both a cartoon turtle and a human man, "Snow White" is both Latina and white, and the Victoria's Secret Angel is both "good" and "bad," both virgin and whore.

In short, these students are learning, and teaching, the critical lessons of complexity and the fluidity and constructedness of both group and individual identity.

Change, complexity, nonlinearity, and fluidity are the hallmarks of postmodern society. Therefore students entering into the contemporary global village will need to arm themselves with the intellectual tools of imagination and experimentation, the social tools of adaptation, performance, and direct interaction, and the psychological tools of identificatory flexibility.

The most important preparation for "real life" we can hope to offer contemporary college students is an ability to recognize and accept internal and external contradiction. Therefore the academy should not be so quick to condemn college carnivals such as Halloween in Isla Vista, which not only serve as vibrant expressions of students' paradoxical position within society, but as open-air laboratories where students can experiment with various ways of conceptualizing and coping with contradiction. Rather, these events should be at least *tolerated* if not outright celebrated as radical acts of grassroots intellectualism.

And though things may look bleak for the U.S. carnivalesque, the college campus, and indeed large-scale gatherings more generally in this time of enforced social distancing, if there is one thing I've learned in the course of my research it's that the revelers always find a way. I look forward to discovering what new forms the carnivalesque will take in the future, what rules will be broken and which reified, and what creative circumnavigations revelers will invent to get around these formidable spatial and social challenges.

The show, after all, must go on.

PART VII
REFERENCE

BIBLIOGRAPHY

dler, Patricia A. & Peter Adler, eds. *Constructions of Deviance: Social Power, Context, and Interaction*, Belmont, CA: Wadsworth Publishing, 1997.

Aching, Gerard. *Masking and Power: Carnival and Popular Culture in the Caribbean*, Minneapolis: University of Minnesota Press, 2002.

Arnett, Jeffrey Jensen. *Emerging Adulthood: The Winding Road From the Late Teens Through the Twenties*, Oxford: Oxford University Press, 2004.

Association for the Anthropological Study of Play. Meeting (8th: London, Ont.) *The Masks of play*, New York: Leisure Press, 1984.

Axelrod, Mark. "Beauties and Their Beasts & Other Motherless Tales from the Wonderful World of Walt Disney," in Ayres, Brenda, ed. *The Emperor's Old Groove: Decolonizing Disney's Magic Kingdom*, New York: Peter Lang, 2003: 29-38.

Ayres, Brenda, "The Poisonous Apple in *Snow White:* Disney's Kingdom of Gender," in Ayres, Brenda, ed. *The Emperor's Old Groove: Decolonizing Disney's Magic Kingdom*, New York: Peter Lang, 2003: 39-52.

Ayres, Brenda, ed. *The Emperor's Old Groove: Decolonizing Disney's Magic Kingdom*, New York: Peter Lang, 2003.

Bakhtin, Mikhail. *Rabelais and His World*, Trans. Helene Iswolsky, Cambridge: M.I.T. Press, 1965.

--------------------. *The Dialogic Imagination: Four Essays*, ed. Michael Holquist, trans. Caryl Emerson and Michael Holquist. Austin: University of Texas Press, 1981.

Bean, Kellie. "Stripping Beauty: Disney's 'Feminist' Seduction," in Ayres, Brenda, ed. *The Emperor's Old Groove: Decolonizing Disney's Magic Kingdom*, New York: Peter Lang, 2003: 53-64.

Belk, Russell W. "Carnival, Control, and Corporate Culture in Contemporary Halloween Celebrations," in Santino, Jack, ed. *Halloween and Other Festivals of Life and Death*, Knoxville: The University of Texas Press, 1994: 105-132.

Bell, Elizabeth, "Somatexts at the Disney Shop: Constructing the Pentimentos of Women's Animated Bodies," in Bell, Elizabeth, Lynda Haas, & Laura Sells, eds. *From Mouse to Mermaid: The Politics of Film, Gender, and Culture*, Bloomington: Indiana University Press, 1999: 107-124.

Bell, Elizabeth, Lynda Haas, & Laura Sells, eds. *From Mouse to Mermaid: The Politics of Film, Gender, and Culture*, Bloomington: Indiana University Press, 1999.

Bhabha, Homi K. *The Location of Culture*, London: Routledge, 1994.

Bloustein, Edward. *The University and the Counter-Culture; Inaugural and Other Addresses*, New Brunswick, NJ: Rutgers University Press, 1972.

Brake, Mike. *Comparative Youth Culture: the Sociology of Youth Cultures and Youth Subcultures in America, Britain, and Canada*, London: Routledge and Kegan Paul, 1985.

Brecht, Bertold. "Alienation Effects in Chinese Acting," in *Brecht on Theatre*, ed. and trans. John Willett, New York: Hill and Wang, 1964: pp. 91-99.

Brode, Douglas. *From Walt to Woodstock: How Disney Created the Counterculture*, Austin: University of Texas Press, 2004.

Brovarney, Dorothy E. "The Seductive Sixties: Isla Vista's Quest for Identity, 1960-1978," dissertation, UCSB, 1998.

Bryman, Alan. *The Disneyization of Society*, London: SAGE Publishers, 2004.

Burke, Peter. *Varieties of Cultural History*, Ithaca: Cornell University Press: 1997.

Burton, Richard D.E. *Afro-Creole: Power, Opposition and Play in the Caribbean*, Ithaca: Cornell University Press, 1997.

Butler, Judith. *Gender Trouble: Feminism and the Subversion of Identity*, London: Routledge: 1999.

---------------. "Imitation and Gender Insubordination" (1990), in Sarah Salih, ed. *The Judith Butler Reader*, Malden: Blackwell, 2004.

Caplan, Lionel, Humphrey Fisher, and David Parkin, eds. *The Politics of Cultural Performance*, Providence: Berghahn Books, 1996.

Carlson, Marvin. *Performance: a Critical Introduction*, London: Routledge, 1996.

Castle, Terry. *Masquerade and Civilization: The Carnivalesque in Eighteenth-Century English Culture and Fiction*, Stanford: Stanford University Press, 1986.

Cohen, Abner. *Masquerade Politics: Explorations in the Structure of Urban Cultural Movements*, Oxford: Berg, 1993.

Cole, Catherine, Harry Nelson, and Walter Yuen. "Final Report on the Isla Vista Action Group," submitted to Chancellor Henry T. Yang, April, 2005.

Cook, Thomas D. and Frank F. Furstenburg Jr. "Explaining Aspects of the Transition to Adulthood in Italy, Sweden, Germany, and the United States: A Cross-Disciplinary Case Synthesis Approach," in Alan W. Heston, ed. *The Annals of the American Academy of Political and Social Science: Early Adulthood in Cross-National Perspective*. March 2002, vol. 580

Cowley, John. *Carinval, Canboulay, and Calypso: Traditions in the Making*, Cambridge: Cambridge University Press, 1996.

Crumrine, Ross, Marjorie Halpin, eds. *The Power of symbols: masks and masquerade in the Americas*, Vancouver, B.C.: University of British Columbia Press, 1983.

DaMatta, Roberto. *Carnivals, Rogues, and Heroes: An Interpretation of* *the Brazilian Dilemma*, translated by John Drury, Notre Dame: University of Notre Dame Press, 1991.

Danesi, Marcel. *My Son is an Alien: A Cultural Portrait of Today's Youth*, Lanham: Rowman & Littlefield, 2003.

Davis, Mike. *City of Quartz*, New York: Verso, 1990.

Debord, Guy. *The Society of the Spectacle*, trans. Donald Nicholson-Smith, New York: Zone Books, 1995.

De Certeau, Michel. *The Practice of Everyday Life*, Berkeley: University of California Press, 1984.

DeGroot, Gerard J., ed. *Student Protest: The Sixties and After*, London: Longman, 1998.

Demarest, Michael. "Halloween as an Adult Treat: An Escapist Extravaganza Outdazzling Mardi Gras." *Time* 122 (31 Oct.): 110.

Deninth, Simon. *Bakhtinian Thought: An Introductory Reader*, London: Routledge, 1995.

Desforges, Luke. "Checking Out the Planet: global representations / local identities and youth travel," in Tracy Skelton and Gill Valentine, eds., *Cool Places: Geographies of Youth Culture*, London: Routledge, 1998: 175-194.

Douglas, Mary. *Purity and Danger: An Analysis of Concepts of Pollution and Taboo*, New York: Frederick A. Praeger, 1966.

Drewal, Margaret Thompson. *Yoruba Ritual: Performers, Play, Agency*, Bloomington: Indiana University Press, 1992.

Eagleton, Terry. "Bakhtin, Schopenhauer, Kundera," in Ken Hirschkop and David Shepherd (eds), *Bakhtin and Cultural Theory* (Manchester University Press, 1989): 178-88.

Eco, Umberto. "Frames of Comic 'Freedom'," in Eco et al, *Carnival!* New York: Mouton, 1984: 1-10.

Eco, Umberto, V.V. Ivanov, Monica Rector, edited by Thomas A. Sebeok, assisted by Marcia E. Erickson. *Carnival!* New York: Mouton, 1984.

Elias, James, ed. *Porn 101: Eroticism, Pornography, and the First Amendment*, Amherst, NY: Prometheus Books, 1999.

Epstein, Jonathon S., ed. *Adolescents and Their Music: If It's Too Loud, You're Too Old*, New York: Garland, 1994.

---------------- ed. *Youth Culture: Identity in a Postmodern World*, Oxford: Blackwell, 1998.

Faubion, James. *Michel Foucault: Power*, Essential Works of Foucault 1954-1984, Volume 3, New York: The New Press, 1994.

Flacks, Richard and Jack Whelan. *Beyond the Barricades, The Sixties Generation Grows Up*, Philadelphia: Temple University Press, 1989.

Foucault, Michel. *The History of Sexuality: Volume I, An Introduction*, New York: Vintage Books, 1990.

----------------. *Discipline and Punish: The Birth of the Prison*, New York: Vintage Books, 1995.

Fulassi, Alessandro. *Time out of Time: Essays on the Festival*, Albuquerque: University of New Mexico Press, 1987.

Gault-Williams, Malcolm. *Don't Bank on Amerika: The History of the Isla Vista Riots of 1970*, Santa Barbara, CA: Malcolm Gault-Williams, 1987.

Geertz, Clifford. *The Interpretation of Cultures*, New York: Basic Books, 1973.

Gibson, Pamela Church and Roma Gibson, eds. *Dirty Looks: Women, Pornography, Power*, London: BFI, 1993.

Giroux, Henry A. "Teenage Sexuality, Body Politics, and the Pedagogy of Display," in Jonathon S. Epstein, ed. *Youth Culture: Identity in a Postmodern World*, Oxford: Blackwell, 1998: 24-55.

---------------------. *The Mouse That Roared: Disney and the End of Innocence*, Lanham: Rowman & Littlefield Publishers, Inc., 1999.

------------------- **and Kostas Myrsiades, eds.** *Beyond the Corporate University: Culture and Pedagogy in the New Millennium*, Lanham: Rowman & Littlefield, 2001.

Graubard, Mark. *Campustown in the Throes of the Counterculture (1968-1972)*, Minneapolis: Campus Press Scope, 1974.

Haas, Lynda. "Eighty-Six the Mother: Murder, Matricide, and Good Mothers," in Bell, Elizabeth, Lynda Haas, & Laura Sells, eds. *From Mouse to Mermaid: The Politics of Film, Gender, and Culture*, Bloomington: Indiana University Press, 1999: 193-211.

Hardt, Antonio & Michael Negri. *Empire*, Cambridge: Harvard University Press: 2000.

Harris, Max. *Carnival and Other Christian Festivals: Folk Theology and Folk Performance*, Austin: University of Texas Press, 2003.

Hebdige, Dick. *Subculture: The Meaning of Style*, London: Routledge, 1979.

Hegel, G.W. *The Phenomenology of Spirit*, trans. A.V. Miller, Oxford: Oxford University Press, 1977.

Heywood, Leslie & Dworkin, Shari L. *Built to Win: The Female Athlete as Cultural Icon*, Sport and Culture Series, Vol. 5, Minneapolis: University of Minnesota Press, 2003.

Heineman, Kenneth J. *Put Your Bodies Upon the Wheels: Student Revolt in the 1960s*, Chicago: I.R. Dee, 2001.

Ivanov, V.V. "The Semiotic Theory of Carnival as the Inversion of Bipolar Opposites," in Eco et al, *Carnival!* New York: Mouton, 1984: 11-36.

Jackson, Stevi and Sue Scott, eds. *Feminism and Sexuality: A Reader*, New York: Columbia University Press, 1996.

Jagodzinski, Jan. *Youth Fantasies: The Perverse Landscape of the Media*, New York: Palgrave Macmillan, 2004.

Jeffords, Susan. "The Curse of Masculinity: Disney's *Beauty and the Beast*," in Bell, Elizabeth, Lynda Haas, & Laura Sells, eds. *From Mouse to Mermaid: The Politics of Film, Gender, and Culture*, Bloomington: Indiana University Press, 1999: 161-174.

Kelley, Robert. *Transformations: UC Santa Barbara 1909-1979*, Santa Barbara: The Associated Students of the University of California, 1981.

Levin, Bob. *The Pirates and the Mouse: Disney's War Against the Counterculture*, Seattle: Fantagraphics Books, 2003.

Levi-Strauss, Claude. *The Savage Mind*, London: Weidenfeld and Nicolson, 1966.

Liverpool, Hollis Urban. "Origins of Rituals and Customs of the Trinidad Carnival: African or European?" *TDR*, Vol. 42, No. 3 (Fall 1998), pp. 24-37.

Lott, Eric. *Love and Theft: Blackface Minstrelsy and the American Working Class.* New York: Oxford University Press, 1993.

MacKinnon, Catherine A. *Only Words*, Cambridge: Harvard University Press, 1993.

McGowan, Philip. *American Carnival: Seeing and Reading American Culture*, Westport: Greenwood Press, 2001.

McIntosh, Mary and Lynne Segal, eds. *Sex Exposed: Sexuality and the Pornography Debate*, New Brunswick, NJ: Rutgers University Press, 1993.

McKenzie, Jon. *Perform or Else: From Discipline to Performance*, London: Routledge, 2001.

Mulvey, Laura. "Visual Pleasure and Narrative Cinema." *Screen* 16.3 (1975): 6-18. Rpt. in *Visual and Other Pleasures*. Bloomington: Indiana UP, 1989. 14-27.

Munt, I. "The 'Other' postmodern tourism: culture, travel and the new middle classes," *Theory Culture and Society* 11: 101-23

Nellis, Michelle. "A Profile of Downtown Isla Vista," Masters thesis, UCSB, 1989.

Ogersby, Bill. " 'A Caste, a Culture, a Market:' Youth, Marketing, and Lifestyle in Postwar America," in Ronal Strickland, ed., *Growing up Postmodern: Neoliberalism and the War on the Young*, Lanham, Rowman & Littlefield, 2002.

Olson, Gayle Clark. "Twenty-four Years of Policing: Law Enforcement at UCSB and in Isla Vista 1954 to 1978," Masters thesis, UCSB, 1978.

Parekh, Pushpa Naidu. "*Pocahontas:* The Disney Imaginary," in Ayres, Brenda, ed. *The Emperor's Old Groove: Decolonizing Disney's Magic Kingdom*, New York: Peter Lang, 2003: 167-178.

Pinsky, Mark I. *The Gospel According to Disney: Faith, Trust, and Pixie Dust*, Louisville: Westminster John Knox Press, 2004.

Postman, Neil. *The Disappearance of Childhood*, New York: Delacorte, 1981.

Potter, Potter and James J. Sullivan. *The Campus By the Sea Where the Bank Burned Down: A Report on the Disturbances at UCSB and Isla Vista, 1968-1970*, Santa Barbara: Faculty and Clergy Observer's Program, 1970.

Prato, Alison. "Playboy's Top 25 Party Schools." *Playboy.* November 2002: 89.

Pratt, Jane and Kelli Pryor. *For Real: the Uncensored Truth About America's Teenagers,* New York: Hyperion, 1995.

Pratt, M.L. *Imperial Eyes: Travel Writing and Transculturation,* London: Routledge, 1992.

Prosterman, Leslie. *Ordinary Life, Festival Days: Aesthetics in the Midwestern County Fair,* Washington: Smithsonian Institution Press, 1994.

Riggio, Milla Cozart, ed. *Carnival: Culture in Action—the Trinidad Experience,* Worlds of Performance Series, London: Routledge, 2004.

Riggs, Marlon T. *Ethnic Notions,* video distributed by California Newsreel, San Francisco, 1986.

------------------. *Color Adjustment*, video distributed by California Newsreel, San Francisco, 1991.

Roach, Joseph. *Cities of the Dead: Circum-Atlantic Performance,* New York: Columbia University Press, 1996.

Roediger, David. *The Wages of Whiteness: Race and the Making of the American Working Class,* New York: Verso, 1991.

Rogers, Nicholas. *Halloween: From Pagan Ritual to Party Night,* Oxford: Oxford University Press, 2002.

Rose, Margaret A. *Parody: ancient, modern, and post-modern,* Cambridge: Cambridge University Press, 1993.

Rushkoff, Douglass. *The GenX Reader,* New York: Ballantine, 1994.

------------------. *Playing the Future: How Kids' Culture can Teach us to Thrive in an Age of Chaos,* New York: HarperCollins, 1996.

Russo, Mary. "Female Grotesques: Carnival and Theory," in Teresa de Lauretis, ed., *Feminist Critical Studies,* Theories of Contemporary Culture Vol. 8, Bloomington: Indiana University Press, 1987: 213-229.

Rutherford, Paul. *The New Icons? The Art of Television Advertising,* Toronto: University of Toronto Press, 1994.

Salih, Sarah, ed. *The Judith Butler Reader,* Malden: Blackwell, 2004.

Santino, Jack, ed. *Halloween and Other Festivals of Life and Death,* Knoxville: The University of Texas Press, 1994.

Sarlo, Beatriz. *Scenes From Postmodern Life*, translated by Jon Beasley-Murray, Cultural Studies of the Americas, Vol. 7, Minneapolis: University of Minnesota Press, 2001.

Scott, James C. *Domination and the Arts of Resistance: Hidden Transcripts*, New Haven: Yale University Press, 1990.

Schechner, Richard. "Carnival (Theory) After Bakhtin," in Milla Cozart Riggio, ed. *Carnival: Culture in Action—the Trinidad Experience*, Worlds of Performance Series, London: Routledge, 2004: 3-11.

Scher, Philip W. *Carnival and the Formation of a Caribbean Transnation*, Gainesville: University of Florida Press, 2003.

Schweizer, Peter & Rochelle. *Disney, The Mouse Betrayed: Greed, corruption, and children at risk*, Washington D.C.: Regnery Publishing, Inc., 1998.

Sells, Laura, " 'Where Do the Mermaids Stand?' Voice and Body in *The Little Mermaid*," in Bell, Elizabeth, Lynda Haas, & Laura Sells, eds. *From Mouse to Mermaid: The Politics of Film, Gender, and Culture*, Bloomington: Indiana University Press, 1999: 175-192.

Simon, Roger I. "The University: A Place to Think?" in Henry A. Giroux and Kostas Myrsiades, eds., *Beyond the Corporate University: Culture and Pedagogy in the New Millennium*, Lanham: Rowman & Littlefield, 2001: 45-56.

Skal, David J. *Death Makes a Holiday: A Cultural History of Halloween*, New York: Bloomsbury, 2002.

Smoodin, Eric, ed. *Disney Discourse: Producing the Magic Kingdom*, New York: Routledge, 1994.

Sponsler, Claire. *Ritual Imports: Performing Medieval Drama in America*, Ithaca: Cornell University Press, 2004.

Stallybrass, Peter, and Allon White. *The Politics and Poetics of Transgression*, London: Metheun, 1986.

Stickney, John. *Actions, Alternatives, Raps*, New York: G.P. Putnam's Sons, 1971.

Storey, John. *An Introductory Guide to Cultural Theory and Popular Culture*, Athens: University of Georgia Press, 1993.

---------------. *Inventing Popular Culture*, Oxford: Blackwell Publishing, 2003.

Strand, J.H. "Maximum Freedom and The Limits of Community: Isla Vista, CA, 1925-1975," dissertation, UCSB, 1994.

Strickland, Ronald, ed. *Growing up Postmodern: Neoliberalism and the War on the Young*, Lanham, Rowman & Littlefield, 2002.

Suljak, Nedjelko. *Campus Disorder and Cultural Counter-Revolution*, Davis, CA: Inst. of Governmental Affairs, U. of California, 1970.

Sutton-Smith, Brian. "What Happened to Halloween?" *Parents* 58 (Oct.): 63-64.

-------------- and Diana Kelly-Byrne, eds. *The Masks of Play*, New York: Leisure Press, 1984.

Tallant, Robert. *Mardi Gras...As It Was*, Gretna, LA: Pelican Publishing, 1989 (first published 1947).

Toll, Robert C. *Blacking Up: The Minstrel Show in Nineteenth-Century America*, New York: Oxford University Press, 1974.

Trowe, Martin et al. "Report of the Commission on Isla Vista," submitted to UC President Charles J. Hitch, October, 1970.

Turner, Victor. *The Ritual Process: Structure and Anti-Structure*, Chicago: Aldine Transaction, 1995 (originally published 1969).

Twitchell, James B. *Carnival Culture: The Trashing of Taste in America*, New York: Columbia University Press, 1995.

Wasko, Janet. *Understanding Disney: The Manufacture of Fantasy*, Cambridge: Blackwell Publishers, Ltd., 2001.

Whelan, John James. "Echoes of Rebellion: the Liberated Generation Grows Up," dissertation, UCSB, 1984.

Wilson, Peter J. *Crab Antics: The Social Anthropology of English-Speaking Negro Societies of the Caribbean*, New Haven: Yale University Press, 1973.

Zipes, Jack. "Breaking the Disney Spell," in Bell, Elizabeth, Lynda Haas, & Laura Sells, eds. *From Mouse to Mermaid: The Politics of Film, Gender, and Culture*, Bloomington: Indiana University Press, 1999: 21-42.

MEDIA SOURCES

Audiovisual recordings

Dateline: Campus Porn, NBC, November 2, 2003, videocassette.

Halloween, 2003, Bruce Gordon (UCSB student), 2003, digital video recording.

Halloween, 2003, Isla Vista Foot Patrol, 2003, videocassette.

I.V. T.V. Sevan Matossian and Greg Shields (UCSB students).

- Tape 1, Episodes: "The Night You Forgot," "The Sack," "Halloween [1999]," Sex Ed Part I: Dance, Dance, Dance," 1999, videocassette.
- Tape 2, Episodes: "Sex Ed Part II: Sex and Violence," "Spit or Swallow?" "Froggy Style," "Let's Get it On," 1999, videocassette.
- Tape 3, Episodes: "Self Seduction," "Halloween [2000]," "Foster Freeze," 2000, videocassette.

Halloween 2004 and *Halloween 2005*, Robert Lewis (Local videographer), 2004 and 2005, digital video recordings.

. . .

Newspaper / Magazine Articles

93106 (UCSB administrative publication):

March 1, 2004 (Vol. 14, no. 12)

Cole, Catherine and Harry Nelson. "Faculty Must Become Part of I.V.'s 'Solution,'" available at: http://www.instadv.ucsb.edu/93106/2004/March1/faculty.html

EL GAUCHO (UCSB student publication):

October 27, 1954

Christy Lord, "All Aboard for All-U Game, Rally, Dance Set": 1

October 4, 1963 (Vol. 44, #10)

"Rally? Yes Really": 1

October 25, 1963 (Vol. 44, #19)

"Homecoming Queen Contest Signup Due": 6

November 1, 1963 (Vol. 44, #22)

"Homecoming Queen Finalists Announced": 1

November 8, 1963 (Vol. 44, #?)

"Not University Conduct": 2

November 13, 1963 (Vol. 44, #26)

Denis Green, "Open Forum" (Discussion of "Halloween High jinks"): 2

"Humor Highlights GGR (Galloping Gaucho Review)": 6

October 23, 1964 (Vol. 45, #16)

Tom Bulgin, "The Isla Vista Problem": 2

November 2, 1964 (Vol. 45, #20)

"Student Talent Featured in GGR": 1

November 9, 1964 (Vol. 45, #23)

Photo page, Homecoming parade: 5

October 18, 1965 (Vol. 46, #18)

"GGR Talent Show Set for Festivities": 3

October 29, 1965 (Vol. 46 #25)

"Halloween High Life Gives Officers Overtime Chance": 1

. . .

THE DAILY NEXUS (UCSB student publication):
October 28, 1977
Weintrab, Rachel. "Halloween Costumes Link Kids to Gloomy Past": 2.
Lillington, Karlin J. "Getting Spooked On and Off Campus": 5.
October 30, 1978
Green, Kim, and Kim Kavanagh. "Del Playa Party Becomes a Halloween Riot: Four of those arrested face felony charges": 1.
--------------. "Disagreements in Accounts of DP 'Mini Riot'": 1.
Gaswirth, Mitchell M. "VIEWPOINT: Night on the Town": 4.
Webster, Marnie. "VIEWPOINT: DP Halloween Party": 4.
November 2, 1979
Herman, Dennis. "DP Disturbance Mars Celebration": 1.
October 27, 1980
Alburger, Jonathan. "IV Patrols Increased to Prevent Halloween Riot": 1.
November 3, 1980
Alburger, Jonathan. "Halloween Ends With Few Arrests": 1.
November 6, 1980
Brown, Paul. "OPINION: Halloween": 10.
November 10, 1980
Brown, Paul. "OPINION: Halloween" (extended version of the original, listed above).
November 2, 1981
DiBartolomeo, Steve. "Halloween Eve Reported Calm By Foot Patrol": 1.
November 1, 1982
Coe, Wendy. "Students Picket IV Market": 1.
November 3, 1982
Halloween photo spread: 10.
November 2, 1983
"Calm Halloween This Year": 1.
October 31, 1985
Siegel, Amy. "Foot Patrol Plans for Halloween Crowd Control": 1.
"This Week in UCSB History": 4.

November 4, 1985
Arellanes, Doug. "Halloween Revelers Crowd Del Playa: Despite high arrests, police say DP partyers [sic] cooperate": 1.
November 3, 1986
Hampton, Phil. "30,000 Flock to IV Streets for Halloween; No Major Mishaps": 1.
November 2, 1987
Wyland, Chris. "Crowds Smaller Than Officials' Prediction": 1.
----------------. "Checking Out the Scene on All Hallows Eve": 10.
October 28, 1988
Cottrell, Allen. "Taking Back The Night": 1.
Skelton Veronica. "Halloween: What It Is: What It Was: What It Shall Be": 10.
October 30, 1989
Donnelley, Maxwell C. "Halloween Antics Bring Fun and Danger: Isla Vista Revellers Get Just a Tad Bit Wacky": 1.
Editorial: "Annual Hellraising": 10.
November 1, 1989
Donnelley, Maxwell C. "I.V. Bash Does Not Rival Past Years' Rowdy Affairs": 1.
October 29, 1990
Hornberger, Charles. "Pre-Halloween Revelry Bigger Than Expected: Out-of-Town Partier Falls From IV Bluffs": 1.
November 1, 1990
Hornberger, Charles. "Fright Night: IV's Costume Party Calmer Than Saturday: Fewer Arrests, Incidents": 1.
November 1, 1991
French, Ross. "Police Arrest Over 350 During Halloween Bash: Two Injured in Falls From Isla Vista Cliffs": 1.
Adams, Jennifer. "Downtown Refuge From DP": 4.
November 4, 1991
French, Ross. "Violence Ends Halloween Weekend": 1.
"WEEKEND TOTALS": 11.
October 30, 1992

Ortega, Diana. "Some Fear Mob Scene, Others Welcome Party": 10.

November 2, 1992

Acevedo, Edward and Lisa Nicolaysen. "Halloween 1992: Sure It Was Huge, But Some Were Left Unsatisfied By The Anticlimax": 1.

Epler, Kimberly. "Condoms, Cows, and Cretins": 4.

October 26, 1993

Wisnes, Julianna. "Halloween Crackdown Leads to Higher Fines: Officials Say they Plan on Increased Arrests": 1.

October 27, 1993

Epler, Kimberly. "Isla Vista's Youth Take Trick-or-Treating in Stride Despite the Yearly College Party": 1.

October 28, 1993

Sato, Lisa. "Police, UCSB Attempt to Ward Off Invasion: Media Helps to Spread 'No Tolerance' Message": 1.

October 29, 1993

"College Media React to Weekend Laws": 3.

November 1, 1993

Chapman, Brett. "I.V. Partiers Inhibited by Police Suppression: More Arrests, Fewer Citations, Less Revelry": 1.

October 31, 1994

Robertson, Nick. Cover Story: "What if There Was a Halloween and Nobody Came?": 1.

November 1, 1994

Robertson, Nick. "Locals Celebrate Traditionally as Holiday Reaches the Final Night": 1.

October 31, 1996

"Going, Going Gone: I.V. Halloween's Dying Wishes: Continue Your Quest for Revelry, but Watch Your Back": 6.

October 30, 1997

"Halloween 1997" 1B-4B.

"Five Year Plan? Halloween Is No Longer the Huge Party It Once Was, So It's Time for a Smaller Police Presence": 6A

November 2, 1998 (Vol. 78 #28)

Mason, Sarah and Christine Putnam. "Holiday Gives Revelers Haunting Opportunities": 1.

October 29, 1999

McGrady, Shawn. "I.V.'s Frightfully Quiet Night": 1.

Lupo, Jeff. "Halloween in Isla Vista": 4.

Sarria, Henry. "Tales From the Ghost of Halloween Past": 7.

November 1, 1999

Andersen, Ted. "Partiers Enjoy Halloween Weekend of Fun": 1.

November 1, 2000

Keehn, Laura and Jennifer B. Siverts. "I.V. Celebrates With Festival, D.P. Parties": 1.

Photo Spread: 8-9.

November 3, 2000

Siverts, Jennifer B. Halloween Crime Statistics: 3.

October 12, 2001

Ruszczycky, Steven. "It's the Noisy Apes That Get Noticed." Available at: http://www.dailynexus.com/opinion/2001/1466.html

October 31, 2001

Bai, Christine and Matt Cohen. "IVRPD Provides Alcohol Free Alternative," available at: http://www.dailynexus.com/news/2001/1625.html

Lagos, Marisa. "Foot Patrol Anticipates Big Crowd: Police Expect Over 15,000 Party-Goers in Isla Vista for Halloween Festivities," available at: http://www.dailynexus.com/news/2001/1624.html

November 1, 2001

Lagos, Marisa, Ladan Moeenziai and Rebecca Turek. "Isla Vista Celebrates Halloween," available at: http://www.dailynexus.com/news/2001/1643.html

Photo spread: 4.

February 22, 2002

Jennifer B. Siverts, "Student Prepares Play Based on I.V. Tragedy," available at: http://www.dailynexus.com/news/2002/2435.html

April 25, 2002

Downs, David. "Heavy Mettle: 'Sidewalks and Better Light' tackles the toughest topic on the Sabado Tarde block," available at: http://www.dailynexus.com/artsweek/2002/2909.html

October 16, 2002

Buhler, Brendan. "Why Are There [So] Many Cops in Isla Vista? A Brief History of Halloween in Isla Vista," available at: http://www.dailynexus.com/feature/2002/3596.html

Lagos, Marisa. "Isla Vista Gears up for Halloween," available at: http://www.dailynexus.com/news/2002/3591.html

October 28, 2002

Ramirez, Armand. "A Ghost of Halloween Past: The Secret to a Great Halloween Lies in the Community," available at: http://www.dailynexus.com/opinion/2002/3707.html

October 31, 2002

Baldwin, Tiye. "Police Prepare for Halloween," available at: http://www.dailynexus.com/news/2002/3756.html

Baldwin, Tiye. "Party Like It's 1989: Isla Vista has a Wild but Exciting Halloween History," available at: http://www.dailynexus.com/opinion/2002/3750.html

November 5, 2002

Anthony, Cory. "Drugstore Cowboy: Thanks for All the Memories; Next Time Keep Your Hands Off," available at: http://www.dailynexus.com/opinion/2002/3808.html

September 25, 2003

McInerney, John. "Police, UCSB Get Ready for Wild Halloween," available at: http://www.dailynexus.com/news/2003/5527.html

September 26, 2003

Haier, Daniel. "UCSB Divided by Porn," available at: http://www.dailynexus.com/news/2003/5555.html

October 21, 2003

Haier, Daniel. "I.V. Gets a Chance to Ask Cops About Halloween," available at: http://www.dailynexus.com/news/2003/5812.html

October 24, 2003

Dozier, Matt. "I.V. Hears Halloween Security Plans," available at: http://www.dailynexus.com/news/2003/5864.html

October 28, 2003

Haier, Daniel and Kristina Ackermann. "He Said, She Said: Are Cop Costumes a Good Idea?" available at: http://www.dailynexus.com/opinion/2003/5889.html and http://www.dailynexus.com/opinion/2003/5890.html

October 30, 2003

Freeman, Jay. "Halloween Could Be Fun if I.V. Were a Democracy," available at: http://www.dailynexus.com/opinion/2003/5916.html

October 31, 2003

Brown, Ashley. "Fun Runs Dry at On-Campus Parties," available at: http://www.dailynexus.com/news/2003/5945.html

Haier, Daniel. "Officials Urge Safe Partying to Protect Students, Reputation," available at: http://www.dailynexus.com/news/2003/5948.html

------------. "Police Brace for I.V. Halloween: Law Enforcement To Increase Presence for Holiday Crowd," available at: http://www.dailynexus.com/news/2003/5947.html

Pritchard, Seth. "I.V., SB Offer Sober Halloween Fun," available at: http://www.dailynexus.com/news/2003/5944.html

November 3, 2003

Haier, Daniel. "I.V. Draws Diverse Crowd, Crime: Swamped Streets Result in Property Damage, Injuries," available at: http://www.dailynexus.com/news/2003/5960.html

Holladay, Bonnie. "Volunteers Pick Up Revelers' Refuse," available at: http://www.dailynexus.com/news/2003/5958.html

November 5, 2003

Haier, Daniel. "Teen Center Fear Impact of Party Behavior," available at: http://www.dailynexus.com/news/2003/5979.html

November 12, 2003

Flannery, Devon. "I.V. Halloween Review Faults Visiting Revelers," available at:

http://www.dailynexus.com/news/2003/6048.html

February 20, 2004

Cole, Catherine and Harry Nelson. "The Isla Vista Action Group," available at: http://www.ucsbdailynexus.com/opinion/2004/6790.html

October 27, 2004

Franseze, Dave. "A Golden Halloween: Piss Your Way to Freaky Tricks and Treats," available at: http://www.dailynexus.com/opinion/2004/8175.html

Haier, Daniel. "Halloween Subtext Kills Inner Child," available at: http://www.dailynexus.com/feature/2004/8182.html

October 29, 2004

Austinson, Rachel, and Michelle Kuhn. "Even Kinky Fetishes Need Consent," available at: http://www.dailynexus.com/opinion/2004/8216.html

November 1, 2004

Dozier, Matt. "Revelers Enjoy Well-Monitored Halloween Scene," available at: http://www.dailynexus.com/news/2004/8228.html

Haier, Daniel and Jason La. "Chancellor Visits Locals, DP Haunts," available at: http://www.dailynexus.com/news/2004/8229.html

November 2, 2004

Dozier, Matt. "Cops Express Relief Over Holiday's End," available at: http://www.dailynexus.com/news/2004/8243.html

McFadden, Kevin. "No More Treats, Just More Tricks," available at: http://www.dailynexus.com/opinion/2004/8249.html

November 8, 2004

Pike, Kaitlin, "Fall Defensive Set to Even the Score," available at: http://www.dailynexus.com/news/2004/8324.html

January 26, 2005

Elshorafa, Khalid. "Housing Fair Offers Info on I.V. Options," available at: http://www.ucsbdailynexus.com/news/2005/8749.html

February 9, 2006

Stephanie Cain, "Artist in Profile; Adam de Boer."

LOS ANGELES TIMES:

October 23, 2003

Overend, William. "Working to Tame the Wild Party," B6.

. . .

MAXIM MAGAZINE:
October, 2004
Mike Damone, "Fright Night" (Part 2. Monster Bashes), 63.

THE MILWAUKEE CHANNEL:
November 3, 2003
"Minnesotan Blamed for Madison Halloween Riot: Will Annual Bash be Canceled Next Year?" available at: http://www.themilwaukeechannel.com/news/2605673/detail.html

MUSTANG DAILY (San Luis Obispo):
February 25, 2004
Zwakenberg, Eric. "Riots Plague Mardi Gras," available at: http://www.orion-online.net/vnews/display.v/ART/2004/02/25/403c04bf30b0f
February 7, 2002
Pietzer, Scott. "Mardi Gras Isn't Debated Only in SLO," available at: http://www.mustangdaily.calpoly.edu/archive/20020207/opinion/op2.html
October 16, 2002
Hopping, Nick. "SLO stops the party before it starts," available at: http://www.mustangdaily.calpoly.edu/archive/20021016/index.php?story=op5

PLAYBOY MAGAZINE:
Alison Prato, "Playboy's Top 25 Party Schools," November 2002, p. 89.
Someone, "Girls of the Top Ten Party Schools," May 2006, p. 109.

ROLLING STONE MAGAZINE:

"College Porn Nightmare: Students Seduced into XXX movies,"
September 18, 2003

SAN FRANCISCO CHRONICLE:
February 26, 2004
Kim, Ryan. "Mardi Gras' Rowdy Revelers Arrested," available at:
http://sfgate.com/cgi-bin/article.cgi?f=/c/a/2004/02/26/
BAGQN58LF71.DTL.

SANTA BARBARA NEWS PRESS:
February 24, 1960
Petition (??)
November 1, 1962
"Vandals Throw Water Bombs, Tomatoes; Youths Arrested": B-1
October 31, 1963
"Homecoming Queen Finalists": A-7
"Safety Rules for a 'Harmless Halloween'": A-18
November 1, 1963
"Near Riot, Broken Windows, Vandalism Mark Halloween": A-1
"Parents Should Set Curfew, Chief Says": B-7
"Not University Conduct"
October 30, 1964
"College Freshmen Put Fun First": A-5
"No License to Destroy: Fair warning given on Halloween pranks":
B-1
"Added City Police Patrol is Endorsed": B-4
November 1, 1964
"Halloween Activity Routine, and Area Officers Relax": A-1
"Homecoming at UCSB Thursday": B-1
October 29, 1965
"6 Coeds Candidates for College Queen": B-7
October 30, 1965
"Homecoming Parade Given a 'Big Hand'": 1-A

November 1, 1979
"Isla Vista Party Turns into Melee; 20 are Arrested."
October 29, 1987
O'Hara, Karen. "Isla Vista ready for Halloween's rabble-rousers,": B-2.
October 26, 1988
Weston, L.P. "Isla Vista bracing for devil of a Halloween,": B-1.
October 29, 2003
"University Officials, Police Hope Halloween Stays Dry."
November 1, 2003
"The Party's Over."
November 2, 2003
"Wet and Wild Halloween."
February 23, 2004
Associated Press. "SLO's Mardi Gras Party Turns Ugly": A6.

SANTA MARIA TIMES :
Curran, Stephen. "Violent SLO Mardi Gras Celebration Turns 'Very Ugly,' available at: http://msnbc.msn.com/id/4349799/

THE WASHINGTON POST:
November 2, 1978
Shirley, Don. "Halloween for Grown-Ups."

LaCumbre Yearbook Halloween Coverage:
1985, Vol. 65, David L. Rickabaugh, ed.: 36.
1986, Vol. 66, Mary A. Doll, ed.: 84-85.
1989, Vol. 69, Kevin Thomas Haugh, ed.: 40-43.
1990, Vol. 70, Giovanni Baldassarre, ed.: 47.

Websites cited:

http://www.islavistahistory.com
http://www.santaynezchumash.org/history.html
http://hep.ucsb.edu/people/hnn/present.pdf

WEBLOGS CITED:

JARVIS, Jeff. "Should New Orleans be Rebuilt?" Posted Tuesday, August 30th, 2005, 4:58 pm on *Buzz Machine*. Available at: http://www. buzzmachine.com/index.php/2005/08/30/should-new-orleans-be-rebuilt/

HUNTER, Marnie. "Mardi Gras to fatten New Orleans tourism," CNN.com, Monday, February 27, 2006; Posted: 11:04 a.m. EST (16:04 GMT). Available at: http://www.cnn.com/2006/US/02/23/nola. tourism/?section=cnn_latest

"NAGIN APOLOGIZES FOR CHOCOLATE CITY COMMENTS," CNN.com, Wednesday, January 18, 2006; Posted: 3:42 a.m. EST (08:42 GMT). Available at: http://www.cnn.com/2006/US/01/17/nagin.city/

QUESTIONNAIRE RESPONDANTS

*N*OTE: names in quotation marks are false or modified names used by request of the respondents:

2003: Carrie Awalt, Jenna Baker, "Barbie," "Bob," "Colleen," Stephanie Chan, "Dragon," Tony DiNoto, Kurt Duggleby, Anika Hartounian, Shelby Hensler, Jessica Hejna, "Ivanna Humpalot," "Jenn," "Jimmy Johnny," Dan Leelachat, "Mike," "Moon Unit," "Nick," Christina Ossa, "Ophelia," Myles Peck, Drew Porter, "Penishead," Erica Reisig, "Sarah," Courtney Toretto, Laura Updegrove, "B.W.", J. Warm, Tyler Whalen.

2004: "Ace," "Allie," "Alex," "Alisha," Tiffany Apel, "Arianna," "Lisa B.," Mica Bell, "Bob," Brett Bradshaw, "Bren," "Briana," Ashley Brown, London Burns, Anna Campistrous, Diana Chang, Amanda Chiopa, "Christian," Katie Cohn, Parisa Dana, "Daniel," Chole Davis, "Jimmy Dean," "John Doe," Sierra Drucker, Anthony Duong, "E.I.B.," Dave Eircleson, "Elizabeth," "Enrique," Burt Farrell, Michael Figge, Graham Fischer-Ortiz, Greg Fish, Martha Franco, Joshua Freeman, Sandra Gibson, "Maria Gonzales," Jessica Gorman, "Grace," "Halloween Madness," Sarah Harman, Anthony Hewitt, Lindsey Hinzo, Kelsey Hoppe, Stephanie Jackson, Kelsey James, "Jamie," "Jessica," "Jimmy," "Joy," "Tina K.," Meghan Kennedy, Jonathan Kluger, Hannah Laiken,

Amber Larkin, "Lauren," Mike Levy, Kim Li, Jennifer Long, Christy Lozano, Ilene Mamiya, Angela Marseguerra, Caitlin McClelland, Lisa McClelland, "John McDougle," Krista McIntosh, "Susana Meadows," Shaina Mervis, Efrain Michel, Shannon Mulcahy, Meghan Ng, Stanley Nzessi, Kellie Ragusano, Kara Robarts, Kathryn Rube, "Ryan," "Michael S.," "Sally," "Jaycee San Miguel," Kim Schwartz, Erica Seele, "Sheena," "Shi-Ann," Stephen Oswald Smith, Jessie Steinberg, Brittney Stinner, Kathleen Swanson, Tracy Taylor, "Tiana," "Tumor Torbjorn," Emily Wanser, Britney Weinberg-Lynn, "Willie," Rebecca Wonaman, Ashley Young, Taryn Zigterman,

INTERVIEWS:
"Supertramp," Nov. 4, 2003.
Bruce Gordon and Carrie Awalt: February 19, 2004.
Jenn Lotz: March 3, 2004.
Alison Zuber: April 3, 2004.
Catherine Cole: April 21, 2004.
Stan Hoffman: March 25, 2005.
Michael Andrews: March 29, 2005.
Ethan Roberts: March 31, 2005.
Lieutenant Sol Linver: October 18, 2005.
Robert Bernstein: October 31, 2005.
"Mardi Gras Bob": February 27, 2006.
Carol Mosley: March 14, 2006

EMAIL CORRESPONDENCE:
Patti Newman Crandall: April 3, 2004.
Genesis Lodise: March 23-25, 2005.
Glen Lazof: March 24, April 4, 2005.
Jill Kelly-Moore: March 23, 2005.
Janet Langley: March 25, 2005.
Malcolm Gault-Williams, March 26, 2005.
Michael Katz, March 24, 2005.

Mitchell Stockton: March 28, 2005.
Tom Stone: March 23, 2005.
Erika Thost: November 24, 2005.

Halloween Field notes submitted for Dr. Cole's DA 251 (Performance Studies Seminar), Fall 2004 by:

- John Carnwath
- Xaio Che
- Anne Garcia-Romero
- Andrew Gibb
- Tracy Jamison
- Wen-ling Lin
- Ottiliana Rolandsson
- Hal Ross
- Jessica Sanders
- Jason Davids Scott
- Emily Weisberg
- Hank Willenbrink

HALLOWEEN QUESTIONNAIRE 2003

1. How many times have you attended Halloween in I.V.?

If you have never attended, please briefly explain why):
    If you have attended more than once, which year would you say was the most successful celebration and why?

1. Did you experience any of the following during the Halloween festivities? (Please check all that apply)
2. ___ Freedom from normal social restrictions
3. ___ Reduction of social inhibitions
4. ___ Communitas (a spontaneous sense of solidarity among strangers or near-strangers)
5. ___ Amusement / fun / enjoyment
6. ___ Indulgence in excesses
7. ___ Experience of an alternate reality or of possible alterations to your everyday life
8. ___ Sexual titillation / excitement / desire
9. ___ Desirable attention from fellow revelers
10. ___ Pressure to conform / participate in unwanted activities

11. ___ Fear of violence or undesirable attention from fellow revelers
12. ___ Actual violence or undesirable attention from fellow revelers
13. ___ Fear of violence or undesirable attention from authority figures
14. ___ Actual violence or undesirable attention from authority figures
15. ___ Feeling of disgust or revulsion at excesses / grotesqueries witnessed
16. ___ Other (please describe)

If you would like to go into detail about any of the above-mentioned experiences, please do so now:

1. Please list at least five adjectives describing your experience of Halloween in I.V.:
2. What is your fondest memory of Halloween in I.V.?
3. What is your least fond memory of Halloween in I.V.?
4. Are you looking forward to next Halloween? Why / Why not?
5. If there is anything else you would like to add regarding your experience of or feelings about Halloween in I.V., please do so now:

Should I decide to use any of your responses in my paper, may I use your real name?

Y, Name: N, False name:

THANK YOU SO MUCH FOR YOUR TIME!!

- Adrienne M. MacIain, PhD candidate in Dramatic Art, UCSB

HALLOWEEN QUESTIONNAIRE 2004

Appendix B: Halloween Questionnaire 2004

1. Please describe how you spent Halloween weekend this year (2004):
2. What did you hope to get from the weekend; did you achieve your goal(s)?
3. Please describe your costume:
4. How do you think your costume choice affected your own behavior?
5. Please describe any noteworthy reactions you received:
6. Please describe your favorite costume(s) witnessed:
7. Please describe any remarkable behavior or interaction witnessed:
8. What is your fondest memory of Halloween in I.V.?
9. What is your least fond memory of Halloween in I.V.?
10. What improvements would you like to see made to the Halloween experience?
11. If there is anything else you would like to add regarding your experience of or feelings about Halloween in I.V., please do so now:

12. Should I decide to use any of your responses in my dissertation, may I use your real name?

Yes, Name: No, False name:

THANK YOU SO MUCH FOR YOUR TIME!!
- Adrienne M. MacIain, PhD candidate in Dramatic Art, UCSB

NOTES

1. FINDING NEMO ON DEL PLAYA DRIVE

1. Isla Vista is the neighborhood adjacent to the University of California, Santa Barbara.
2. "Nemo," a black and orange striped fish, is the protagonist of Pixar's 2003 computer animated film *Finding Nemo*, directed by Andrew Stanton and Lee Unkrich.
3. These images of the 2003 Halloween celebration have been compiled from video footage taken by UCSB student Bruce Gordon, and by the Isla Vista Foot Patrol, from memory, and from anecdotes shared by participants.

2. THE SPECTER OF POST-ADOLESCENT YOUTH

1. Jan Jagodzinski, *Youth Fantasies: The Perverse Landscape of the Media*, New York: Palgrave Macmillan, 2004: 32.
2. Jeffrey Jensen Arnett, *Emerging Adulthood: The Winding Road From the Late Teens Through the Twenties*, Oxford: Oxford University Press, 2004: 3.
3. Marcel Danesi, *My Son is an Alien: A Cultural Portrait of Today's Youth*, Lanham, Rowman & Littlefield, 2003.
4. Jagodzinski, 2004: 36.
5. Jagodzinski, 2004: 33.
6. Jagodzinski, 2004: 33-34.
7. Bill Osgerby, "'A Caste, a Culture, a Market:' Youth, Marketing, and Lifestyle in Postwar America," in Ronald Strickland, ed., *Growing up Postmodern: Neoliberalism and the War on the Young*, Lanham, Rowman & Littlefield, 2002.
8. Jagodzinski, 2004: 46.
9. Jagodzinski, 2004: 34.
10. Danesi, 2003: 5.
11. For example, Arnett charts the median marriage age in the United States as having risen by approximately five years between 1950 and 2000. Arnett 2004: 5.
12. It is worth noting that Danesi sees the spread of adolescence as working backwards as well, so that children are increasingly eager to mature into teenagers. "Tweenies," argues Danesi, are older children who have already begun to adopt the style of dress and manner popularly associated with adolescents.
13. Another objection I have to the terms "middlescence" and "tweeniehood" is that they both emphasize a perceived seepage of adolescence—forward into the later twenties, and backward into the pre-teen years. While I do not deny that the pop-cultural connection between youth and fun has had a profound impact on the whole of U.S. society, I find it problematic to characterize adolescence as *spreading*,

as if it were some sort of highly-contagious social disease that everyone seems a bit too eager to catch.

14. Although research on youth culture in the U.S. appears to be on the rise, these inquiries are mainly focused on the mid-early teen years, when young people are still residing with their parents. Epstein 1998 is an excellent resource for this area. See also: M. Brake, *Comparative Youth Culture: the Sociology of Youth Cultures and Youth Subcultures in America, Britain, and Canada* (London: Routledge and Kegan Paul, 1985); J. Epstein, ed., *Adolescents and Their Music: If It's Too Loud, You're Too Old* (New York: Garland, 1994); N. Postman, *The Disappearance of Childhood* (New York: Delacorte, 1981); J. Pratt and K. Pryor, *For Real: the Uncensored Truth About America's Teenagers* (New York: Hyperion, 1995); Douglass Rushkoff, *The GenX Reader* (New York: Ballantine, 1994) and D. Rushkoff, *Playing the Future: How Kids' Culture can Teach us to Thrive in an Age of Chaos* (New York: HarperCollins, 1996).

15. Arnett, 2004: 8. Emphasis in original.

16. Thomas D. Cook and Frank F. Furstenburg Jr., "Explaining Aspects of the Transition to Adulthood in Italy, Sweden, Germany, and the United States: A Cross-Disciplinary Case Synthesis Approach," in Alan W. Heston, ed. *The Annals of the American Academy of Political and Social Science: Early Adulthood in Cross-National Perspective*. March 2002, vol. 580: 281.

17. Arnett 2004: 140.

18. See Arnett 2004, pp. 128-130 for an excellent discussion of racial differences in educational opportunity in the U.S.

19. "Profile of 'New' Freshmen entering UCSB in Fall quarter 2002, 2003, and 2004," UCSB office of Budget and Planning.

20. Sal Castillo, interview with author, April 27, 2005.

21. Martin Heidegger, *The Essence of Reason*, tr. Terrence Malick, Evanston: Northwestern University Press, 1969. For a more thorough explanation of Dasein, see Martin Heidegger, *Being And Time (Sein und Zeit)*, Translation by John Macquarrie and Edward Robinson (San Francisco: Harper, 1962). Originally published 1927.

22. Arnett, 2004: 10.

23. See particularly John Cowley, *Carnival, Canboulay, and Calypso: Traditions in the Making*, Cambridge: Cambridge University Press, 1996; and Richard D.E. Burton, *Afro-Creole: Power, Opposition and Play in the Caribbean*, Ithaca: Cornell University Press, 1997.

24. See Aching (2002), M. Bakhtin (1965), Burton (1997), Crumrine & Halpin (1983), Eco et al (1985), Harris (2003), Liverpool, H.U. (1998).

25. Studies focused on the U.S. college campus as a coherent cultural space are still relatively few, and are overwhelmingly focused on the counter-cultural movement of the 1960s [P. A. Adler & P. Adler, eds., *Constructions of Deviance: Social Power, Context, and Interaction* (Belmont, CA: Wadsworth Publishing, 1997); E. Bloustein, *The University and the Counter-Culture; Inaugural and Other Addresses* (New Brunswick, NJ: Rutgers University Press, 1972); G. J. DeGroot, ed., *Student Protest: The Sixties and After* (London: Longman, 1998); M. Graubard, *Campustown in the Throes of the Counterculture (1968-1972)* (Minneapolis: Campus Press Scope, 1974); K. J. Heineman, *Put Your Bodies Upon the Wheels: Student Revolt in the 1960s* (Chicago: I.R. Dee, 2001); N. Suljak, *Campus Disorder and Cultural Counter-Revolution* (Davis, CA: Inst. of Governmental Affairs, U. of California, 1970)].

5. THE CARNIVALESQUE AS A GLOBAL
PHENOMENON

1. Russell W. Belk, "Carnival, Control, and Corporate Culture in Contemporary Halloween Celebrations," in Jack Santino, ed., *Halloween and Other Festivals of Life and Death*, Knoxville: The University of Texas Press, 1994: 105.

2. Here I would include: Gerard Aching, *Masking and Power: Carnival and Popular Culture in the Caribbean*, Minneapolis: University of Minnesota Press, 2002; Richard D.E. Burton, *Afro-Creole: Power, Opposition and Play in the Caribbean*, Ithaca: Cornell University Press, 1997; Abner Cohen, *Masquerade Politics: Explorations in the Structure of Urban Cultural Movements*, Oxford: Berg, 1993; John Cowley, *Carinval, Canboulay, and Calypso: Traditions in the Making*, Cambridge: Cambridge University Press, 1996; Ross Crumrine & Marjorie Halpin, eds., *The Power of Symbols: Masks and masquerade in the Americas*, Vancouver, B.C.: University of British Columbia Press, 1983; Roberto DaMatta, *Carnivals, Rogues, and Heroes: An Interpretation of the Brazilian Dilemma*, translated by John Drury, Notre Dame: University of Notre Dame Press, 1991; Alessandro Fulassi, *Time out of Time: Essays on the Festival*, Albuquerque: University of New Mexico Press, 1987; Max Harris, *Carnival and Other Christian Festivals: Folk Theology and Folk Performance*, Austin: University of Texas Press, 2003; Milla Cozart Riggio ed., *Carnival: Culture in Action—the Trinidad Experience*, Worlds of Performance Series, London: Routledge, 2004; Joseph Roach, *Cities of the Dead: Circum-Atlantic Performance*, New York: Columbia University Press, 1996; Philip W. Scher, *Carnival and the Formation of a Caribbean Transnation*, Gainesville: University of Florida Press, 2003; Claire Sponsler, *Ritual Imports: Performing Medieval Drama in America*, Ithaca: Cornell University Press, 2004.

3. See for example Roach, 1996; Scher, 2003.

4. Leslie Prosterman, *Ordinary Life, Festival Days: Aesthetics in the Midwestern County Fair*, Washington: Smithsonian Institution Press, 1994: 35-41.

5. James B. Twitchell, *Carnival Culture: The Trashing of Taste in America*, New York: Columbia University Press, 1995.

6. Philip McGowan, *American Carnival: Seeing and Reading American Culture*, Westport: Greenwood Press, 2001: 1.

7. Umberto Eco, "The frames of comic 'freedom,'" in Umberto Eco, V.V. Ivanov, and Monica Rector, *Carnival!* New York: Mouton, 1985: 1-10.

8. Bakhtin, Mikhail, *Rabelais and His World*, trans. Helene Iswolsky, Cambridge: M.I.T. Press, 1968: 10.

9. Bakhtin, 1968: 8.

10. Mary Douglas, *Purity and Danger: An Analysis of Concepts of Pollution and Taboo*, New York: Frederick A. Praeger, 1966: 36.

11. Douglas, 1996: 134.

12. Douglas, 1996: 96-97.

13. Douglas, 1966: 7.

14. Douglas, 1966: 36.

15. See for example: Adler and Adler, 1997; Castle, 1986; Crumrine and Halpin, 1983; Fulassi, 1987; Scott, 1990; Stallybrass and White, 1986; Peter J. Wilson, *Crab Antics: The Social Anthropology of English-Speaking Negro Societies of the Caribbean*, New Haven: Yale University Press, 1973.

16. Simon Dentinth, *Bakhtinian Thought: An Introductory Reader*, New York: Routledge, 1995: 74.

17. "Natural" refers here to any cherished classification within a given culture, and is not intended to imply any relationship to nature as it is conceived of in the Judeo-Christian tradition.

18. V.V. Ivanov, "The Semiotic Theory of Carnival as the Inversion of Bipolar Opposites," in Eco et al, 1985: 11,12.

19. Brian Sutton-Smith and Diana Kelly-Byrne, *Masks of Play* (New York: Leisure Press, 1985): 74.

20. Eco et al, 1985: 6.

21. Eco et al, 1985: 7.

22. Richard Schechner, "Carnival (theory) after Bakhtin," in Milla Cozart Riggio, ed., *Carnival: Culture in Action – the Trinidad Experience*, Worlds of Performance Series, New York: Routledge, 2004: 3.

23. Baz Kershaw, *The Radical in Performance: Between Brecht and Baudrillard*, London: Routledge, 1999: 6.

24. Kershaw, 1999: 7.

25. Michel Foucault, *Discipline and Punish: The Birth of the Prison*, Trans. Alan Sheridan, New York: Vintage Books, 1995.

26. Jon McKenzie, *Perform or Else: From Discipline to Performance*, London: Routledge, 2001: 18.

27. Including, though not limited to, the writings of Jean-François Lyotard, David Harvey, Fredric Jameson, and Jean Baudrillard. Kershaw, 1999: 6, 21.

28. Kershaw, 1999: 13.

29. Kershaw, 1999: 6.

30. Jan Jagodzinski, *Youth Fantasies: The Perverse Landscape of the Media*, New York: Palgrave Macmillan, 2004: 33.

31. Jagodzinski, 2004: 65.

32. Jagodzinski, 2004: 69.

33. Jouissance is a tricky term to translate. In general French usage it carries a sexual connotation (*jouir* is a slang term for ejaculation/orgasm), as well as an amoral quality (*jouir de* means to "get off on" something, often something one would be ashamed to admit publicly to taking pleasure in) which is lacking in English terms like enjoyment or satisfaction. In psychoanalytic parlance jouissance refers to a kind of penultimate fulfillment which is impossible to attain but which we continue (unconsciously) to strive for via desire. This inevitable lack of jouissance endows desired objects with what Lacan named *"objet a"* – a sort of magical quality of unconscious desirability. In this sense jouissance encompasses pleasure and pain, fulfillment and lack. Jagodzinski defines jouissance as "libidinal bodily pleasure or *unconscious desire* that harbors within it the paradox of pain-pleasure" (2004: 7). See particularly Jacques Lacan, "The Subversion of the Subject and the Dialectic of Desire in the Freudian Unconscious," in *Ecrits*, trans. Bruce Fink, New York: W.W. Norton & Company, Inc.: 281-312.

34. Kershaw, 1999: 52.

35. Jagodzinski, 2004: 80.

36. Jagodzinski, 2004: 100.

37. Jagodzinski, 2004: 97.

38. Beatriz Sarlo, *Scenes From Postmodern Life*, translated by Jon Beasley-Murray, Cultural Studies of the Americas, Vol. 7, Minneapolis: University of Minnesota Press, 2001: 33.

39. Sarlo, 2001: 33.

40. Jagodzinski, 2004: 91.

41. Jagodzinski, 2004: 93.

42. Riggio, 2004: 4.

43. Riggio, 2004: 6, 10, 28.

44. L.M. Fraser, "History of Carnival," *Colonial Office Original Correspondence, Trinidad* (C.O. 295), vol. 289, Trinidad No. 6460. Quoted in Errol Hill, *The Trinidad Carnival: Mandate for a National Theatre*, Austin: University of Texas Press, 1972: 10.

45. Hill, 1972: 10-11.

46. It is difficult to know how the rest of Trinidadian society felt about Carnival, since non-white and lower-class voices were carefully excised from public record in the colonial period.

47. John Cowley, *Carnival, Canboulay and Calipso: Traditions in the Making*, Cambridge: Cambridge University Press, 1996: 105.

48. Cowley, 1996: 127.

49. Cowley, 1996: 11. Note that "naughty schoolgirl" and "baby" costumes are popular choices at Halloween in Isla Vista. See chapter four.

50. Douglas, 1966: 7.

51. Cowley, 1996: 21.

52. Quoted in Cowley, 1996: 39-40.

53. For example, limiting the annual festival (which had begun a slow but steady backward creep toward January) to the three days prior to Lent and penalizing anyone caught masking outside of that three-day span. Cowley, 1996: 25-26.

54. The following year (1858) saw rumors that governor Robert William Keate planned to ban Carnival altogether. Ultimately, though, he acquiesced to popular demand and allowed the festivities to continue under the current limitations. Cowley, 1996: 52.

55. Philip W. Scher, *Carnival and the Formation of a Caribbean Transnation*, Gainesville: University of Florida Press, 2003: 39.

56. Scher, 2003: 41.

57. Scher, 2003: 42.

58. Cowley, 1996: 61. Note that this is remarkably similar to Isla Vista's "Festival Ordinance," which bans the playing of musical instruments, or any kind of amplified music, out of doors after six p.m., as described in chapter two.

59. Cowley, 1996: 61.

60. Cowley, 1996: 59.

61. Note that the same policy has been adopted at Halloween in Isla Vista.

62. These processions commemorated the common experience among plantation workers of putting out cane fires (called "Canboulay" from the French *Cannes Brûlées*).

63. This sequence of events is eerily similar to the 1979 Halloween "mini-riot" in Isla Vista: see chapter two. Cowley, 1996: 85.

64. See Richard D.E. Burton, *Afro-Creole: Power, Opposition and Play in the Caribbean*, Ithaca: Cornell University Press, 1997: 173-177.

65. See Cowley, 1996: 124, 134-175.

66. Cowley, 1996: 90.

67. Cowley, 1996: 92.

68. Better described as a protest than a riot, the death toll among the protestors was so high that the incident later became known as the "Hosien Massacre." Cowley, 1996: 104.

69. Cowley, 1996: 122-123.

70. Gerard Aching, *Masking and Power: Carnival and Popular Culture in the Caribbean*, Minneapolis: University of Minnesota Press, 2002: 4.

71. As I will argue, similar tensions are ritually acted out in U.S. carnival, with the police publicly acting out their power, as well as (albeit inadvertently) advertising their vulnerability and their need for public recognition.

72. Scher, 2003: 58.

73. Scher, 2003: 43.

74. Scher, 2003: 44.

75. Scher, 2003: 42.

76. Margaret Thompson Drewal, *Yoruba Ritual: Performers, Play, Agency*, Bloomington: Indiana University Press, 1992: 2.

77. Drewal, 1992: 7.

78. Drewal, 1992: 8.

79. Peter Burke, "The Translation of Culture: Carnival in Two or Three Worlds," in *Varieties of Cultural History*. Ithaca: Cornell University Press, 1997.

80. Burton, 1997: 157.

81. Burton, 1997: 157.

82. Aching, 2002: 4. Emphasis in original.

83. Aching, 2002: 9.

84. Aching, 2002: 2.

85. Aching, 2002: 21.

86. For more on *tactics*, see Michel de Certeau, *The Practice of Everyday Life*, Berkeley: University of California Press, 1984.

87. Aching, 2002: 10.

88. Aching, 2002: 6. Emphasis mine.

89. Kershaw, 1999: 18.

6. THE U.S. CARNIVALESQUE

1. See particularly David J. Skal, *Death Makes a Holiday: A Cultural History of Halloween*, New York: Bloomsbury, 2002.

2. Skal, 2002: 33; 34.

3. Skal, 2002: 53.

4. Michael Demarest, "Halloween as an Adult Treat: An Escapist Extravaganza Outdazzling Mardi Gras." *Time* 122 (31 Oct., 1983): 110; See also Sutton-Smith, Brian. "What Happened to Halloween?" *Parents* 58 (Oct. 1983): 63-64.

5. Nicholas Rogers, *Halloween: From Pagan Ritual to Party Night*, Oxford: Oxford University Press, 2002: 137.

6. Belk, Russell W. "Carnival, Control, and Corporate Culture in Contemporary Halloween Celebrations," in Santino, Jack, ed. *Halloween and Other Festivals of Life and Death*, Knoxville: The University of Texas Press, 1994: 118.

7. Skal, 2002: 153.

8. "Hollywood Halloween: Some Came as Vandals and Looters," *L.A. Times*, Nov. 2, 1988: Metro, 1, 8.

9. Mike Davis, *City of Quartz*, New York: Verso, 1990: 260.

10. "Boulder's Riot History," *The Daily Camera*, Nov. 1, 2004: A7

11. As a Boulder native and a current Isla Vista resident, I feel quite comfortable drawing parallels between I.V. and "The Hill": both neighborhoods are known for hard partying, both have specific ordinances regarding couch burning, and the student populations of both have an infamously antagonistic relationship to local police. However, The Hill is much more integrated into the surrounding community than is Isla Vista, and therefore less easily isolated and marginalized. Also, the Mall Crawl, which took place downtown, was an event which appealed to a wide range of community members. Therefore its passing is still mourned by Boulderites of all stripes, not just students.

12. "Mayor May Impose Martial Law on Halloween," Channel 3000.com, posted 8:58 pm CST October 31, 2005. http://www.channel3000.com/station/5218472/detail.html. I predict even larger crowds for Halloween, 2006 in Madison, thanks to the U. of Wisconsin's number one spot in *Playboy*'s May 2005 pictorial "The Girls of the Top Ten Party Schools," which explicitly mentions the annual bash.

13. Scott Peitzer, "With Liberty and Breasts for All," *The Daily Texan* (University of Texas, Austin), Feb. 6, 2002.

14. Sarah R. Buchholz, "45 arrested, scores hurt at off-campus disturbance," *The Campus Chronicle* (University of Massachusetts, Amherst), Vol. XVIII, Issue 32, May 9, 2003.

15. David Schweingruber, "Campus Riots at Iowa State and Across the Nation," Iowa State University, Department of Sociology seminar series, Feb. 24, 2005: http://www.public.iastate.edu/~dschwein/
        riotseminar.pdf.

16. Eric Zwakenberg, "Riots Plague Mardi Gras," *The Mustang Daily* (California Polytechnic, San Luis Obispo), Feb. 24, 2004; "Mardi Gras Update," *The Cal Poly Report*, Jan. 12, 2004: http://calpolynews.calpoly.edu/cpreport/05reports/Jan12.htm.

17. Mike Davis, *City of Quartz: Excavating the Future in Los Angeles*, New York: Verso, 1990: 315.

18. Sarlo, 2001: 16.

7. MORE THAN JUST A PARTY

1. Brendan Buhler, "Why Are There [So] Many Cops in Isla Vista? A Brief History of Halloween in Isla Vista," *Daily Nexus*, October 16, 2002.

2. The largest Halloween crowds recorded by the *Daily Nexus* were in 1987 (see Skelton, Veronica, "Halloween: What it is: What it Was: What it Shall Be," Oct. 28, 1988), 1992 (see Epler, Kimberly, "Condoms, Cows, and Cretins," Nov. 2, 1992), and 2003 (see Daniel Haier, "I.V. Weekend Draws Diverse Crowd, Crime," Nov. 3, 2003). Notably, in all three cases, October 31st fell on a weekend.

3. Mike Damone, "Fright Night," *Maxim*, October 2004: 63.

8. ORIGINS: 1962-1970

1. Robert Kelley, *Transformations: UC Santa Barbara 1909-1979*, Santa Barbara: The Associated Students of the University of California, 1981: 21.
2. Kelley, 1981: 21.
3. Christy Lord, "All Aboard for All-U Game, Rally, Dance Set," *El Gaucho*, Oct. 27, 1954: 1.
4. "Not University Conduct," *Santa Barbara Newspress*, Nov. 1, 1963.
5. Denis Green, "Open Forum," *El Gaucho*, Nov. 13, 1963.
6. "Halloween High Life Gives Officers Overtime Chance," *El Gaucho*, Oct. 29, 1965.
7. Gayle Clark Olson, "Twenty-four Years of Policing: Law Enforcement at UCSB and in Isla Vista 1954 to 1978," Masters Thesis in History, UCSB, 1978: 41.
8. Sergeant David Cordero, interviewed by Gayle Clark Olson in Olson, 1978: 41.
9. Carmen Lodise, "Building a Community," chapter four of "Isla Vista, A Citizen's History," available at: http://www.islavistahistory.com/ivhistory/chapter4.1.html

9. THE EARLY YEARS: 1971-1977

1. Alison Zuber, telephone interview, April 3, 2004.
2. Stan Hoffman, interview with author, March 25, 2005.

10. THE MINI-RIOTS: 1978-1979

1. Kim Kavanagh and Kim Green, "Del Playa Becomes a Halloween Riot," *Daily Nexus*, Oct. 30, 1978.
2. In 2003, rioting broke out at the University of Wisconsin, Madison's annual "Killer (Halloween) Party," and at Cal Poly, San Luis Obispo's Mardi Gras celebration.
3. Eco et al, 1985: 7.
4. See section three for further details on the Isla Vista riots.
5. See section three for further discussion of Isla Vista as a ghetto.
6. The "fall defensive" mounted by concerned students in 2004 provides a recent example. See Kaitlin Pike, "Fall Defensive Set to Even the Score," *Daily Nexus*, Nov 8, 2004.
7. Kim Kavanagh and Kim Green, "Disagreements on Accounts of DP Mini-Riot," *Daily Nexus*, Monday, Oct. 30, 1978.
8. Kim Kavanagh and Kim Green, "Del Playa Becomes a Halloween Riot," and "Disagreements..." *Daily Nexus*, Oct. 30, 1978.
9. James C. Scott, *Domination and the Arts of Resistance* (New Haven: Yale University Press, 1990): 4, 2.
10. Henry Giroux, "Teenage Sexuality, Body Politics, and the Pedagogy of Display," in Jonathan S. Epstein, ed. *Youth Culture: Identity in a Postmodern World*, Oxford: Blackwell, 1998: 25.
11. Aching, 2002: 2.
12. G.W. Hegel, *The Phenomenology of Spirit*, trans. A.V. Miller, Oxford: Oxford University Press, 1977: 111-119.

13. "Supertramp," interview with author, Nov. 4, 2003.

14. Kim Green and Kim Kavanagh. "Del Playa Party Becomes a Halloween Riot: Four of those arrested face felony charges": *Daily Nexus*, Oct. 30, 1978: 1.

15. Although the "history" Gaswirth refers to here is likely a class he and his interlocutor will attend together the following Monday, the phrase provides an interesting *double entendre*: although the two appear to doubt, at least on some level, the reality of the event in which they have taken part, they are nonetheless aware of its significance. They are, in fact, "in history" now, along with everyone else who took part in that "mini-riot." Mitchell M. Gaswirth, "Night on the Town," *Daily Nexus*, Oct. 30, 1978.

16. It is worth noting that this rebellion, apparently perpetrated by high school students, was much more easily dismissed than the college students' mutiny of the year before. Automatically assumed to be mindlessly aping the actions of their elders, the intentions of these young rioters were never investigated.

11. THE GOLDEN ERA: 1980-1986

1. See, for example, Brendan Buhler, "Why Are There [So] Many Cops in Isla Vista? A Brief History of Halloween in Isla Vista," *Daily Nexus*, Oct. 16, 2002.

2. Robert Bernstein, interview with author, October 31, 2005.

3. Amy Siegel, "Foot Patrol Plans for Halloween Crowd Control," *Daily Nexus*, Oct. 31, 1985: 1.

4. Doug Arellanes, "Halloween Revelers Crowd Del Playa," *Daily Nexus*, Nov. 4, 1985: 1.

5. Chris Wyland, "Checking Out the Scene on All Hallows Eve," Nov. 2, 1987: 10.

6. Zuber interview, April, 2004.

7. Erika Thost, email correspondence, Nov 21, 2005.

8. Harry Nelson, informal conversation on October 31, 2005.

9. Michael Katz, email correspondence, March 24, 2005.

12. AFTER THE FALL: 1987-1992

1. Bernstein interview, Oct., 2005.

2. Karen O'Hara, "Isla Vista ready for Halloween's rabble-rousers," *Santa Barbara News Press*, Oct. 29, 1987: B-2.

3. L.P. Weston, "Isla Vista bracing for devil of a Halloween," *Santa Barbara News Press*, Oct. 26, 1988: B-1.

4. These estimates are issued by the Santa Barbara Sheriff's Department and reported in the *Daily Nexus*.

5. "Weekend Totals," *Daily Nexus*, Nov. 4, 1991: 11.

6. Ross French, "Violence Ends Halloween Weekend," *Daily Nexus*, Nov. 4, 1991: 1.

7. "Going, Going, Gone," *Daily Nexus*, Oct. 31, 1996: 6.

8. Ross French, "Police Arrest Over 350 During Halloween Bash: Two Injured in Falls From Isla Vista Cliffs," Nov. 1, 1991: 1.

9. Jennifer Adams, "Downtown Refuge From DP," *Daily Nexus*, Nov. 1, 1991: 4.

10. "Going, Going, Gone," *Daily Nexus*, Oct. 31, 1996: 6.

13. NO TOLERANCE: 1993-2002

1. Sarah Mason and Christine Putnam, "Holiday Gives Revelers Haunting Opportunities," *Daily Nexus*, Nov. 2, 1998: 1.
2. Lisa Sato, "Police, UCSB Attempt to Ward Off Invasion: Media Helps to Spread 'No Tolerance' Message," *Daily Nexus*, Oct. 28, 1993: 1. "College Media React to Weekend Laws," *Daily Nexus*, Oct. 29, 1993: 3.
3. "Halloween 1997," (retrospective of the Five Year Plan) *Daily Nexus*, Oct. 30, 1997: 2B.
4. "Get Out of Town!" *Daily Nexus*, Oct. 31, 1996: 1.
5. "Five Year Plan?..." *Daily Nexus*, Oct. 30, 1997.
6. "Going, Going, Gone; I.V. Halloween's Dying Wishes: Continue Your Quest for Revelry, but Watch Your Back," *Daily Nexus*, Oct. 31, 1996: 6.
7. Genesis Lodise, email correspondence with author, March 23, 2005.
8. I will deal with the "UCSB admissions theory" in more depth in section four, but for now let me say that while it is an intriguing explanation, and a popular one among long-term residents, the evidence that I've been able to gather on the matter is inconclusive.
9. Zuber interview, April, 2004.
10. Andersen, Ted. "Partiers Enjoy Halloween Weekend of Fun," *Daily Nexus*, Nov. 1, 1999.
11. Bourbon Street is the site of the most infamous annual street party of the New Orleans Mardi Gras celebration. See conclusion for further parallels between Mardi Gras and Halloween in I.V.
12. Tiye Baldwin, "Party Like it's 1989," *Daily Nexus,* Oct. 31, 2002. The missing section of this quote appears later in this section.
13. Baldwin, "Party..." Oct. 31, 2002.
14. Emily McCoy, interview with author, October 1, 2005.
15. As explained in section five, all Halloween costumes in I.V. come with that unspoken prefix, "sexy."
16. Vikki Bowles, "Haunting DP," LaCumbre Yearbook, 1990, Vol. 70, Giovanni Baldassarre, ed.: 47.
17. See Maureen Fan, "Halloween Santa Barbara Style," LaCumbre Yearbook, 1986, Vol. 66: 84-85; L.P. Weston, "Isla Vista Bracing for a Devil of a Halloween," *Santa Barbara News Press*, Oct 26, 1988; Veronica Skelton, "Halloween: What it is: What it was: What it shall be," *Daily Nexus*, Oct 28, 1988: 10; Brendan Buhler, "Why Are There Many Cops in Isla Vista?" *Daily Nexus*, Oct 16, 2002 (note that Buhler anomalously cites the Playboy article as having appeared in 1991); Armand Ramirez, "A Ghost of Halloween Past," *Daily Nexus*, Oct 28, 2002.
18. Alison Prato, "Playboy's Top 25 Party Schools," *Playboy*, November 2002, p. 89.
19. **Someone**, "Girls of the Top Ten Party Schools," *Playboy*, May 2006, p. 109.
20. This urban legend is debunked by Rebecca Carrigan, Joe Gross, Angela McCorkle, Leonard McCants II in "1965-1975 at The University of Virginia: A Decade of Fundamental Restructuring," Available at: http://www.virginia.edu/history/courses/courses.old/hius330/decade.html
21. Fan, "Halloween Santa Barbara Style," LaCumbre Yrbk, 1986: 84.
22. Mike Damone, "Fright Night," *Maxim*, October 2004: 62-63.

14. "THE PARTY IS (NOT) OVER"

1. Isla Vista Foot Patrol reports for 10/31 – 11/01, 2003; annual report for 2003; randomly selected reports from the months of February, April, June, September, and December of 2003.
2. Lt. Sol Linver, interview with author, October 18, 2005.
3. Carol Mosely, interview with author, March 14, 2006.
4. Mosely interview, March 2006.
5. Nick Hopping, "SLO Stops Party Before It Starts," *Mustang Daily*, Oct. 16, 2002.
6. Incidentally, the "S.B." in UCSB has also been rumored to stand for "Surfing and Bud," "Sluts on the Beach," "Studs and Babes," and a number of other things.
7. William Overend, "Working to Tame the Wild Party," *L.A. Times*, Oct. 23, 2003: B6.
8. See Daniel Haier, "Officials Urge Safe Partying to Protect Students, Reputation," *Daily Nexus*, Oct. 31, 2003.
9. Quoted in Haier, "Officials…" *Daily Nexus*, Oct. 31, 2003.
10. In the wake of reports that professional pornography companies such as "Shane's World" and "collegefuckfest.com" were throwing parties to which students were lured with promises of free beer, and subsequently filmed engaging in sexual activity with porn stars and with each other, alarmed University administrators sent out a letter warning students about the exploitative nature of these "porn parties." The letter concentrates on warning students of the exploitative nature of the practice, insisting that "We in the UCSB administration have no desire to monitor or regulate your private lives" and stating, "Let's be clear: These films are pornography for sale, and these companies are exploiting students for their profit." Cited in William Overend, "Working to Tame the Wild Party," *Los Angeles Times*, October 23, 2003.
11. "College Porn Nightmare: Students Seduced into XXX movies," *Rolling Stone*, September 18, 2003; *Dateline: Campus Porn*, NBC, November 2, 2003; For a good discussion of the debate over porn companies' activities in I.V., see Daniel Haier, "UCSB Divided by Porn," *Daily Nexus*, Sept. 26, 2003.
12. Quoted in Haier, "Officials…" *Daily Nexus*, Oct. 31, 2003.
13. Daniel Haier, "Teen Center Fear Impact of Party Behavior," *Daily Nexus*, Nov. 5, 2003.
14. Haier, "Teen Center…" *Daily Nexus*, Nov. 5, 2003.
15. Linver, Oct. 2005 interview.
16. This policy prompted a number of students to create what they called the "fall defensive," a student rights advocacy group, in the fall of 2004.
17. Quoted in Haier, "Officials…" *Daily Nexus*, Oct. 31, 2003.
18. Baldwin, "Party…" 2002. Baldwin does not mention when and where UCSB was listed as "one of the top three party schools."
19. 2003 Questionnaire, "Courtney."
20. 2003 Questionnaire, Tyler Whalen.
21. Jennifer Adams, "Downtown was Refuge from DP," *Daily Nexus*, Nov. 1, 1991.
22. Devon Flannery, "I.V. Halloween Review Faults Visiting Revelers," *Daily Nexus*, Nov. 12, 2003.
23. Overend, "Working to Tame…" *L.A. Times*, Oct. 23, 2003. See also Marisa Lagos, "Foot Patrol Anticipates Big Crowd," *Daily Nexus*, Oct. 31, 2001, which discusses

Yang's annual Del Playa walk. As noted earlier, the first year Chancellor Yang attended Halloween in Isla Vista was 1994. Footage of Chancellor Yang and his wife on Del Playa can be seen on I.V. T.V.'s "Halloween [2000]" episode.

24. Daniel Haier, "I.V. Weekend Draws Diverse Crowd, Crime," Nov. 3, 2003.

25. Linver, Oct. 2005 interview.

26. Linver, Oct. 2005 interview.

27. Devon Flannery, "Halloween Review Faults Visiting Revelers," *Daily Nexus*, Nov. 12, 2003.

28. Maxwell C. Donnelly, "Halloween Antics Bring Fun and Danger: Isla Vista Revelers Get Just a Tad Bit Wacky," *Daily Nexus*, Oct. 30, 1989: 4.

29. Devon Flannery, "I.V. Halloween Review Faults Visiting Revelers," *Daily Nexus*, Nov. 12, 2003; Allen Cottrell, "Officials Hope Precautions Lead to Safe Halloween Weekend," *Daily Nexus*, Oct. 28, 1988.

30. Sevan Matossian and Greg Shields, I.V. T.V., "Halloween (2000)".

31. "College Porn Nightmare…" *Rolling Stone*, Sept. 18, 2003.

32. Overend, "Working to Tame…", 2003.

33. Haier, "Officials…" *Daily Nexus*, Oct. 31, 2003.

34. 2003 Questionnaire, Christina Ossa.

35. Carrie Awalt, interview with author, Feb. 19, 2003.

36. Catherine Cole, Harry Nelson, and Walter Yuen, Final Report of the Isla Vista Action Group, 2005: 5.

37. Taken from an email forwarded from Catherine Cole; the student chose to remain anonymous.

38. This attitude is indicative of the ongoing hostilities between probients and police officers in Isla Vista.

39. I can't help but note that the crowded conditions on Del Playa, which law officials cite as the most dangerous aspect of the celebration, is at least partly due to the surrounding community's desire to see Halloween corralled; in other words, kept out of the backyards of the (largely wealthy) population of the city of Santa Barbara. Downtown festivities are thus confined to the commercial space of bars and clubs, while the Isla Vista celebration, like the "Isla Vista problem" more generally, has become quarantined onto two parallel streets: Del Playa Drive and Sabado Tarde (though the major concentration of people is still on Del Playa). If an effort were to be made to spread out the festivities, say by offering sanctioned entertainment in nearby Anis'q Oyo park, the danger of stampeding would be considerably lessened, and officers would be better able to circulate among revelers and assist those in need of attention.

40. Ethan Roberts, interview with author, March 31, 2005.

41. An excellent book on the subject is Sharon Mazer's *Professional Wrestling: Sport and Spectacle*, Jackson: University of Mississippi, 1998.

42. Sol Linver interview, October 2005.

43. Catherine Cole, Harry Nelson, and Walter Yuen. "Final Report on the Isla Vista Action Group," submitted to Chancellor Henry T. Yang, April, 2005.

44. As the Graduate Student Association representative to the IVAG, I attended, and actively participated in, all of these meetings.

45. Matt Dozier, "Revelers Enjoy Well-Monitored Halloween Scene," *Daily Nexus*, Nov. 1, 2004: 1.

46. Although, as I discovered after my assault, that does not necessarily mean that no violent crime *occurred*.
47. Dozier, "Revelers Enjoy…", 2004.
48. Sol Linver quoted in Mollie Vandor, "Police Kept Busy During Weekend," *Daily Nexus*, Oct. 31, 2005: 1.
49. Although there are a sizeable number of Latino families living in Isla Vista, it is quite rare to see more than a handful of non-white probients on Del Playa outside of Halloween weekend.
50. Field notes, Oct. 29, 2005.
51. Linver, Oct. 2005 interview.
52. Linver, Oct. 2005 interview.

15. THE BEGINNING OF THE "PARTY AT THE END…"

1. I was exceptionally granted entrance to the 2005 debriefing by Lt. Linver, and sat with the press in the rear of Embarcadero Hall for this much-anticipated opening statement. Disappointingly enough, it was less than two minutes in length and included no pertinent information whatsoever.

16. ISLA VISTA: ON THE EDGE

1. Eco et al, 1985: 6.

17. RADICAL FREEDOM AND THE MARGINALIZATION OF MASQUERADE

1. Sarlo, 2001: 32.
2. It is no coincidence that it was the L.A.P.D.'s Special Forces unit which was called in to "restore order" in Isla Vista after the riots of 1970, nor that the brutality these "peacekeepers" inflicted on the community is nothing short of legendary (see section four). Isla Vistans were primarily guilty of *trespassing*: refusing to respect private space (i.e. breaking into, and eventually burning down, the Bank of America), and refusing to stay out of public space when instructed (i.e. the Perfect Park curfew protest). Therefore the "space police" were the logical choice to restore (spatial) order to the neighborhood.
3. The injudiciousness of this policy was amply proved during the chaotic aftermath of Hurricane Katrina (August, 2005), when martial law reigned, and yet the innocent remained without basic necessities and in continual peril.
4. Sarlo, 2001: 32.
5. Eco et al, 1985: 6.
6. Credit for this insight goes to Professor Leo Cabranes-Grant of the UCSB Dramatic Arts and Spanish departments.

7. Timothy Bewes, *Reification, or The Anxiety of Late Capitalism*, London: Verso, 2002: xiii.

8. Bewes, 2002: xi.

9. A series of movies directed by Larry and Andy Wachowski in which human beings are trapped in a virtual world created by artificial life forms in order to keep humankind enslaved. Most people accept "the matrix" as reality but a few recognize it as a simulation and are able to escape and struggle against it.

10. Jagodzinski, 2004: 58.

11. Bewes, 2002: xiii.

12. Bewes, 2002: xiv.

13. Judith Butler, "Imitation and Gender Insubordination" (1990), in Sarah Salih, ed. *The Judith Butler Reader*, Malden: Blackwell, 2004: 125.

14. Salih, 2004: 128.

15. Judith Butler, *Gender Trouble: Feminism and the Subversion of Identity*, London: Routledge: 1999: 181.

16. See: http://www.caribana.ca/history.HTM

17. Claire Sponsler, *Ritual Imports: Performing Medieval Drama in America*, Ithaca: Cornell University Press, 2004: 68.

18. Sponsler, 2004: 68.

19. Sponsler, 2004: 69.

18. THE END OF THE WORLD

1. John Stickney, *Streets, Actions, Alternatives, Raps*, New York: G.P. Putnam's Sons: 17.

2. Una Chaudhuri, *Staging Place: The Geography of Modern Drama*, Ann Arbor, University of Michigan Press, 1995: 6.

3. Michel de Certeau, *The Practice of Everyday Life*, Berkeley: University of California Press, 1984. See particularly part III, "Spatial Practices": 91-130.

4. De Certeau, 1984: 95.

5. Martin Heidegger, *Being And Time (Sein und Zeit)*, Translation by John Macquarrie and Edward Robinson, San Francisco: Harper, 1962.

6. De Certeau, 1984: 98.

7. De Certeau, 1984: 93.

8. De Certeau, 1984: 96.

9. See Sarlo, 2001: 12-13 on the similarity of shopping malls to casinos, and the similarity of both to a sealed space capsule.

10. Sarlo, 2001: 9.

11. Isla Vista's lack of sidewalks will be discussed in more detail later in this section.

12. Stephanie Cain, "Artist in Profile; Adam de Boer," *Daily Nexus*, Thurs. Feb. 9, 2006.

13. See also "The judgers and the judged" section of part five, which explores the Isla Vistan practice of rating costumes and revelers as they pass by on Del Playa.

14. Davis, 1990: 226.

15. Laura Mulvey, "Visual Pleasure and Narrative Cinema," *Screen* 16.3 (1975): 6-18. Rpt. in *Visual and Other Pleasures*. Bloomington: Indiana UP, 1989: 14-27.

16. Mulvey, 1975: 19.

17. IVFP Report, Monday, April 9, 2006

18. IVFP Report, April 9, 2006

19. Alison Zuber, interview with author, April 3, 2004.
20. Catherine Cole, informal discussion with author, October, 2004.
21. Hebdige, 1979: 53-54.
22. See especially: Henry A. Giroux and Kostas Myrsiades, eds., *Beyond the Corporate University: Culture and Pedagogy in the New Millennium*, Lanham: Rowman & Littlefield, 2001; and John A. Flower, *Downstairs, Upstairs: The Changed Spirit and Face of College Life in America*, Akron: University of Ohio Press, 2003.
23. Chaudhuri, 1995: 12.
24. Potter & Sullivan, 1970: 44.
25. I. Munt, "The 'Other' postmodern tourism: culture, travel and the new middle classes," *Theory Culture and Society* 11: 104.
26. Luke Desforges, "Checking Out the Planet: global representations / local identities and youth travel," in Tracy Skelton and Gill Valentine, eds., *Cool Places: Geographies of Youth Culture*, London: Routledge, 1998: 178.
27. M.L. Pratt, *Imperial Eyes: Travel Writing and Transculturation*, London: Routledge, 1992: 29-30.
28. J.H. Strand, "Maximum Freedom and The Limits of Community: Isla Vista, CA, 1925-1975," UCSB dissertation, 1994: 2-3.
29. For further details on the history of I.V. I highly recommend Lodise's website: www.islavistahistory.com and Malcolm Gault-Williams, *Don't Bank on Amerika*, Santa Barbara: self published, 1987. Other helpful studies include: J.H. Strand, "Maximum Freedom and the Limits of Community: Isla Vista, California, 1925-1975"; D.E. Brovarney, "The Seductive Sixties: Isla Vista's Quest for Identity, 1960-1978," Dissertation, UCSB, 1998; Robert Potter and James J. Sullivan, *The Campus By the Sea Where the Bank Burned Down: A Report on the Disturbances at UCSB and Isla Vista, 1968-1970*; and the Trowe Commission Report (submitted October 9, 1970). Also useful, though not always directly related to Isla Vista, is Robert Kelley's *Transformations: UC Santa Barbara 1909-1979*, which traces the evolution of UCSB from a small teacher's college overlooking downtown Santa Barbara, to its current incarnation as a research one institution, sprawling across the isolated Goleta Bluff.
30. Malcolm Gault-Williams, 1987: 48.
31. From the Santa Ynez band of Chumash Indians website: http://www.santaynezchumash.org/history.html
32. For more information about the early years of the "Santa Barbara College," and a useful discussion of its transformation from a small teacher's college to a branch of the University of California, see Kelley, 1981, prologue through chapter II.
33. J.H. Strand, 1994: 13.
34. Lodise, www.islavistahistory.com
35. This now-famous quote was part of Jack Schwartz's speech before the County Board of Supervisors. Quoted in Lodise, "From Indian Settlement to Student Ghetto," available at: http://www.islavistahistory.com/ivhistory/chapter1.7.html
36. Today, there are areas which do exceed Isla Vista's population density: San Francisco's China Town, for example, is home to nearly 50,000 people per square mile. But 25,000 people per square mile is still a high number, even in comparison with major West Coast cities, and Isla Vista is not part of a city at all, but remains an unincorporated area of Santa Barbara County.

37. Photographic examples of the conditions existing in many Isla Vista apartment buildings are available at: http://hep.ucsb.edu/people/hnn/present.pdf.

38. Khalid Elshorafa, "Housing Fair Offers Info on I.V. Options," *Daily Nexus*, Jan. 26, 2005.

39. Cole et al, 2005: 24.

40. After Feb. 23, 2001, when UCSB student David Attias plowed into a group of pedestrians, killing four students and seriously injuring a fifth, Dramatic Arts and English Major Sarah MacKay wrote and directed the award-winning play, *Sidewalks and Better Light*, based on interviews she conducted with those connected to the tragedy. The play, which sent a clear message to the county about the need for amenities (particularly the two named in its title) premiered at UCSB's Studio Theatre on April 27, 2002. See Jennifer B. Siverts, "Student Prepares Play Based on I.V. Tragedy," *Daily Nexus*, Feb. 22, 2002, and David Downs, "Heavy Mettle," *Daily Nexus*, April 25, 2002.

41. Strand, 1994: 2.

19. WHERE THE SIDEWALKS END

1. Michel de Certeau, *The Practice of Everyday Life*, trans. Steven Rendall, Berkeley: University of California Press, 1984: 34. Emphases in original.

2. Tom Bulgin, "The Isla Vista Problem," *El Gaucho*, Oct. 23, 1964: 2.

3. Dorothy E. Brovarney notes that even in the heyday of *in loco parentis*, "collegians may not have taken it all that seriously." Even Dean Lyle Reynolds recalled the Isla Vista regulations to be "a loose arrangement." It should also be noted, however, that it was much less loosely arranged in the case of female students, who were required to live in supervised housing and to sign in at specified hours until the late 1960's. D.E. Brovarney, "The Seductive Sixties: Isla Vista's Quest for Identity, 1960-1978," 1998: 16.

4. Michelle Nellis, "A Profile of Downtown Isla Vista," Masters thesis, UCSB, 1989: 11-12.

5. The rejected demand called for the firing of Athletic Director Curtice.

6. J.H. Strand 1994: 82-83. The apartment was searched on the pretext of performing an eviction, and marijuana was discovered on the premises.

7. The Educational Opportunity Program, designed to allow minority students from working-class families to attend the University, had met with controversy from the outset. Quoted in Potter and Sullivan, "The Campus by the Sea...," 1970: 7.

8. "Students Form New Free University," *El Gaucho*, Feb. 19 1969.

9. Kelley, 1981: 41.

10. Strand, 1994: 86.

11. Strand, 1994: 88.

12. Kelley, 1981: 42.

13. KCSB News Report, April 11, 1969. Quoted in Gault-Williams, 1987: 61.

14. Strand, 1994: 113-114.

15. Quoted in G.C. Olsen, "Twenty-four Years of Policing Law Enforcement at UCSB and in Isla Vista: 1954 – 1978" Masters thesis, UCSB, 1979: 110.

16. The fact that the officers arrived on a single bus, rather than infiltrating the area in a less conspicuous and easily-targeted manner, is evidence of their lack of training in, and preparation for, riotous conditions.

17. Gault-Williams, 1987: 136.

18. Richard Flacks and Milton Mankoff, "Why They Burned the Bank," *The Nation*, March 23, 1970: 340; quoted in Strand, 1994: 134.

19. Gault-Williams, 1987: 136.

20. John James Whelan, "Echoes of Rebellion: the Liberated Generation Grows Up," Ph.D. dissertation in sociology, UCSB, December 1984: 26.

21. Jack Whelan and Richard Flacks, *Beyond the Barricades, The Sixties Generation Grows Up*, Philadelphia: Temple University Press, 1989: 47-48.

22. John Stickney, *Streets, Actions, Alternatives, Raps*, 1971: 19; quoted in Gault-Williams, 1987: 139.

23. The officers sent in during Isla Vista II were given faulty intelligence which led them to believe that the area was saturated with student snipers. In fact, the Sheriff first blamed Moran's death on a sniper, but later admitted that one of his officer's weapons had accidentally discharged when Moran was shot. A coroner's inquest later found that the safety gauge on the weapon in question was malfunctioning.

24. The Los Angeles Police Department (LAPD) is quite well-known for its hatred of public gatherings, as pointed out by Mike Davis in *City of Quartz*. Davis notes that, "Subconsciously (the LAPD) has probably never recovered from the humiliation of August 1965 when it temporarily was forced to surrender the streets to a rebellious ghetto." Surely that defeat was still fresh in the minds of many of the agents sent to "restore order" to Isla Vista. Davis, 1990: 258.

25. Olson, 1979: 128.

26. Martin Trowe et al, "Report of the Commission on Isla Vista," submitted to UC President Charles J. Hitch, October, 1970: iii.

27. Catherine Cole, Harry Nelson, and Walter Yuen, "Final Report on the Isla Vista Action Group," submitted to Chancellor Henry T. Yang, April, 2005: 5.

28. Tom Hayden, *Ramparts*, July 1970: 55-56; quoted in Strand, 1994: 162.

29. *Isla Vista Viewpoint*, July 3, 1970, IVCC Archives; quoted in Strand, 1994: 160.

30. Although resources come from both the University and the County, the IVFP is ultimately under the jurisdiction of the County Sheriff's department.

31. For a more detailed look at the IVFP's inception and its slow and often painful process of integration into the community, see G.C. Olsen, 1979, Chapter V, "The Isla Vista Foot Patrol – 1970 to 1978": 239-306.

32. "University of California Budget for Current Operations: Departmental Allocations, 1970-71," University Archives UCSB: 831.

33. Statistics courtesy of the Isla Vista Foot Patrol office.

34. Carol Mosely, interview with author, March 14, 2006.

35. Statistics courtesy of the Isla Vista Foot Patrol office.

36. Potter and Sullivan, 1970: 31, 38.

37. Michael Hardt and Antonio Negri, *Empire*, Cambridge: Harvard University Press, 2000: 288.

38. Guy Debord, *The Society of the Spectacle*, trans. Donald Nicholson-Smith, New York: Zone Books, 1995.

39. Hardt & Negri, 2000: 289.

40. Davis, 1990: 232-233.

41. Jamie Birkett, informal conversation with author, June 2005.
42. A couple of Jamie's companions (who declined to give their names) added that they have often felt singled out by police, particularly when they were wearing clothing emblazoned with the UCSB logo. However, they did note that the harassment is far worse for students attending the less affluent Santa Barbara City College, and doubly so for those SBCC students who reside in Isla Vista.

20. PARODY AT PLAY

1. Margaret A. Rose, *Parody: ancient, modern, and post-modern*, Cambridge: Cambridge University Press, 1993: 51.
2. Rose, 1993: 38.
3. M. Bakhtin, *The Dialogic Imagination: Four Essays*, ed. Michael Holquist, trans. Caryl Emerson and Michael Holquist. Austin: University of Texas Press, 1981: 75-6.
4. Clifford Geertz, "Deep Play: Notes on the Balinese Cock Fight," in *The Interpretation of Cultures*, New York: Basic Books, 1973: 448
5. Aching, 2002: 6. See section two for further discussion of this term and Aching's use of it.

21. THE GROTESQUE REALISM
(RE)GENERATION

1. A small group of fellow graduate students working on a field notes assignment for Dr. Cole's Performance Studies class, plus a couple of curious friends.
2. Partial transcription of a conversation recorded on my mini-cassette recorder.
3. Bakhtin, 1968: 19-20.
4. Bakhtin, 1968: 21.
5. Ethan Roberts, interview with author, March 31, 2005.
6. Mark I. Pinsky, *The Gospel According to Disney: Faith, Trust, and Pixie Dust*, Louisville: Westminster John Knox Press, 2004: 3.
7. Elizabeth Bell, Lynda Haas Laura Sells, eds. *From Mouse to Mermaid: the Politics of Film, Gender, and Culture*, Bloomington: Indiana University Press, 1995: 2-3.
8. Sean Griffin, *Tinker Belles and Evil Queens: The Walt Disney Company from the Inside Out*, New York: New York University Press, 2000: 7.
9. Griffin, 2000: 14.
10. Griffin, 2000: 21.
11. Griffin, 2000: 26.
12. Griffin, 2000: 28.
13. Even the implied (though not yet achieved) kiss in *The Little Mermaid*'s musical number "Kiss the Girl" has been severed from Ariel's desire for Prince Eric in that she is "forced" to solicit the prince's kiss by Ursula, the bawdy and evil sea witch.
14. Douglas Brode, *From Walt to Woodstock: How Disney Created the Counterculture*, Austin: University of Texas Press, 2004: xxi, xxvii.
15. Pinsky, 2004: 5-6.
16. Email correspondence, Nov. 2003.

17. Sevan Matossian and Greg Shields , I.V. T.V., "Halloween" 1999.

18. Jenn Lotz, interview with author, March 3, 2004.

19. The most often-rented costumes in 1977 were cited by Sarah Elizabeth Glober, owner and manager of "The Costume Rental Shop," once located at 501 Chapala in Santa Barbara, as the gorilla suit for men and belly-dancer garb for women. The implications of this provocative combination surely merit a separate study, but for my purposes suffice it to say that images of Animal House, I Dream of Genie, and King Kong immediately spring to mind. Rachel Weintraub, "Halloween Costumes Link Kids to Gloomy Past," *Daily Nexus*, Oct. 28, 1977: 2.

20. Walt Disney and Maurice Rapf, quoted in Pinsky, 2004: 55.

21. Elizabeth Bell, "Somatexts at the Disney Shop: Constructing the Pentimentos of Women's Animated Bodies," in Bell, et al 1999: 114.

22. Kellie Bean, "Stripping Beauty: Disney's 'Feminist' Seduction," in Ayres, Brenda, ed. *The Emperor's Old Groove: Decolonizing Disney's Magic Kingdom*, New York: Peter Lang, 2003: 60.

23. From "Milkshake" by Kelis. Interestingly, although self-proclaimed feminist Kelis's chorus does suggest prostitution, she states in the second verse that her "techniques that freaks these boys [...] can't be bought."

24. Ariel of *The Little Mermaid*, Jasmine of *Aladdin*, Belle of *Beauty and the Beast*, and Esmerelda of *The Hunchback of Notre Dame*.

25. Wasko, Janet. *Understanding Disney: The Manufacture of Fantasy*, Cambridge: Blackwell Publishers, Ltd., 2001: 134.

26. Bean, 2003: 54.

27. Laura Mulvey, "Visual Pleasure and Narrative Cinema," *Screen* 16.3, 1975: 6-18. Rpt. in *Visual and Other Pleasures*. Bloomington: Indiana UP, 1989: 14-27.

28. Bean, 2003: 55.

29. Laura Sells, " 'Where Do the Mermaids Stand?' Voice and Body in *The Little Mermaid*," in Bell et al, 1999: 179.

30. Sells, 1999: 183.

31. Luce Irigaray, *This Sex Which is Not One*, Trans. Catherine Porter with Carolyn Burke, Ithaca: Cornell University Press, 1985: 76.

32. Pushap Naidu Parekh, "*Pocahontas*: The Disney Imaginary," in Ayres, 2003: 167-178.

33. For a thorough description of the term "Disneyfication," its origins and usage, see Alan Bryman, *The Disneyization of Society*, London: SAGE, 2004: 7.

34. This observation is based on my own informal costume tally and those of fellow graduate students taking field notes.

35. Ana Vasquez, from a journal assignment in Introduction to Acting, Fall 2004. Cited with permission of author.

36. Susan Jeffords, "The Curse of Masculinity: Disney's Beauty and the Beast," in Bell et al, 1999: 171.

37. Field notes, Sunday October 31, 2004.

38. Sevan Matossian and Greg Shields, "Halloween (1999)," "Halloween (2000)," IV TV.

39. Doug Arellanes, "Halloween Revelers Crowd Del Playa," *Daily Nexus*, Nov. 4, 1985; photo, *Daily Nexus*, Oct. 27, 1980; photos, *Daily Nexus*, Nov. 1, 1990.

40. For example, during the first Gulf War, Saddam Hussein was a frequently lampooned figure (Charles Hornberger, "Fright Night: I.V.'s Costume Party Calmer Than Saturday," *Daily Nexus*, Nov. 1, 1990). Also, the 2004 celebration, falling

directly before a presidential election, was awash with dueling political endorsements and derisions.

41. Dan Hilldale and Chris Ziegler, "I.V. Residents, All Gussied Up, Descend on Del Playa Drive," *Daily Nexus*, Nov. 1, 1991.

42. One notable exception: a number of students did hold up picket signs in imitation of the long-suffering grocery workers, who had recently gone on strike in Southern California, and who would remain on strike until late February, 2004.

43. This is a comment I saw repeatedly, in various forms, in the field notes taken by fellow graduate students after attending Halloween in Isla Vista, 2004.

44. Richard D. E. Burton, *Afro-Creole: Power, Opposition, and Play in the Caribbean* (Ithaca: Cornell University Press, 1997): 210.

45. Burton, 1997: 164.

46. The fallopian swimmers were recorded as being present at two different Halloween celebrations, in 1985 and in 1992. Chris Wyland, "Checking Out the Scene on All Hallows Eve," *Daily Nexus*, Monday, November 2, 1987: 10; Cover photo, *Daily Nexus*, Monday, November 2, 1992.

47. Carol Mosely, interview with author, March 14, 2006.

48. Catherine A. MacKinnon, *Only Words*, Cambridge: Harvard University Press, 1993: 19.

49. Jenn Lotz, interview with author, March 3, 2004.

50. 2003 & 2004 Halloween Questionnaire results.

51. UCSB First-Year Students Opinion Survey, Open-Ended Commends Report, Winter 2005. Courtesy of the UCSB Women's Center.

52. Spring Survey for Sexual Battery, 2005. Courtesy of the UCSB Women's Center.

53. "Kevin," informal conversation with author, October 31, 2001.

54. Catherine Cole, informal discussion with author, May 2005.

55. Quoted in Jennifer Adams, "Downtown Was Refuge From DP", *Daily Nexus*, Friday, November 1, 1991.

56. "Joe," informal conversation with author, April 29, 2006.

57. To be fair, I must implicate myself in this phenomenon: on Halloween, 2003, I dressed as Pippi Longstocking, the 9-year-old heroine of a 1973 film (based on a Swedish children's book by Astrid Lindgren) that was subsequently remade as Disney's *The New Adventures of Pippi Longstocking* (1988). Although my costume was fairly "authentic," the tension created by my 27 year-old body in a dress intended for a pre-pubescent girl does fit the above-described pattern.

58. Field notes, 30 October, 2004.

59. Mary Russo, "Female Grotesques: Carnival and Theory," in Teresa de Lauretis, ed., *Feminist Studies/Critical Studies: Issues, Terms, and Contexts* (Bloomington: Indiana University Press, 1986): 219.

60. These Marley hats were also popular at Mardi Gras 2006.

61. Catherine Cole, *Ghana's Concert Party Theatre*, Bloomington: Indiana University Press, 2001; Ralph Ellison, *Shadow and Act*, New York: Random House, 1964; Eric Lott, *Love and Theft: Blackface Minstrelsy and the American Working Class*. New York: Oxford University Press, 1993; Marlon T. Riggs, *Ethnic Notions*, 1986, and *Color Adjustment*, 1991, videos distributed by California Newsreel, San Francisco; David Roediger, *The Wages of Whiteness: Race and the Making of the American Working Class*, New York: Verso, 1991; Robert C. Toll, *Blacking Up: The Minstrel Show in Nineteenth-Century America*, New York: Oxford University Press, 1974.

62. Homi K. Bhabha, *The Location of Culture*, London: Routledge, 1994: 86.
63. Bhabha, 1994: 79.
64. C. Richard King and Charles Fruehling Springwood, *Team Spirits: The Native American Mascot Controversy*, Lincoln: University of Nebraska Press, 2001: 9. Emphasis in original.
65. Unfortunately, I was unable to make contact with this reveler before he was reabsorbed into the crowd.
66. By the same token, many people living on the west coast of the United States believe themselves to have no accent: because many of the voices they hear on the radio and on television share their dialect, it becomes invisible to them, a standard by which other dialects are to be measured.
67. Edward Said, *Orientalism*, New York: Vintage Books (Random House), 1979 (originally published 1978): 228
68. Sheilds and Matossian, I.V. T.V., "Halloween," 1999; "Halloween," 2000.
69. Dick Hebdige, *Subculture: the Meaning of Style* (London: Routledge, 1979): 139. The quotation is a paraphrase of Jean Paul Sartre from an interview in "New York Review of Books," March 26, 1970.

22. DEFINING WE; DEFINING ME

1. Jagodzinski, 2004: 20.
2. Sarlo, 2001: 32.
3. Jagodzinski, 2004: 32.
4. Field notes, October 28, 2005.
5. Michel de Certeau, *The Practice of Everyday Life*, Berkeley: University of California Press, 1984: 92. I can't help but note here the eerily prophetic language used by de Certeau when he speaks of the inevitability of "an Icarian fall" following this godlike escape to the World Trade Center. Little did he suspect that, nearly twenty years later, the towers themselves would be the tragic heroes of such a fall.
6. Sarlo, 2001: 27.
7. Ethan Roberts, March 2004 interview.
8. Schechner, *Performance Studies*, London: Routledge, 2002: 148.
9. Bertold Brecht, "Alienation Effects in Chinese Acting," in *Brecht on Theatre*, ed. and trans. John Willett, New York: Hill and Wang, 1964: pp. 91-99.
10. Christine Bai and Matt Cohen, "IVRPD Provides Alcohol Free Alternative," *Daily Nexus*, Oct. 31, 2001. Emphasis mine.
11. Kevin McFadden, "No More Treats, Just More Tricks," *Daily Nexus*, Nov. 2, 2004.
12. Jagodzinski, 2004: 238.
13. Jagodzinski, 2004: 239-240.
14. De Certeau, 1984: 29-30. Emphasis in original.
15. De Certeau, 1984: 177.
16. De Certeau, 1984: 178.

VI. CONCLUSION

1. "Mardi Gras Bob," interview with author, February 27, 2006.
2. Kelly Barber, informal interview with author, October 28, 2005.

24. WE'RE NOT GOING ANYWHERE

1. Arthur Hardy's Mardi Gras Guide 2006: 20.
2. Robert Tallant, *Mardi Gras...As It Was*, Gretna, LA: Pelican Publishing, 1989 (first published 1947): 12.
3. Jeff Jarvis, "Should New Orleans be Rebuilt?" Posted Tuesday, August 30th, 2005, 4:58 pm on *Buzz Machine*. Available at: http://www.buzzmachine.com/index.php/2005/08/30/should-new-orleans-be-rebuilt/
4. Arthur Hardy's Mardi Gras Guide 2006: 8.
5. Clifford Geertz, "Deep Play: Notes on the Balinese Cock Fight," in *The Interpretation of Cultures*, New York: Basic Books, 1973: 448
6. Marnie Hunter, "Mardi Gras to fatten New Orleans tourism," CNN.com, Monday, February 27, 2006; Posted: 11:04 a.m. EST (16:04 GMT). Available at: http://www.cnn.com/2006/US/02/23/nola.tourism/?section=cnn_latest
7. "Mardi Gras Bob," interview with author, Lundi Gras (February 27), 2006.
8. Nagin infamously assured the world that New Orleans would soon enough be "Chocolate City again"—in other words, that the devastated black population would once again thrive—a quote which has come back to haunt him and which he has spent a good deal of effort attempting to defend/explain. See "Nagin Apologizes for Chocolate City Comments," CNN.com, Wednesday, January 18, 2006; Posted: 3:42 a.m. EST (08:42 GMT). Available at: http://www.cnn.com/2006/US/01/17/nagin.city/
9. In reference to the fact that approximately 25,000 flood refugees were given emergency shelter in the New Orleans Superdome, and later the Houston Astrodome, following hurricane Katrina.
10. In reference to the blue tarps covering houses whose roofs were blown off in the storms.
11. Everyone attending a Mardi Gras parade, whether they are located on a float or somewhere along the street, is a participant. It is impossible to be a passive observer since one is constantly being bombarded with beads and other projectiles which can cause physical injury if one is not prepared to catch, deflect, or dodge them. I learned this important lesson the hard way, by getting hit full in the face with a bag of beads while attempting to take a photograph of a float in the Iris parade.
12. Victor Turner, "Liminality and Communitas" in *The Ritual Process: Structure and Anti-Structure*, Chicago: Aldine Transaction, 1995 (originally published 1969): 94-130.

25. THE U.S. CARNIVALESQUE

1. Hardt & Negri, 2000: 189.
2. Carmen Lodise, "Building a Community," chapter four of "Isla Vista, A Citizen's History," available at: http://www.islavistahistory.com/ivhistory/chapter4.1.html
3. Martin Heidegger, *Being And Time (Sein und Zeit)*, Translation by John Macquarrie and Edward Robinson, San Francisco: Harper, 1962: 296.
4. Heidegger, 1962: 315.
5. Jon McKenzie, *Perform or Else: From Discipline to Performance*, London: Routledge, 2001: 18.
6. See section three for a more thorough discussion of Drewal's theory. Margaret Thompson Drewal, *Yoruba Ritual: Performers, Play, Agency*, Bloomington: Indiana University Press, 1992
7. Note particularly the transparency of Hegel's writing process in *The Phenomenology of Spirit*, trans. A.V. Miller, Oxford: Oxford University Press, 1977.
8. Roger I. Simon, "The University: A Place to Think?" in Henry A. Giroux and Kostas Myrsiades, eds., *Beyond the Corporate University: Culture and Pedagogy in the New Millennium*, Lanham: Rowman & Littlefield, 2001: 47.
9. Henry Giroux, "Teenage Sexuality, Body Politics, and the Pedagogy of Display," in Jonathan S. Epstein, ed. *Youth Culture: Identity in a postmodern world*, Oxford: Blackwell, 1998: 25.
10. Schechner, 2002, 64.